With kind r[illegible]

Henry Moff[illegible]

an old friend and colleague

Con Callahan

AF510773

The Search For Truth

THE SEARCH FOR TRUTH

AN INTRODUCTION TO THE JURY TRIAL PROCESS

CORNELIUS P. CALLAHAN

SEXTANT PRESS, INC.

Published by Sextant Press, Inc.

© 1997 Cornelius P. Callahan

All rights reserved

Printed in the United States of America

No part of this book may be used or reproduced in any manner without written permission except in the case of brief quotations embodied in critical articles and reviews.

For information, address Sextant Press, Inc.
P. O. Box 1416, Chicago, IL 60690-1416
1-800-399-7533

Library of Congress Cataloging-in-Publication Data

Callahan, Cornelius P.
The search for truth: an introduction to the jury trial process/
Cornelius P. Callahan
p. cm.—(instruction in trying civil jury cases)

Includes index.

1. Law. 2. Trial, civil – trying jury cases.

ISBN: 0-9658769-1-8 (alk.paper)
347.73075 97-92212
CIP

10 9 8 7 6 5 4 3 2 1

To the thousands who were called
and the hundreds who were chosen
to serve as jurors in my cases.

A trial is a search for truth; an appeal is a search for error.
— Saying

Contents

Preface and Acknowledgements

A number of people have helped me to bring this book to publication. Arthur L. Foster and Stephen A. Milwid were the first ones to recognize the value of a book like this to law students and beginning lawyers. They provided many stories and insights. In the end we agreed that we would have liked to have had such a book ourselves when we were starting out.

My editor, Kathleen Fitzgerald, took time from a very busy schedule to read the draft from cover to cover. The reader has been well served as a result of her editing and of the addition of needed explanatory notes. Her assistant editor, Patricia Burt, spent much time and patience with me in carefully going over the manuscript.

My true and loyal secretary of many years, Tina Theisen, has gone through many rewrites, additions, subtractions and what have you. She began doing drafts long before we reached the point where we really believed we had something that would be worthy of publication.

In addition, I owe a debt of gratitude to many who contributed to the book in a number of different ways: William P. Butler, Calvin K. Hubbell, Robert P. Schmidt, William F. DeYoung, Barry E. Yavitz, David M. Macksey, Thomas L. Samuel, M. Frances McNamara and Michael W. Rathsack.

And of course we all learn from our opponents. It was from my opponents after all that I learned how to put on a plaintiff's case when the time to do so came along. I believe that although all my cases were hard fought, I never made an enemy among the attorneys whom I tried cases against—or as I really prefer to say, "tried cases with." I vividly remember the first case I tried with the redoubtable James A. Dooley, who later went on to serve as a member of the Supreme Court of

Illinois. After we finished our final arguments and the jury had retired to the jury room to begin its deliberations, he offered his hand and said, "Nice working with you." In Chicago the concept is that unless you are in court with a jury in the box you are not really working, no matter what else you may be doing and no matter how important it may be.

I will mention only a few of those with whom I tried a number of cases: John D. Hayes, my opponent in the case followed throughout the book, Louis G. Davidson, the above mentioned James A. Dooley, Philip H. Corboy, William D. Maddux (now a prominent judge) and Robert A. Clifford. I could tell wonderful stories about each of them and a few do appear in some of the anecdotes running throughout the book. They probably did not realize that they were being so helpful when we were slugging it out toe to toe during those many trials.

Introduction

The history of what the law has been is necessary to the knowledge of what the law is.

— Holmes, *The Common Law*

When the beginning trial lawyer enters the courtroom for the first time it seems to him that everything is set in stone, that things have been the way they are for eons and that everyone involved, except himself, knows exactly what is going on at all times. Experience alone will in due course bring him to a sense of belonging and being an equal participant in the trial process. While a knowledge of the history of the legal process will not of itself bring to the beginner a feeling of equality with his more experienced adversaries, it will serve to put into perspective the fact that he is but one in a long line of lawyers stretching back in time for more than two thousand years.

In accordance with Justice Holmes's urging that a history of the law is necessary to a true understanding of it, however, it seems appropriate to precede the substance of this book with a summary, however brief, of some commonly known highlights in the development of the law. I hold myself out as a trial lawyer, not as a legal history scholar. Nevertheless, the student of any discipline, particularly one stretching back so very far in history, can only benefit from some understanding of how he takes his place in the evolution of such a great profession. And this is particularly true for the hesitant and unsure lawyer who is entering into the trial process for the first time. It places the whole situation in an historical perspective. So let us begin.

The great source for the study of law, of judges and of justice is the Bible. The first law is that issued by God to Adam in the second chapter of Genesis:

> *And the Lord God took the man, and put him into the garden of Eden to dress it and to keep it. And the Lord God commanded the man, saying, Of every tree of the garden thou mayest freely eat: But of the tree of the knowledge of good and evil, thou shalt not eat of it: for in the day that thou eatest thereof thou shalt surely die. (Gen. 2:15-17)*

And so it came to pass.

One of the most beautiful Biblical passages is found in the Judgment of Solomon, which appears in the Book of Kings. Solomon, son of David and one of the great kings of Israel asked for and was given by God a wise and understanding heart and great powers of discernment. In the Judgment of Solomon we are given an example of brilliance in the rendering of a judgment demonstrating stunning insight into the human heart.

Two harlots, who resided together in the same house, came before King Solomon, each claiming to be the true mother of the same infant child. Unable to determine from the testimony before him which of the women was the mother, Solomon ordered that a sword be brought and that the living child be divided in two. The false mother agreed that the child should be so divided; the true mother pleaded that the child not be killed but that it be given to the other woman. Solomon then judged that the child be given to the woman who wished it not to be killed; ruling, "she is the mother thereof."

"And all Israel heard of the judgment which the King had judged; and they feared the King: for they saw that the wisdom of God was in him, to do judgment." (1 Kings 3:16-28) This lucid and compelling story, with its insight into human nature so profound yet so readily understood, is always included in collections of Bible stories for children.

The most famous trial in history is that of Jesus Christ before Pontius Pilate. Even though this trial long precedes the development of the trial by jury, it presents a scene in which the judge turns over to laymen the power to make the ultimate determination as to guilt or innocence—whether the accused is to be set free or crucified. Notwithstanding his own finding of "no fault" in the accused, Pilate accedes to the willfulness of the chief priests and elders of Jerusalem, and turns the judgment of Christ over to them. The priests, the elders and the people of Jerusalem, not the judge, are given the power to decide Christ's fate—to be Christ's jury.

One of the oldest legal codes, the Code of Hammurabi, was discovered in 1901 by a French scholar and scientist excavating in Susa in modern Iran. Although fragments of even more ancient codes have been found since that time, such as one discovered in Ebla in western Syria, dating to approximately 2400 B.C., the Code of Hammurabi is the most extensive, elaborate and complete. Several of its provisions can be identified in various Biblical passages.

Hammurabi was king of Babylon from 1792 to 1750 B.C. The code developed during his reign deals with criminal and civil law, property (including slaves), and various commercial laws pertaining to prices, tariffs and trade. The code also contains some primitive survivalist provisions relating to family solidarity, direct personal responsibility, trial by ordeal, and the *lex talionis* (law of retaliation: "eye for eye, tooth for tooth"), also found in the Bible.[1]

Thus, from the Bible, the Dead Sea Scrolls, the Code of Hammurabi, and other historical writings, it appears that early societies developed rules and regulations pertaining not only to criminal offenses but also to property rights, contracts, marriage, trade and other matters requiring regulation and control. It is generally accepted that prior to the institution of written legal codes there existed a body of traditional "common law" in ancient Western Asia.

The need for a fair and consistent application of justice is a fundamental requirement of any stable society. Every society has developed and established customs, practices and rules governing their members, as well as granting certain rights and privileges. These obligations and entitlements came to constitute the common law of these societies and they were retained and extended as the societies became more complex. The succeeding written laws, such as those of Babylon, Egypt and Palestine, with variations due to cultural, geographic and economic differences, came from this source.

Certainly, diverse and complex civilizations could exist and even flourish without formal written codes or laws. Just as today, for example, people who can neither read nor write are fully expected to conform to the numerous laws of our far more complex societies. Common sayings such as, "Everyone is presumed to know the law"

---

[1] *Although the lex talionis is considered primitive and extreme by modern standards, it has been asserted that it was originally designed as a moderating influence. As such it was intended to restrain excessive retaliatory punishment for crimes and to repay in kind rather than mete out more severe penalties of torture and death for offenses which, though significant, did not warrant such extreme retribution.*

and "Ignorance of the law is no excuse," are routinely accepted and enforced.

Roman Law

The Romans, in the Institutional Treatise published under the Emperor Justinian (527-565), described their legal system as consisting of two elements: "All nations who are ruled by laws and customs, are governed partly by their own particular laws, and partly by those laws which are common to all mankind. The law which a people enacts is called the Civil Law of that people, but that which natural reason appoints for all mankind is called the Law of Nations, because all nations use it." The Law of Nations came in time to be called the Law of Nature—natural law.

Modern legal systems are deeply indebted to the development of Roman law. More than any other civilization, Rome brought law to a level of order, sophistication and acuity that enriched those legal systems which borrowed so heavily from it. It is the Roman legal system, for example, which developed the distinction between public law, in which the state is directly involved, and private law, concerned with disputes between individual citizens.

The Jury System

Although its specific development is unknown, the jury system appears to spring from Anglo-Saxon or Frankish precedents during the Middle Ages. Used by the Norman Dukes, it is believed to have been brought to England by them. There are two types of juries: the grand jury and the petit jury. The grand jury is referred to as the jury of accusation; the petit jury as the jury of trial. While the grand jury and the petit jury developed from a common root, the criminal petit jury is preceded in historical development by the grand jury and evolved from it. Similarly, the civil petit jury is preceded by the criminal petit jury.

While the evidence is unclear, it seems that the jury system may have developed in the course of having a judge travel to remote villages only once or twice a year. Upon his arrival, the elders of the place assembled to advise him of crimes or offenses committed in the intervening period. In time this group became the grand jury, consisting of from twelve to twenty-three members. As the jury of accusation, it issued criminal charges and indictments. The grand jury's longevity is testified to by Shakespeare in *Twelfth Night*: "There have been grand jurymen since before Noah was a sailor."

The petit jury, or jury of trial, consists of twelve members. It was originally composed of the peers of the parties, those who had personal knowledge of the dispute and who would be most able to determine the truth of the matter. It may be that the petit jury grew out of the dilemma confronting visiting judges. With no personal knowledge of the disputing parties or their witnesses, these judges may have had difficulty distinguishing between the truth and falsehood of those testifying. Over time, they may well have come to rely on peers of the disputing parties and witnesses to advise them how to weigh each person's testimony.

Judging

Judging is the process of forming an opinion or making an evaluation by discerning and comparing. It is not something reserved exclusively for judges. It is done by ordinary people, including very young children, hundreds of times each day. "Even a dog," Justice Holmes observes, "distinguishes between being stumbled over and being kicked."[2] In trials, judging involves deciding whether the testimony of a witness is trustworthy and can be relied on, and whether his testimony when compared to all the other evidence in the case stands unshaken.

A lie consists in speaking a falsehood with the intent of deceiving. It is the most direct attack on the truth. The trial is rare indeed which does not involve testimony that is false to one extent or another. While on some occasions it involves merely an excess such as overstating the extent of an injury or disability, on many other occasions it goes to the very heart of the case and involves a presentation that is knowingly, intentionally and willfully false.

There are times when one gets the feeling that a witness is lying and there are times one feels that a witness is telling the truth. And

[2] *The Common Law*, 7

there are still other times when one simply cannot tell. It is then that the weighing, balancing, analyzing and intuitive perceiving can decide the outcome of a trial.

In cases tried by jury, the process of evaluating and weighing the testimony of the various witnesses is solely the jury function. The standard jury instruction on credibility reads as follows:

> You are the sole judges of the credibility of the witnesses and of the weight to be given to the testimony of each of them. In determining the credit to be given any witness you may take into account his ability and opportunity to observe, his memory, his manner while testifying, any interest, bias or prejudice he may have, and the reasonableness of his testimony considered in the light of all the evidence in the case.

The thinking and weighing process of jurors is often very simply expressed:

* * * * * *

> We just couldn't buy the plaintiff's story. That expert witness gave a lot of double talk whenever he was asked tough questions.

* * * * * *

> We couldn't figure out what really happened, but the way the defendant tried to get us to believe it happened just wasn't so.

* * * * * *

> We were never able to put it all together. In the end we just figured that the plaintiff got hurt and it was as much the defendant's fault as anyone's. So we came down for the plaintiff—but we cut the damages.

* * * * * *

Studies show that in virtually every case there are differing viewpoints among the jurors, sometimes about quite tangential matters. Some differences are resolved by the give and take of argument and persuasion, some by negotiation, and still others by the wear and tear of time and the disinclination to disrupt one's life because of one's convictions. All this is part and parcel of the search for truth.

No Appeals in Ancient Law

The Bible provides for the appointment of judges and frequently calls for fairness in the application of justice; it makes no reference to appeals. It is clear from the Judgment of Solomon and the trial of Jesus Christ before Pontius Pilate that in early legal systems there was no appeal. Judgment was carried out forthwith: Solomon's ruling was immediate and final; Christ was executed by torture the very day of His trial.

In the Book of Deuteronomy, Moses tells his people that because their number has increased so greatly he alone cannot continue to be their sole judge. Setting the standards for their selection, he directs them to select other judges:

> *Take you wise men, and understanding, and known amoung your tribes, and I will make them rulers over you....captains over thousands and captains over hundreds, and captains over fifties, and captains over tens, and officers amoung your tribes. (Deut. 1:13-15)*

He gives the new judges their commission:

> *Hear the causes between your brethren, and judge righteously between every man and his brother, and the stranger that is with him. Ye shall not respect persons in judgment; but ye shall hear the small as well as the great; ye shall not be afraid of the face of man; for the judgment is God's: and the cause that is too hard for you, bring it unto me, and I will hear it. (Ibid., 1:16-17)*

These newly appointed judges were to be trial judges. There is no mention of appellate judges. Moses says that if a matter seems too difficult it should be referred to him to hear—not to review.

Root of Appeals

Challenges to judgments appear in the Roman law. If a party thought that the judge neglected his duty, or was guilty of partiality, the judge could be charged *quasi ex maleficio.*[3] The party could also move for a rehearing of the case in the same court, usually on equitable grounds such as excusable failure to appear at trial. A rehearing also could be sought in a situation in which the judgment was alleged to have been procured by bribery or false testimony. As the Roman Empire grew and a need for a unified and coherent application of the law became apparent, certain appeals to higher judges culminating with a hearing before the emperor were allowed. Such an appeal, however, was not a review of the lower court record, but rather a complete rehearing of the cause, *de novo* (anew; afresh; a second time).

At its height in the second century, the Roman Empire ruled virtually all of Europe, Britain to the Scottish Highlands, the African countries bordering the Mediterranean Sea, and to the East, Arabia, Palestine, Mesopotamia and Armenia. With the fall of the Roman Empire in the fifth century, this vast, cohesive judicial system, administered in a single language, also came to an end.

Canon Law

It appears, however, that the Roman Catholic Church developed a sophisticated ecclesiastical appellate procedure embellishing and expanding the provisions of the Roman Law. The Church created ecclesiastic courts throughout Christendom which provided an appellate review process to succeeding higher courts. By the twelfth century, after a matter had been heard and ruled upon by the Archdeacon, there was a right of appeal to the Bishop, from the Bishop to the Archbishop and from the Archbishop to the Pope.

To develop a uniform law for the entire Church, statutes and decretals were published, judges trained, and interlocutory referrals of issues of importance were ruled upon by the Pope. Thus, there was formed a sophisticated appeal procedure at almost every stage of ecclesiastical court proceedings. Ancient Vatican documents demon-

[3] *As if growing out of wrongdoing or an illegal act. A separate action could be instituted against the judge.*

strate that the system of citing authority in the course of written opinions was first used in canon law.

Development of English Appellate System

Appellate procedure in canon law later became the primary influence on the development of an appellate system in English law. Initially English common law did not have a right to appeal; rather, challenges to a judgment were sought through parallel attacks in other courts of competing jurisdiction. Various writs were available to cause removal of a case before or after judgment to another court.

The judge or the jury was required to defend the verdict and record on review in the other court. Eventually the proceedings by which a judge was accused of a false judgment became a proceeding to correct errors in the record of inferior courts. In time, the prevailing party, rather than the judge or jury, became responsible for defending the record. A desire for uniformity and control came to cause the King's Court to stand in relationship to the other courts as the papal court did to the lower ecclesiastical courts. However, it was not until the seventeenth century after merging common law and equity that the system of writs was replaced by an appeal procedure from the trial court to an appellate court in England.[4]

United States Legal System

The American colonies modeled their procedures after the system in England. The crown's desire to maintain control of the colonies and to establish uniform law (similar to the objective of the Church in developing the canon law), required that the Privy Council in England be the court of last resort for all of the colonies. This appellate structure ceased with the American Revolution. Thereafter, appellate procedure in the United States was developed with state court systems and the formation of the federal courts.

Under our current state court systems, there is an absolute right of appeal from the trial court, usually to an intermediate appellate court,

[4]*More than a century later a witty English Common Pleas judge, Sir William Henry Maule (1788-1858), observed, "Everybody is presumed to know the law except His Majesty's judges, who have a Court of Appeal set over them to put them right." See Williams, Criminal Law, 386 (1953).*

and a process of further appeal to the supreme court of a state, usually by a process of leave to appeal. The leave to appeal procedure gives the higher court the discretion to accept or refuse the appeal, except in certain limited and clearly specified cases where the appeal is taken as a matter of right. Thereafter, on an even more restrictive basis, there is a procedure for further appeal to the Supreme Court of the United States. The granting of such an appeal is wholly discretionary in that Court.

The federal system is quite similar. An appeal lies as a matter of right from the trial court, the United States District Court, to the United States Court of Appeals. Thereafter, appeals to the Supreme Court of the United States are discretionary in that court except in certain cases.

Even from this brief summary, one can see that the law and the legal process is rooted in man's experience and spans his entire history. In the opening passage of Lecture I of his epic work, Justice Holmes comments on this phenomenon:

> The life of the law has not been logic; it has been experience. The felt necessities of the time, the prevalent moral and political theories, intuitions of public policy, avowed or unconscious, even the prejudices which judges share with their fellow-men, have had a good deal more to do than the syllogism in determining the rules by which men should be governed. (Oliver Wendell Holmes, *The Common Law*, Little Brown, 1881, p.5)

In 1921, forty years after the publication of his historic treatise, Justice Holmes again pronounced time and experience as the elements fundamental to the life of the law: "A page of history is worth a volume of logic." (*New York Trust Co. v. Eisner*, 256 U. S. 345, 349 [1921})

The trial of a jury case requires much more than a law degree and a keen mind. It demands tact, restraint, courage, insight, endurance, tenacity and a sense of humor. It is demanding, exhilarating work. It can be great fun. It is in the trial of a jury case that work comes closest to play.

The vast majority of civil jury trials conducted in the United States are those in the field of personal injury. They comprise more than 90 percent of all such trials. Usually the plaintiff has suffered an injury, sometimes a devastating injury, leaving him crippled and dependent. The defendant is customarily a corporation or similar entity with funds adequate to satisfy any judgment which may be entered against it. The plaintiff's injury and the defendant's ability to pay combine to create the concept known as the "deep pocket." This concept assumes that when presented with a choice, the jury will more commonly find in favor of the injured plaintiff and against the wealthy defendant.

To be sure, the wealthy defendant has funds with which to defend itself, either its own corporate funds or, commonly, insurance funds. And it is ready, willing and able to defend itself, not only against false and frivolous claims but, in many cases, to treat each and every claim, including meritorious ones, as false and to seek to defeat them in any way possible. So while the term "deep pocket" is a provocative and descriptive phrase, it does not at all mean that such defendants are sitting targets.

The purpose of this book is to provide a description and explanation of what a jury trial involves. While it should prove interesting to more seasoned lawyers, and might well engage the public with its growing interest in jury trials, it was conceived to be of particular benefit to the lawyer who has never tried a jury case. It is that lawyer, the lawyer I once was, to whom this exposition is dedicated.

Chapter One

The Conduct of a Trial

Tell the truth and shame the Devil.

— Shakespeare, *Henry IV*

Initial Concepts

First, at some time well before the commencement of the trial, you should think about how you can argue your case to the jury at the final argument stage. Consider how you will articulate your version of the evidence and, perhaps more important, how you will overcome, explain or otherwise put to rest the evidence which will go in against you. A common mistake of an inexperienced lawyer is to think only of the evidence which is beneficial to his case while ignoring or deprecating the evidence to be presented in opposition. One way to defend against this tendency is to write out your opponent's closing argument making the most telling points just as you expect him to do. The whole exercise will help you evaluate the case and prepare you to deal with the adverse evidence which will be introduced.

Understand too, that no case tries exactly the way it reads in the file. Just because you thoroughly know your case, do not assume that the evidence will go in precisely as you think it will. There are always unanticipated changes and variations. Each trial presents occurrences of one kind or another which are totally unexpected and to which the attorneys must respond. There is no training for this, of course, and your response should be made with grace. The best way to approach these unexpected happenings is by not taking yourself too seriously.

Second, you are constantly under the scrutiny of the jury. This does not mean that you should cater or pander to it, but simply that you should comport yourself accordingly. By reason of their constant observation of you and your demeanor in the course of the trial, the jury will develop certain feelings and opinions about you. You wish those impressions to be beneficial to you in the jury's rendering of its verdict.

Third, a jury trial in one respect is like a basketball game. No one wins a basketball game 100 to 0. No matter how good your case may be, the other side will score on you and score repeatedly. It is important to recognize this because you must be prepared to have things occur which are damaging to your case and which will be disheartening to you. It's all a necessary part of the process. Bearing this in mind will help you keep your equilibrium.

Fourth, do not make the mistake of showing off before the jury. You will be on stage enough because of your position as an advocate. Let me give an example. Suppose one of the witnesses requires an interpreter and you happen to be somewhat fluent in his language. Because of this bilingual ability which by chance comes into play in your case, you may be tempted in your closing argument to refer to the testimony of the witness in its original and in translation. "He testified that the weather was *muy mala*—very bad." Avoid pretentious displays.

Take the lawyer in an airplane crash case who has been trained as a military pilot and is also qualified as a commercial pilot. In his direct and cross-examination of the witnesses and his argument to the jury, he should be careful to keep the language understandable to the jury. Of course, he should explain through questioning of witnesses all technical terms that may be used, but at no time should he reveal to the jury that he has special training in the field. Not only does it not enhance his credibility to do so, it may be viewed by the jury as an attempt to use his personal experience to bolster the weaknesses in his case or to otherwise promote himself. Use your expertise to articulate all the more clearly and persuasively your position. Keep yourself in the background.

Terms of Engagement—Semantic Incursion

You must be careful about the language of the debate in a trial. Your opponent will try to control the case by establishing the terminology to be used. If he is successful and you adopt his language, what happens is a process referred to in diplomatic negotiations as "semantic incursion." If your opponent persuades you to adopt his terms in litigating the case, you may already have lost.

Let me give an example. In litigation involving railroads there is a class of suits known as "crossing cases." These cases deal with those accidents which occur between railroad trains and vehicular traffic at railroad grade crossings. Of the thousands of such crossing in the United States, about 15 percent are protected by automatic flashing railroad warning lights and crossing gates. The other 85 percent, sometimes referred to as "country crossings," are protected by railroad crossbuck signs and state highway signs warning the driver of a vehicle that he is approaching a railroad crossing.

When you are defending the railroad in a case involving an accident at a country railroad crossing, particularly if the suit is filed in a city where all crossings have gates and flashing lights, your opponent will begin to refer to the crossing as an "unprotected" crossing. Accepting this terminology in referring to the crossing results in semantic incursion and places your side of the case in extreme prejudice. These railroad crossings are not unprotected crossings. They are crossings protected by railroad crossbuck signs and by state highway warning signs. Any driver who approaches such a crossing will have been fully apprised that he is approaching a railroad crossing well before he reaches it. This should be repeated and emphasized to the jury to offset the effects of plaintiff's semantic incursion.

In the course of a trial you will find yourself coming up with good ideas and persuasive jury arguments, often in the middle of the night. Keep a note pad next to your bed to jot these ideas down. If you don't, you may find in the morning that you have forgotten them. You can forget even great ideas. The only thing you remember in the morning is that they were great.

Another caution: never complain to the jury about your exhaustive efforts in preparing or trying your case. The jury's unspoken response to such a plea can be punitive: "If you don't like this work then do something else; we didn't choose to be here but you did; do your job and stop complaining."

Pay Attention To The Witness

It is rare at trial for witnesses to be called whose depositions have not been taken in the course of the trial preparation. The inexperienced lawyer, wishing to appear busy and knowledgeable, reaches for the deposition transcript as each witness appears on the stand and avidly follows the testimony from the deposition as it is adduced on direct examination. This should not be done. Have instead an abstract of the witness' deposition and an even briefer summary of his essential testimony, perhaps merely a sentence or two covering the key elements. You do not need the entire deposition.

Watch and listen to the witness. See what kinds of impressions are being made on the jury. Hear and evaluate his testimony just the way the jury does. After all, you are going to have to discuss this testimony with the jury at the conclusion of the case. It is not at all unknown for a witness to give an entirely different impression at trial than he gives in his deposition even though his trial testimony is fully consistent with his deposition testimony. Many witnesses are simply nervous. Others are intimidated by testifying in a courtroom before a judge and a jury. Either instance can cause a witness to appear uncertain or untruthful, impressions which may be directly contrary to those given at the deposition. In any case a witness's bearing and the impression he gives is important and you cannot be aware of it if you are following the testimony by reading the witness's deposition.

A trial produces intense emotion. The judicial process has ways of controlling any improprieties which may arise in court. Once outside the courtroom, however, things can get out of hand. For this reason it is wise not to fraternize with your opposing counsel. This means that it is generally advisable to avoid talking with or even approaching him while outside of the courtroom in order to prevent the possibility of an untoward exchange.

More experienced lawyers may have things better under control and need not concern themselves about such exchanges with their opposing counsel. Still, they generally do not fraternize with them in the presence or observation of the jury; there is a school of thought that suggests jurors may draw an adverse inference if counsel is seen fraternizing with an adversary.

To the extent that you can do so, you will need to relax and follow the case with interest and enjoyment. It is important that you convey to the jury a sense of confidence and equanimity. If you exhibit apprehension or concern, you may reveal a sense of uncertainty as to the virtue of your case. You may unintentionally telegraph to the jury that you do not believe that yours is the winning side. Your demeanor may speak more persuasively than your argument.

Never Miss Sleep

The trial of a lawsuit can be physically and emotionally draining. It is necessary to be fully rested at the commencement of each day's trial. Do not miss sleep. Allow an absolute minimum of eight hours for this. If additional research or preparing motions or other pleadings is necessary, have someone else do it. Loss of sleep is never helpful. Prolonged loss of sleep affects one's judgment; a person whose judgment is not sound cannot responsibly try a lawsuit.

Moreover, at the beginning of the case you say to the jury in your opening statement, "At the conclusion of all the evidence in this case, I'm going to ask you to return a verdict in favor of my client and against my opponent and I fully expect you to do so." If, then, at the conclusion of the case, you stand before the same jury and argue for their verdict while at the same time having dark circles under your eyes and looking exhausted, you will not appear to be the same relaxed and confident advocate you were at the beginning. Your appearance can defeat anything you may say.

To remain in command of yourself it is necessary to organize your time rigorously during a trial. This is particularly so if the case is going to take a week or more to try. You will find that the demands on your time are such that you wish you had a forty-eight hour day. Some things will have to be done in much less time than you would prefer. The simple fact is that you never have as much time as you would like when you are involved in a trial. Nevertheless, somewhere throughout all of this you should have some time to yourself. You should read the newspaper and be aware of what is going on in the world. You should get some exercise and not think about your case all the time. This will enable you to step back and see the case in better perspective. It can also enhance your appearance and demeanor.

Some lawyers feel that it is necessary to order what is called "daily copy" from the court reporter attending the trial. This transcription of the prior day's proceedings delivered to your office by 9:00 the following morning is usually a waste of time and money. Since you do not have time to conduct a trial and at the same time read over the transcript of the previous day's proceedings, there is no advantage in having it available. It either becomes a distraction or is totally ignored. You can keep your own record of the important admissions, concessions and statements for reference in your closing argument.

Moreover, it is improper to quote or read from the transcript in your closing argument because it has not been reviewed by your opponent or certified as to its correctness by the trial judge. However, if there is a special passage or an important series of concessions on cross-examination that you wish to examine more carefully, it may be appropriate to order only that portion of the trial transcript written.

Preparing For Your Closing Argument

Contrary to common belief, you don't want your case, including your opening statement and closing argument, to go so smoothly as to appear rehearsed. Rather, you want it to appear natural, spontaneous. Jurors suspect that which appears too rehearsed as being contrived and false.

The best time for reducing and summarizing the trial proceedings is in the evening of each day. You should take only the most important parts of the testimony of each witness and write them in a separate note pad to be used for the outline of your closing argument. Never wait to do this until the end of the week, or worse, until the end of the trial. If you do, you will find that you cannot remember the witnesses very well and cannot understand your own notes of their testimony.

Keeping notes on cross-examination can be done by an associate or assistant, particularly since you cannot and should not take notes while cross-examining. At day's end your associate can give you his notes of your cross-examination to incorporate with your own summary. Look for the vivid expression, the particular phrase or word choice or gesture that may be used to your advantage in your closing argument; understand that persuasive points can come as often from an adverse witness as from your own. Your closing may be more telling if you quote from an opposing witness, thus making his testimony the basis of your argument.

The trial of jury cases involves winning and losing. No one wins all the time. Winning exhilarates; losing discourages. "If you can meet with Triumph and Disaster and treat those two impostors just the same,"[1] you can go from a loss to a win and from a win to a loss. Play each game and try each case as if it were your last.

[1] *These lines by Kipling are inscribed over the doors to the center court at Wimbledon.*

Chapter Two

Commencing the Trial

Truth, the mother of justice.

— Coke, *Second Institute*, 524 (1628)

Before a case is reached for trial there is a complex and convoluted world of investigation, interrogation, document production and deposition, referred to generally as "discovery." Because the vast majority of lawsuits, perhaps 98 percent, are settled before trial, and this book deals with only the actual trial process, there will be no attempt to cover the pre-trial discovery procedures nor the maneuvering involved in discovery and motions prior to trial. Matters developed by discovery, however, must be given full consideration in the preparation of your case.

There is an important difference between "litigators" and trial lawyers: all trial lawyers are litigators, but all litigators are not trial lawyers. Litigators settle their cases as they approach or reach trial. There is nothing wrong with this. Since the vast majority of cases are settled before trial, the litigation process serves the important function of revealing to the parties to a suit certain weaknesses in their cases, thus encouraging the litigants to be more reasonable about settlement.

Trial lawyers try cases to verdict. Nevertheless, most often settlement discussions are entered into before trial, continue during the trial of a case, and may well go on after a verdict has been returned and while the case is on appeal. Things that occur during the trial have a direct effect on those negotiations.

* * * * * *

Two businessmen were involved in a lawsuit and one of them was represented during the trial by two attorneys. The other was represented by a single attorney, and he was concerned by the fact that his lawyer was outnumbered. He kept bringing up the discrepancy and his lawyer, who felt the case was going well, repeatedly reassured him. Nevertheless, he continued expressing his concerns. Finally, his exasperated lawyer asked, "What is the problem?" "The problem," he replied, "is that there are two of them and only one of you. When one of them is talking, the other one is thinking. But when you're talking, no one is thinking."

* * * * * *

Because the author's principal trial experience has been in the state and federal courts of Cook County, Illinois, that will serve as the scene for the various trial practices discussed and described. The jury trial process throughout the United States is essentially the same and the elements that come into play in the course of a trial are quite similar.

Parties

There are often multiple parties to a lawsuit. There can also be:

- Counterclaims — A defendant counter sues a plaintiff.
- Cross claims — A defendant files a complaint against another party defendant.
- Third party claims — A defendant impleads into the suit by a separate complaint a party not a party to the original suit.

For clarity and simplicity, all references in this book will be to a suit in which a single party plaintiff brings suit against a single party defendant.

The parties to a lawsuit and their lawyers are entitled to be present at all stages of the litigation. In the case of a corporate party, it is represented through an appropriate officer or employee of the corporation.

Court Personnel

In addition to the judge, court personnel includes a clerk and a bailiff. The clerk maintains the court docket and files, and also may act in the capacity of a secretary to the judge. The bailiff's responsibility involves keeping order in the court, taking care of the jury, and handling related matters the judge may ask of him. The clerk administers oaths to the jury and the various witnesses, and is usually the person to whom the verdict is handed by the jury foreman. There is a court reporter who transcribes the proceedings and also marks exhibits in the course of trial.

Court Rooms

Two tables for the attorneys and the parties are provided and are generally placed end to end lengthwise facing the jury box from across the courtroom. On the far side of each table are three chairs, two for the attorney and his associate and the third for the client. Traditionally, the plaintiff and his attorney occupy the counsel table closest to the judge's bench. This is considered to be a subtle advantage.

In federal courtrooms the tables are placed side by side in front of the judge's bench and there are four chairs on each side of each table. In that configuration the plaintiff occupies the table closest to the jury box. That is considered an even greater advantage, creating the "us against them" concept: the "us" in this case being the jury and the plaintiff and his attorney, the "them" being the defendant and his attorney.

Jury Selection

Traditionally, the jury consists of twelve jurors and its verdict must be unanimous. In a few jurisdictions verdicts of ten to two or nine to three are now the rule. Illinois follows the traditional rule of a twelve juror unanimous verdict. In the federal courts the jury consists of six rather than twelve jurors. At some point, usually before the jury selection process begins, the Court will inquire of counsel if they can agree to the return of a verdict of no fewer than ten jurors, or whether they would prefer to choose an additional two jurors, since one or two jurors may become ill, or for some other compelling reason be unable to serve throughout the entire trial. It seems the preferable choice to agree to a verdict of no fewer than ten jurors. The other choice requires two additional chairs and puts a strain on the jury room which is designed for the use of twelve rather than fourteen jurors. Nevertheless, a verdict of ten jurors must still be unanimous.

The jury selection process, *voir dire*,[1] is commenced by bringing in the jury venire. The jury venire consists of some thirty to forty prospective jurors. It is hoped the parties will be able to choose twelve out of that group who will constitute the jury for the case. If it becomes necessary, additional prospective jurors are available.

The jury venire is first seated at the rear of the courtroom. The judge welcomes them and makes them comfortable. He tells them the names of the parties to the case and informs them in a general way of the nature of the suit. This may often be by a brief statement which has been agreed to in advance by the attorneys. The judge next introduces the parties, or, when a corporation is involved, its representative, and the lawyers for the parties. If any of the prospective jurors know any of the parties or the attorneys they are excused. (This is not done in smaller jurisdictions where it is impractical.) If any of the prospective jurors have a suit pending in the Circuit Court of Cook County they are excused. Certain other initial circumstances may cause a few others to be excused.

The names and juror numbers of twelve of those remaining are called by the clerk or bailiff from jury cards. These cards are furnished to the Court by the administrator of the Circuit Court of Cook County from information furnished by the individual jurors when they are first called for jury duty. They are filled out by each individual prospective juror with pertinent information such as employment, marital status, etc.

When twelve persons have been seated in the jury box, the judge commences his questioning of the first panel of four jurors, the first two in the first row and the first two in the second row. The jury is

[1] *Fr. To speak the truth. This phrase denotes the preliminary examination which the Court may make of one presented as a juror.*

customarily divided into three panels of four each, for the convenience of the jury, the Court, and counsel. As jurors are excused they are replaced by other prospective jurors already in the jury box; they, in turn, are replaced from the venire in the back of the courtroom. When a prospective juror is excused, the others simply move over.

Challenges

There are two ways in which prospective jurors can be excused, (a) preemptory challenges, and (b) challenges for cause. Preemptory challenges are exercised by the attorneys and are based on the attorney's view that a particular juror might not be favorable to his side of the case. In Illinois, the number of preemptory challenges given to each party to a civil lawsuit is five, although the Court may allow a few additional challenges under certain circumstances. A challenge for cause is exercised by the Court, usually by agreement of counsel, and is based on the appearance in a prospective juror of an inability to be impartial or to be otherwise unable to serve on the case.

After the Court has completed its questioning of a panel, the panel is turned over to the lawyers for their questioning. The Court hands the four jury cards to the clerk who gives them to the plaintiff's attorney. The plaintiff always goes first. If a challenge is exercised and a juror is replaced, the attorney exercising the challenge asks the general qualifying questions of the new juror. Ordinarily the questioning does not go back to the judge until the next panel is reached. The plaintiff's lawyer completes his questions and exercises any challenges. When satisfied with a given panel, he "accepts" it on behalf of the plaintiff, and "tenders" it to the defendant's attorney, with the words, "Your Honor, the plaintiff accepts this panel and tenders it to the defendant." He hands the jury cards to the defendant's attorney, who then interrogates the panel.

If no new jurors are placed on the panel in the course of the defendant attorney's questions (no one is challenged), he "accepts" the panel, and it is sworn (an oath is administered) and sent to the jury room. The jury cards are handed back to the clerk. The Court commences questioning the next panel.

If one or more prospective jurors are excused by the defendant's attorney, and new members of a panel are seated, the panel is "accepted" by him, and is "tendered" back to the plaintiff's attorney. The defendant's attorney hands the jury cards to the plaintiff's attorney who may then ask additional questions and exercise challenges. His challenges are not limited to the newly seated jurors. When the defendant's attorney tenders the panel back, the plaintiff's attorney has the right to challenge those jurors who were on the panel he had accepted earlier. This is sometimes called "back-striking." The questioning and challenging process goes on until both attorneys accept a panel. The panel is then sworn, sent to the jury room and the Court begins questioning the next panel.

In a number of jurisdictions the jury is selected as a whole and not divided into panels. This means that if the jury as constituted is accepted by one party and tendered to the other party and that party then excuses a juror, the entire jury is open for challenges. The fact that you may not have challenged a juror in the first instance does not preclude you from doing so if your opposing counsel excuses one or more jurors and tenders the jury back to you.

Judge's Questioning

While they differ from one another in many ways, trial judges all cover certain basic areas of inquiry in putting questions to individual jurors. These involve questions as to whether the jurors or their relatives or close friends have been involved in a lawsuit, whether they have ever appeared in a courtroom for any reason, whether or not they were ever involved in making a claim against someone, or whether someone has made a claim against them. The judge customarily inquires as to whether the nature of the case, which has already been briefly described, would prevent them from being fair and impartial.

The prospective jurors are questioned as to whether they will be able to wait until all the evidence is in before reaching any opinions or conclusions. They are asked if they will be able to follow the law as given to the jury by the Court, even though they may not like it, or may even disagree with it. They are asked about their present and past employment and that of their relatives, including not only their spouses, but their parents and children, and often the employment of their brothers and sisters. Some judges ask whether there is any reason that they feel they could not serve as a juror. Other judges do not use this question because it may be interpreted as an opportunity to avoid serving. Somewhere in the series of questions each juror is asked whether he or she can decide the case without sympathy or prejudice and give both sides a fair hearing.

The responses to these questions prompt additional questions and, as a result, the qualifying of a jury can be a tedious and time-consuming process. To set out the questions of the trial judge and the answers of more than a few jurors would take more space than would be practical. Nevertheless, set out at some length in the next chapter are examples of actual questioning of jurors by the trial judge and by the lawyers representing each of the two parties. The repetitive nature of the questions necessarily put to each prospective juror will be noted.

Since there is so much myth and pretense about the selection of a jury, it should be observed that most questions are common and unspectacular. Certain questions cannot be asked: "What political party do you belong to? How did you vote in the last election?" Still other questions, though technically not improper, cannot be asked because they may seem too personal or offensive for some other reason.

Chapter Three

Impaneling the Jury

The jury has the power to bring in a verdict in the teeth of both law and facts.

— Holmes, J., *Horning v.District of Columbia*, 224 U.S. 135, 138 (1920)

The process of impaneling the twelve jurors who will sit on the case is most commonly referred to as "picking the jury." This phrase is inaccurate and misleading. By the use of challenges, the attorneys for the parties are able to eliminate by "challenging" or "excusing" some of those jurors they do not want to sit on the jury. So you do not in fact "pick" the jury. Rather, you choose by elimination. But because of the limited number of your challenges, your choice is restricted.

On occasion the entire jury venire may not appeal to you. One quick glance can tell you that this is not a group which is sympathetic to your side of the case, a circumstance which makes the entire selection process unappealing and considerably dicey and one which could cause you to begin immediately to re-evaluate your case and your trial tactics. Before you can spend much time on that, though, the prospective jurors are called, placed in the jury box, and the Court begins questioning the first panel. You list the names of those called, watch, listen and make notes.

Desirability of Jurors

At the risk of oversimplifying, in the case where there is evidence of contributory negligence by the plaintiff (his own act caused or contributed to cause the accident), and the injuries are severe, the attorney for the plaintiff is looking for sympathetic, non-judgmental jurors. A person who is easily moved by the misfortune of another and is reluctant to hold an injured person responsible for being a cause of his own injuries would be very appealing. Such a juror would be inclined either not to consider or to discount the evidence of the plaintiff's own fault for the occurrence.

The attorney for the defendant, on the other hand, is looking for a hard-headed, practical juror who has made his way over obstacles and difficulties in his life. He wants someone who will take the view that a person at fault for his own injuries should not recover any damages but must bear responsibility for the consequences of his own acts no matter how severe those consequences.

First Impressions

Lawyers gain a number of immediate impressions about prospective jurors in the course of the questioning by the Court. They may decide in favor or against certain jurors in the course of those questions. Nevertheless, the lawyers will still put questions to each juror. On occasion a juror will admit to being unable to be impartial and will be excused for cause. And repeating your questions to each juror will solidify your concerns about your side receiving a fair trial in the minds of the other prospective jurors.

Various considerations go into the decision to excuse a juror. They are based on the lawyer's perception of how certain jurors may react to his view of the case. A successful defense of a product liability case (the product is allegedly inherently dangerous because of faulty design or manufacture), for example, may rest almost entirely on the extent to which the jury understands some very technical mechanical concepts. Accordingly, unless qualification questions prove otherwise, the defense attorney may reason that prospective jurors who are not generally considered adept at grasping such mechanical technicalities be excused.

Decisions may be made on the basis of a juror's occupation, education, age and marital status. The evaluation process includes race, gender and national and ethnic origin. Of course there are exceptions to every rule, and in the process of questioning prospective jurors attorneys can change their initial impressions and accept some jurors they first had intended to excuse, and vice versa.

As jurors are excused and the roll of prospective jurors in the back of the courtroom diminishes, you may also factor the appearance of the remaining prospective jurors into your decision whether or not to exercise a challenge. If they look as if they might be sympathetic to your side of the case, you might choose to challenge. If they do not look sympathetic, you may chose not to challenge.

Exercising Challenges

There are a number of common and troublesome problems in exercising a challenge. For instance, the juror replacing the one you just excused may be found to be far worse than the one he replaced. Thus you may be compelled to use not one challenge but two. You have lost ground. You must husband your challenges and at the same time not be reluctant to exercise them when necessary. Both sides often see nothing to dislike in the same prospective juror. Those are the ones who remain. When either side favors a prospective juror, that juror will usually be excused by the opposing side. The jury selection process is never easy and at its end no one is certain just what the mixture will produce.

You should never be caught with no challenges left when the last panel is reached. While this is not an absolute rule, you must recognize that a prospective juror in the final panel may respond to a question in a way that reveals something adverse to your side of the case. With no challenges left, if the information does not furnish the basis for a challenge for cause, you are stuck with that juror.

Be sure you listen to the questions asked by the judge and ask follow-up questions about things that occur to you in the course of the judge's questioning. You should be asking about matters that you are simply curious about. Every question should not be momentous. You are simply getting acquainted. Do not over-intellectualize the process.

Certain sensitive areas must sometimes be touched upon in *voir dire* to preclude the possibility of unknowingly accepting jurors with some bias which could prejudice them against your client or your case. Suppose the plaintiff was struck by an automobile which drove off the street and onto the sidewalk where he was standing. Suppose further that he had had a few drinks before the accident. While it may be clear from the facts that his drinking contributed nothing to the occurrence, his attorney must nevertheless ask questions of the jury to identify those prospective jurors who have feelings against the use of alcohol. If a juror readily admits to such a feeling, he can be excused for cause. If a juror appears equivocal, it might be best to excuse him by using a preemptory challenge. This is the manner in which these questions can be raised:

> Q: I believe there will be evidence that the plaintiff had been drinking at a bar shortly before the accident. Do you have any feelings against people having a drink or two?

> Q: I believe the evidence will also show that the drinking had nothing to do with the occurrence. In your consideration of who was responsible for the accident, could you set aside any consideration of the plaintiff's drinking to the extent that it might adversely affect you in being objective about the actual cause of the accident?

At the beginning you should keep it simple, but as you become more experienced you can do more sophisticated things in picking a jury. An example of a level of sophistication that few lawyers achieve, and fewer still should even attempt, may be found in the following story about James A. Dooley, a well known plaintiff's personal injury attorney, who later served on the Supreme Court of Illinois.

* * * * * *

The case involved serious burns to a locomotive engine repairman who received his injuries while re-lighting a fire in a coal burning stove located in a locomotive repair area. The accident was caused by an explosion of gasoline put on the allegedly cold coals of the fire before the attempt to reignite it. The cause of the explosion was critical to the determination of liability.

After he had exercised one of his challenges, Mr. Dooley was examining the new member of the jury panel who had just been seated. The initial information was that the man was a professional chemist with a master's degree in chemical engineering. Clearly this was a juror who would dominate any discussion of causation of the explosion. This was a man whom the plaintiff's attorney did not want on the jury; the defendant's attorney most definitely did. After other information had been developed, Dooley stepped over behind his opposing counsel and whispered, "Do you like this guy?" Surprised and flattered by the attention of the old war-horse, the opposing counsel nodded a vigorous affirmative. Dooley returned to his own table and asked a few more questions of the prospective juror. He then turned to the judge and said, "Your honor, we will excuse this juror."

It would be some time before the opposing counsel realized that in nodding his head affirmatively to the whispered question, he appeared to be agreeing with Dooley that the chemist should be excused. The "we" in "we will excuse this juror," usually meaning the attorney and his client, was interpreted by the jurors in this situation to mean that opposing counsel and Dooley had agreed to excuse the juror.

* * * * * *

Unexpected, often amusing things happen in the jury selection process. A jury was being selected in a case pending in New York City. The judge was conducting the preliminary examination of a young woman. Looking at her jury card on which she had written her occupation as "actor" he questioned her as follows:

Q: It says here that you are an act*ress*?

A: Act*or*!

Q: Well . . . could you please tell me the difference?

A: Could you please tell me what you call a lady judge?

* * * * * *

Judges

It is important to understand that every judge is different from every other judge; no two are the same. When you are in their courtroom, you do things their way—not the way you think they should be done, nor the way they are done in some other judge's courtroom—you do them the way the judge whose courtroom you are in wants them to be done. In that judge's courtroom, that way is the right way.

The following is an extended excerpt from the jury selection process in

Mohler v. Blanchette, et. al,[1] which was tried before the Honorable Irving R. Norman in the state court in Chicago, and which illustrates how the Court and the attorneys for the parties participate in the selection of the jury.

THE COURT: Mr. Clerk, fill the panel.

THE CLERK: 1822, 2225, 2224, 1823.
2123, 2806, 2120, 2303.
2804, 1858, 2219, 1879.

(The other 25 or so prospective jurors remain seated in the back of the courtroom).

THE COURT: Good afternoon, ladies and gentlemen. This courtroom, Room 2404, is where you will be reporting unless discharged or otherwise excused.

First of all, permit me to offer my thanks to you for your willingness to give the benefit of your time to help us resolve the matter that is presently pending before this Court. I don't think it would be an unfair assumption on my part if I were to suggest that when you first received your summons to appear for jury service, you were not particularly pleased about the idea. And this is understandable.

We recognize, of course, that it can be an inconvenience to take time away from your jobs, your businesses, families and your everyday activities, to come into the strange surroundings of a courtroom and give us your time. We recognize that and thank you for it. I think I can safely assure you, however, that by the time you have completed your service, your tour of duty, you will consider it a most rewarding and satisfying experience. Consider this, if you will: that there is no place throughout the civilized world, other than this country, where a citizen is granted the privilege of sitting in judgment on his fellow man. And that is the true test of it. We try to make your experience as comfortable as we can for you, as has already been demonstrated today.

[1] *106 Ill.App. 3rd 545, 435 N.E.2d 1161 (1982).*

Cases are not tried with any mathematical certainty. Unfortunately, there are delays from time to time. There will be some delays, perhaps, in waiting for witnesses. We try to accommodate witnesses, some of whom may have to travel great distances to get to court. It is difficult to know how long the witness will remain on the witness stand. So, in our efforts to accommodate people, we do incur some delays. We'll try to keep them to a minimum as it is certainly not our intention to prolong these proceedings.

Do any of you ladies and gentlemen, in or out of the jury box, have any religious or moral scruples against anyone who seeks medical aid and treatment as a result of injury or disease? If the answer to that is in the affirmative, would you please indicate.

By your silence, I take it that none of you have any such feelings.

Ladies and gentlemen, I have a few general observations, which I should like to clarify with you first. As most of you probably know, the party who brings a lawsuit into court is designated as a plaintiff. The party against whom the lawsuit is brought is designated as a defendant. I would like to introduce you, very briefly, to the nature of this lawsuit and the parties who are involved in it. To begin with, it arises out of an occurrence that took place on December 28, 1967.

This is a civil lawsuit for money damages. The plaintiff in this case is a lady named Virginia Mohler. And I believe that is the lady seated at the first counsel table.

MR. HAYES: It is, your Honor.

THE COURT: She brings this suit in her capacity as the Administrator of the Estate of Harold Mohler, deceased, who was her husband. Under the law, when a party is deceased, a lawsuit in his behalf can only be brought by a legal representative, known as an administrator. And Mrs. Mohler has been appointed administrator, and acts in that capacity. She brings this suit in her capacity, then, as the Administrator of the Estate of her husband Harold Mohler, deceased, and also brings it not only on behalf of herself, individually, as the surviving spouse or wife of Harold Mohler, but also on behalf of their surviving children. Their names are Kathleen, Caroline, Thomas, William, Lee, Mary Jo, and Michael, the children of the decedent.

The defendant in this case is the Trustee of the Penn Central Transportation Company, into which the New York Central Railroad merged following the events in this case; and which later was merged into the Consolidated Railway Corporation, which is commonly known as Conrail. Perhaps that name is familiar to many of you. And so the defendant, commonly referred to as Conrail, is accountable for whatever liability or responsibility, if any there is, which may have been that of the New York Central Railroad, which was in existence at the time of the occurrence that I related to you.

The plaintiff, Mrs. Mohler, on her own behalf, and on behalf of the Estate and further on behalf of the children whose names you've heard me mention, claims that on the date December 28, 1967, her husband Harold Mohler was then employed as a brakeman by the New York Central Railroad Company and that on that day while he was engaged in the performance of his duties within the caboose of the train near a town called Reddick, Illinois, the coupler on the train failed to function properly, causing the train to separate into two parts and automatically bringing the train to a stop. She claims, further, that as a result of that occurrence her husband was injured. She claims further that on January the 19th, 1968, her husband passed away. Very briefly and very generally, it is then the claim of Mrs. Mohler that the injuries and death of her husband were caused in whole or in part by the occurrence which I've related to you, and that occurrence is the failure of the coupler to function properly.

That, generally is the basis of their claim.

The defendant railroad has denied all of the allegations or charges which I've just related to you, and thus, we have a lawsuit. We're going to ask the twelve of you who will be selected, to judge for the benefit of all of the parties.

You will recall that I mentioned earlier that the events in this occurrence took place in December of 1967 and that the death of Mr. Mohler occurred in January of 1968. The fact that this case comes before a court and jury for trial now, in 1980, is not and should not be a matter with which you should concern yourselves. Suffice it to say, the reasons for the delay had nothing to do with the merits of the case. I instruct you, therefore, that you are not to speculate upon the reasons nor allow your determination of the facts in this case to be in any way influenced by the recital of the facts that I've just given you. If any of you are selected as jurors in this case, would you be willing to accept that proposition which I've placed before you?[2]

Would anyone refuse to accept that proposition? I take it, by your silence, that none of you have a problem with that.

That, ladies and gentlemen, of course, is a very brief outline of the nature of this proceeding. The attorneys, at a more appropriate time, will have an opportunity to give you further details of what they feel the evidence will present to you. But, at this time, by way of identifying the parties, and the nature of the case, that is all that the Court is prepared to place before you now.

The plaintiff, Mrs. Mohler, in her own behalf and as administrator of her husband's estate, as well as on behalf of the children, whose names I've mentioned, are represented by attorney John Hayes, the counsel at the first table.

MR. HAYES: (standing) Thank you, your Honor.

THE COURT: Defendant railroad is represented by attorney Cornelius Callahan.

MR. CALLAHAN: (standing) Good morning.

THE COURT: Do any of you ladies and gentlemen know Mrs. Mohler, the decedent, or know any of those whose names I've mentioned, or any of the children whose names you've heard me mention? Do any of you know anyone connected, in any capacity or way, with either the New York Central, Penn Central Railroad, or Conrail?

By your silence I take it that none of you know anyone connected either with the plaintiff or her family or with the defendant or its predecessors.

[2] *The plaintiff's complaint was originally filed in 1970. In 1974, the Circuit Court entered an order dismissing the case for want of prosecution. The order of dismissal granted leave to the plaintiff to refile the action within one year. Plaintiff refiled in 1975 and the case reached trial in 1980.*

Do any of you ladies and gentlemen know either of the attorneys who you see present here in court? Again, by your silence I take it that none of you know any of the attorneys. In our efforts, ladies and gentlemen, to secure twelve people who can be fair to both sides, we find that that is a very good start.

I'm sure that most or all of you have experienced, through the medium of television or the motion picture screen, dramatic portrayals of trials or courtroom scenes. And while, depending upon one's point of view, they may serve as entertainment, I assure you that very little of what is portrayed on the television or motion picture screen is an accurate representation of a trial in an American court of law under prescribed rules of evidence.

I'm sure, also, that most if not all of you know that during the course of trial lawyers will make objections to evidence which they address to the Court. It is not only a lawyer's right to do so, but it's their sworn obligation to their client to object to evidence if they feel that it is being offered improperly or contrary to our rules. And so you are asked not to keep a scorecard, as it were, to determine which lawyer makes more objections than the other, because that will have absolutely no bearing on the case.

As I informed you a few moments ago, counsel and I were engaged in some preliminary discussion. We do this so that they can acquaint the Court with the nature of this lawsuit. As a result of these discussions, I'm informed, and I can inform you that this case may take most or all your duty this next ten day, or two-week period. Consequently, for those of you who will be selected as jurors, if you should encounter either of the parties or their representatives or the attorneys during recess or after adjournment time, in any of the public corridors or elevators of Daley Center, or perhaps during a noon recess in any of the restaurants, and they don't engage in conversation, please do not be offended. They are simply following the rules. They are required to refrain from doing so.

The functions of the Court and jury, ladies and gentlemen, are divided by our rules. It will be my responsibility to pass on all propositions of law as they are involved in this proceeding. It will be the responsibility of the twelve of you, who will be asked to serve as jurors, to be judges no less than I, except that you will be judging the facts of the case. And that is the sharp division of our responsibilities. The law is presented to this side of the bench, and the facts will be presented to that side of the jury bar. And, of course, the facts will be given to you by way of testimony from witnesses who will be testifying from this witness chair to my right, or from any documents or exhibits offered for the consideration of the jury.

It goes without saying, ladies and gentlemen, that we recognize that you come to us from various backgrounds and experiences. While I'm on the subject, perhaps you may be interested in knowing how you come to us as prospective jurors. Your names are selected at random from the registered voting list in Cook County. And because the process is in that form, perhaps you may have members of your own family or neighbors, perhaps some of you have been called to jury service several times, while others may live here a lifetime and never be called at all. It's kind of "the luck of the draw." No one has ever claimed that the system under which we operate is a perfect one, as is nothing that is manmade. But until someone develops something better, it's been working pretty well for a couple of hundred years.

Perhaps some of you may have questions. Unfortunately, the rules do not permit me to respond to them at this time. But I think I can assure you that, as we proceed, they will be answered satisfactorily with the proceedings that will follow immediately. As I started to say, because you come to us from various backgrounds and experiences, we're permitted under the rules to put questions to you dealing with those backgrounds and dealing with your experiences. Admittedly, many of the questions which will be put to you by the Court and counsel may appear to be personal, and indeed they are. But you have my assurance that it is neither our purpose nor intention to embarrass or offend anyone. You will soon see these questions are quite necessary.

As you may know, a jury is divided into sections. We call them panels. And the first panel will consist of two gentlemen in the first row, and two ladies in the second row; the second, the middle four, and the third panel, the last four. There's no particular reason for this, except that it serves everyone's convenience to talk to four people at one time rather than to talk to twelve, which would be quite burdensome.

We're going to be asking each of you ladies and gentlemen in connection with your background and experiences about any accidents or injuries or claims that you or members of your families have been involved in through the years. If in fact you have experienced such occurrences, and it has been some years since it happened, it is possible that it may have slipped your minds. While we're talking to the first juror, the rest of you will have an opportunity to search your minds about those experiences of yours and your families.

That concludes the general remarks I wanted to make at this time. Again, I invite you to be as comfortable as you can. If it gets too cold or too hot in the courtroom, I want you to know that we're quite aware of it. We have been trying for a long time to have it adjusted. They've had some difficulty. I trust that you will not be too unduly inconvenienced.

Thank you ladies and gentlemen.

HELEN SKYE, called as a juror herein, having been first duly sworn, was examined and testified as follows:

VOIR DIRE EXAMINATION BY THE COURT (referring to the jury card):

Q. This lady is Mrs. Helen—is that Skye, S-k-y-e?

A. Yes.

Q. Thank you. And your address, ma'am, is 1918 West Armitage Avenue?

A. Yes, sir.

Q. That is in Chicago?

A. Yes, sir.

Q. Mrs. Skye, you are employed at the Sun Electric Company as an inspector?

A. Yes, sir.

Q. And you have been there for ten years?

A. Yes, sir.

Q. I notice that you recorded here that you are a widowed lady?

A. Yes.

Q. I notice that. And with regret, ma'am, permit me to ask some questions. I don't mean to recall the incident but I'm required to put some questions to you. I hope you don't mind my doing so. What was the nature of Mr. Skye's work?

A. He was a painter.

Q. Was he a painting contractor, or was he employed by a painting company?

A. He was employed by a contractor.

Q. Is that as a house painter, or was he employed in the construction industry?

A. The construction.

Q. For how long had he been doing that kind of work?

A. Oh, maybe ten years.

Q. Did he work on commercial buildings rather than houses or homes?

A. More on commercial buildings.

Q. Do you know the name of the contractor who employed him?

A. No, I don't.

Q. May I ask whether his death was natural or accidental?

A. Natural.

Q. You have two children, ages thirty-five and thirty-six, ma'am?

A. Yes, sir.

Q. Can you tell us briefly what they do?

A. The oldest is an art teacher in California.

Q. An art teacher?

A. In California.

Q. Is that a lady, the oldest, a lady?

A. No, they're both boys.

Q. Yes, ma'am. And the younger one?

A. The younger one is an electronic technician.

Q. Employed by whom?

A. Right now he's not working.

Q. Okay. Does he have some academic degree in electronics or anything of that nature? Is he an electronic engineer?

A. Yes.

Q. Did he get a degree in school on that?

A. No, just worked himself up.

Q. I see, and as an inspector, what kind of products do you work on, ma'am?

A. Automotive parts, circuit boards.

Q. Okay. With reference to the matter of injuries or claims we have been talking about, what has been your experience in your family? Have you yourself ever been injured in any way?

A. No.

Q. Have you ever been injured on the job in any way?

A. No.

Q. How about during his lifetime, Mr. Skye, was he ever injured on the job or in any other fashion?

A. No.

Q. May I ask when was it that he passed away?

A. In '58.

Q. And the two children, have they ever been injured in any way at all?

A. No.

Q. Have you made a lawsuit, a claim, or a lawsuit filed against a party for any reason?

A. No.

Q. Have you ever been called to jury service before?

A. Yes.

Q. When was that?

A. About ten years ago.

Q. Was that in this building here?

A. No, I don't quite remember.

Q. All right. Was it in the downtown area, or was it 26th and California in the Criminal—

A. Probably was the downtown area.

Q. Did you serve on any cases?

A. No.

Q. Never got that far?

A. No.

Q. You see, you're making progress already. What happened, were you excused from service at that time?

A. Yes.

Q. At your request?

A. Yes, sir.

Q. So then you never actually served as a juror before, is that right?

A. Yes.

Q. This is first time you've actually been in a courtroom then as a prospective juror?

A. Right.

Q. Are there any doctors or lawyers in your family?

A. No.

Q. Or among your circle of friends?

A. No.

Q. Do you know now or have you in the past known any relatives or friends who were ever employed by a railroad in any capacity?

A. No, sir.

Q. Do you yourself on occasion ride the Conrail trains or cars?

A. Some years back, yes.

Q. Okay. Did you ever have any occasion to ride on the New York Central or the Penn Central?

A. New York Central.

Q. Okay. I take it that that was on more than one occasion. Was that frequently?

A. Yes—no, it's been twenty years ago.

Q. How often would you ride the train those years?

A. Oh, several times to Buffalo, New York.

Q. Buffalo, New York?

A. Uhm, uhm.

Q. Was there anything about those experiences which you feel might be carried over into this lawsuit?

A. No.

Q. Is there anything about this case that I have related so far, Mrs. Skye, which you feel would prevent you from sitting fairly for both sides?

A. No.

Q. If you're asked to sit as a juror, are you the kind of person who's willing to wait until you've heard all of the evidence for both sides before deciding who's right and who's wrong?

A. Yes, sir, I would.

Q. That seems like a fair enough proposition, doesn't it?

A. Sure does.

Q. Would you agree that that is the way a controversy should be decided after you hear both sides?

A. Yes.

Q. Would you be willing to do that if asked to sit as a juror?

A. Yes, sir.

Q. Now, if Mrs. Mohler on her behalf and on behalf of the estate of her husband proves her case against the railroad, is there any reason why you couldn't sign your name to a verdict in her favor?

A. No.

Q. If she failed to prove her case against the railroad, is there any reason why you couldn't sign a verdict for the railroad. Isn't that a fair way to do it?

A. Right.

Q. You don't come to us with any preconceived ideas about how this case should turn out before you'd heard anything about it, do you?

A. No.

Q. All right. The fact that the decedent, Mr. Mohler, was employed by a railroad and that railroad is now being sued by his wife on behalf of her family, does that start you out with some kind of feeling one way or another?

A. No.

Q. As you may know, the law that applies to this case will be given to the jury at the conclusion, at the end of the case. The rules provide that it be handled in that way.

Therefore, it's my obligation to ask each of the jurors if they would be willing to follow the law if selected as a juror when they hear it for the first time at the end of the case. Even though they hear it for the first time, they find that it is something perhaps they think ought to be changed or is something that is different from what they always thought it was, or, if you just plain don't even agree, would you nevertheless follow the law as given to the jury in this case by this Court?

A. Yes, sir.

Q. I can tell you that it would be your sworn obligation to do so; that would be no problem for you?

A. No.

Q. Why don't you sit back and relax. I'm sure that you recognize that we here in court don't make the law. The law is made in Springfield by the general assembly. And whether we like it or not, we are all obligated to follow the law, okay.

There are laws also made by Congress and the federal government. And if they apply to this case, we're all obligated to follow those laws. This is no problem for you?

A. No.

Q. Is there anything about your background or experience, which you think I ought to know insofar as your willingness and ability to sit fairly and impartially for both sides in this lawsuit?

A. No.

Q. Okay. Obviously, Mrs. Mohler is an individual lady. The defendant is a railroad corporation. In the eyes of the law, can you treat them equally?

A. Yes.

Q. Okay?

A. Yes, sir.

Q. We recognize that people come to us who have not spent their lives living in vacuums. We recognize that people have some prejudices, some biases in some degrees about some things. All of us do, I suppose.

But for the purposes of this lawsuit, whatever prejudices or biases you may have, may I ask you to set those aside so that you can judge this case based purely and simply on the evidence that is presented in this Court, from this witness stand, or whatever else is presented to this jury for determination in this case.

Can you do that?

A. I think so.

Q. Without regard to any other feelings?

A. I think so.

Q. Without regard to some sympathy for someone who has lost her husband, without regard to prejudice of any kind, because if we were to permit that to judge our feelings, without regard to the facts and the evidence of the law, we'd all be wasting our time.

Do you feel that you could judge this based on the facts and the law without regard to those human instincts we all have to some degree?

A. I think so.

Q. It may be asking a lot, but I have to ask you nevertheless if you can do it.

A. Yes, sir.

NATHANIEL BECK, a member of the panel of veniremen was examined as to his qualifications and testified as follows:

EXAMINATION BY THE COURT:

Q. This gentleman is Mr. Nathaniel Beck.

A. That's right, sir.

THE COURT: That's B-e-c-k, counsel.

Q. Your address, sir, is 10145 South Sangamon Street?

A. That's right.

Q. That's in Chicago, sir?

A. Yes, sir.

Q. You're married, sir?

A. Yes.

Q. And you're employed by the Ford Motor Company in Chicago as a supervisor?

A. That's right.

Q. You've been with them for thirty years, sir?

A. Yes, sir.

Q. And are you assigned to any particular department or division?

A. The skills trades department.

Q. What, sir?

A. The skills trades department.

Q. The skills trades department?

A.Right.

Q. Before becoming a supervisor, what other function did you have?

A. I was an electrician.

Q. For how long, sir?

A. Twelve years.

Q. Is that your basic trade?

A. That's right.

Q. Did you have some other function in the Ford Motor Company other than that?

A. Well, briefly as assembly.

Q. On the assembly line?

A. On the assembly line.

Q. And as a supervisor, how large a group of personnel do you have working under your supervision?

A. Roughly about seventeen people.

Q. Does Mrs. Beck have some employment outside the home?

A. No, just a housewife.

Q. All right. Has she had some employment in recent years?

A. No, sir.

Q. You have three children, sir?

A. That's right.

Q. Their ages are fourteen, seventeen and nineteen?

A. Right, sir.

Q. The nineteen year-old, would you tell us what he or she does, please?

A. She's in college right now.

Q. What school is she attending?

A. Georgetown University, Washington, D.C.

Q. And is she pursuing a major course of study there?

A. Mathematics.

Q. Mathematics?

A. Yes, sir.

Q. She's now in her first year, is she?

A. She's a sophomore.

Q. Sophomore? And the seventeen year-old?

A. She's in high school.

Q. I take it the fourteen year-old is also in school?

A. Right.

Q. Mr. Beck, through the years, what has been your experience, yours, Mrs. Beck's, or the children's, so far as injuries or claims of any kind are concerned?

A. Well, back in 1968, the whole family was in an accident. A truck hit the car.

Q. Were you driving the car?

A. Everybody except me, I'm sorry.

Q. You were not in the car?

A. I was not in the car.

Q. Who was driving?

A. My wife was driving.

Q. And the children were in the car?

A. That's right.

Q. Was this in the Chicago area?

A. Right, sir.

Q. Was it a collision between the truck and the vehicle in which your family was injured?

A. That's right, sir.

Q. Who was injured?

A. They were all injured.

Q. Slightly or seriously?

A. Slightly.

Q. Were they hospitalized?

A. For a brief time, about two days.

Q. When was it that this occurred?

A. 1968.

Q. Was there a lawsuit that arose?

A. There was a lawsuit.

Q. Did you retain an attorney to represent the interests of your family?

A. I did.

Q. Counsel would be interested in his name. Would you recall the name of the attorney?

A. An attorney by the name of Pritmore.

Q. Pritmore?

A. Right.

Q. Was that in the Chicago area?

A. Right.

Q. Was there a trial in court, or was it disposed of before trial?

A. No, it was disposed of.

Q. Was that disposed of to your satisfaction?

A. It was.

Q. Was it pending for some period of time before it was disposed of?

A. It was.

Q. Several years?

A. Several years.

Q. All right. And was it explained to you by your attorney that the delay was not his fault or the other side's fault?

A. Right.

Q. All right. Is the family all right now? Have they recovered from their injuries?

A. Very much, sir.

Q. Mrs. Beck has recovered from her injuries?

A. Yes, sir.

Q. Was that the only accident or injury experienced in your family that comes to mind?

A. That's the only one that I can recall right now.

Q. Have you yourself ever been injured in any way?

A. No.

Q. Ever been injured on the job?

A. Not seriously. Just small things.

Q. Were you ever injured on the job to the point where you were required to be away from work for any period of time?

A. No, sir.

Q. So that you never received any workmen's compensation benefits as a result of any injuries, did you?

A. No, sir.

Q. Is that the only claim you or members of your family have ever made against any other party?

A. Yes, sir.

Q. Has anyone ever made a claim against you, sir?

A. Not that I can recall.

Q. Have you or any members of your family ever worked for a railroad in any capacity?

A. No, sir.

Q. Is there anything that I have discussed so far about this case, who the parties are and briefly the nature of this lawsuit, that you feel as you sit there now would prevent you from sitting fairly and impartially for both sides?

A. No, sir.

Q. No question in your mind about that, is that right?

A. That's right, sir.

Q. And may I then assume from your response, Mr. Beck, that if Mrs. Mohler proves the case for the plaintiffs under the law in evidence, as she is required to, that you would find no hesitancy in signing your name to a verdict awarding her money damages? Is that correct?

A. That's right, sir

Q. Likewise, if she fails to prove her case under the law and evidence, is there any reason that you can think of which would prevent you from signing your name in favor of the railroad company?

A. No, sir.

Q. That's a fair way of handling any controversy; would you agree with that, sir?

A. Yes, sir.

Q. Would you be willing if selected as a juror to wait until you've heard all of the evidence for both sides before deciding who is right and who is wrong?

A. Yes, sir.

Q. As you sit there now, there is no reason that comes to your mind which would prevent you from acting in that fair manner; is that correct, sir?

A. That's right, sir.

Q. As in any well-ordered society, obviously all parties cannot speak at the same time; and so the rules provide that the plaintiff, the party who brings the case into court, is given the privilege of presenting her evidence first, to be followed by evidence on behalf of the defendant, in this case the railroad company.

Are you the kind of person who is willing to keep an open mind until you've heard the evidence for both sides before determining who is right and who is wrong?

A. Yes, sir

Q. Would you agree that any fair, reasonable person would accept that kind of a fair program, okay?

A. Yes, sir.

Q. The fact that plaintiff is an individual, defendant is a railroad corporation, is that going to make any difference to you in determining the facts in this case?

A. No, sir.

Q. They both start out fair and even with you; is that correct, sir?

A. Right, sir.

Q. Again, you will recall the Court mentioning when this occurrence took place. Is there anything about the delay in this case coming to trial which bothers you in any way?

A. No, sir.

Q. If I were to inform you that the delay is not to be charged against either party here, would you accept that from the Court?

A. Yes, sir.

THE COURT: Thank you, sir.

(The Court then questions prospective jurors Eva Schwertzer and Rosemary Orsi in the same way that he questioned the preceding jurors.)

THE COURT: Mr. Hayes, you may inquire.

MR. HAYES: Thank you, your Honor. Your Honor, the plaintiff will excuse Mrs. Skye. Thank you, Mrs. Skye.[3]

THE COURT: Mrs. Skye, you may step down. Call another juror.

THE CLERK: Patricia Thomas.

THE COURT: Your name is Patricia Thomas?

A. Yes.

(The Court then questions prospective juror Patricia Thomas in the same way as the previous jurors.)

* * * * * *

THE COURT: Mr. Hayes, you may inquire.

NATHANIEL BECK, being examined on behalf of the plaintiff as to his qualifications, testified as follows:

EXAMINATION BY MR. HAYES:

Q. Mr. Beck.

A. Yes, sir.

Q. Have you in connection with your work at Ford Motor Company for thirty years had anything to do with railroads? I assume that there are spur track and things like that.

A. Yeah. Well, sometimes, you know, like unloading boxcars, and that's about the extent of it. They just bring in stock, and sometimes we have a problem with bulkheads, you know; and we have to get certain trades to move them, you know, so the

[3] *The reason for excusing a prospective juror is not always apparent from the juror's response to questions. It may be something in the demeanor of the juror in answering questions, an impression, for example, that the juror is not being candid.*

stock handlers can take the stock out of the boxcar. Other than that, maybe a switch every once in a while; but other than that, nothing.

Q. The Court has inquired of each of you rather thoroughly, and I don't mean to prolong it at all. If there were anything which concerned you or which you felt might make it difficult for you to give both parties to this lawsuit a fair trial, you wouldn't hesitate to tell us now, would you?

A. No.

Q. You've thought it over, and you believe that you can be a fair and impartial juror to both sides?

A. I believe so, yes, sir.

Q. Now the Court specifically has asked each of you and advised you that the case should be decided by the law and the evidence in this case and nothing beyond that. Are you prepared to do that, sir?

A. Yes, sir.

Q. The Court has also asked you if you would accept his statement that the delay in bringing the case to trial at this time has nothing to do with the fault of either party; it doesn't concern you. Is that right, sir?

A. That's right.

Q. Maybe I can save some time: If the last couple of questions about the liability, your own assessment of your ability to be fair and impartial jurors, if I were to ask that question of not only Mr. Beck but the three other ladies, would your answer be the same?

MS. ORSI: Yes.

MRS. SCHWEITZER: It would be.

Q. Mrs. Thomas, the same thing?

MRS. THOMAS: Yes.

MR. HAYES: And if you felt otherwise, you would tell us; is that correct?

MS. ORSI: Correct.

MR. HAYES: Mr. Beck, let me ask you something about the accident involving your family. At the time that the case was disposed of, you were satisfied that the amount of money that your family would receive from the settlement was fair and just; is that correct?

A. That's right.

Q. Do you have any feeling about the jury system, any feeling against the jury system?

A. No, sir, none whatever.

Q. What I'm saying is, if you felt that it had not been fair, would you have hesitated to bring your case to a jury of twelve people and have them make the decision?

MR. CALLAHAN: Your Honor, I object to this line of questioning.

THE COURT: I'll overrule it.

MR. HAYES: If you had felt that you had not been fairly treated, would you have hesitated to bring your case to a jury and have the jury determine, number one, whether you—your wife and children were entitled to recovery of damages, and, if so, have the jury determine what those fair and just damages were?

A. No, I would not hesitate.

MR. HAYES: Thank you, Mr. Beck.

PATRICIA THOMAS, being examined on behalf of the plaintiff as to her qualifications, testified as follows:

EXAMINATION BY MR. HAYES:

Q. Mrs. Thomas, if I were to ask you the same questions which I put to Ms. Orsi, would the answer with respect to your fairness be the same; that you, starting out in this case are going to be fair to the people I represent and you're going to be fair to the railroad?

A. Yes.

Q. Is that correct? And your decision in this case is going to be based upon the evidence in this lawsuit?

A. Yes.

Q. You are not going to allow extraneous matters to concern you?

A. No.

MR. HAYES: Thank you. Your Honor, the plaintiff will excuse Mrs. Schweitzer. Thank you, Mrs. Schweitzer.[4]

THE COURT: Mrs. Schweitzer, you may step down. Call another juror.

THE CLERK: Ellen Driscoll.

EXAMINATION BY THE COURT:

* * * * * *

THE COURT: Thank you, Mrs. Driscoll. Mr. Hayes you may continue your inquiry.

ROSEMARY ORSI, being examined on behalf of the plaintiff as to her qualifications, testified further as follows:

EXAMINATION (cont'd.) BY MR. HAYES:

Q. Ms. Orsi, I want to get back to you on a matter. You mentioned that you have a sister who's in speech pathology—

A. Yes.

Q. —at the University of Illinois?

A. Yes, she is.

Q. What is your understanding of speech pathology?

A. It's to help the physically handicapped as far as speech impediments.

Q. Would you in any way liken it to a clinical pathologist?

[4] *See footnote #3 re juror Skye.*

A No.

Q. You're going to hear clinical pathologist testimony in this case. Is there anything about your sister being engaged in speech pathology—and I don't know how much you know about it; I don't know how close you and your sister are—and a clinical pathologist coming in to testify in any way would that make you think, "Well, I know something about that"?

A. No, sir.

Q. And, incidentally, do you have any trouble with accepting the fact that you're going to be hearing from medical people in this case: pathologists, neurologists?

A. No.

Q. And then lastly, to the four of you folks, each of you has said to the Court that if you find that Mrs. Mohler and the children are entitled to recover a verdict, then you wouldn't hesitate to sign that verdict. You also indicated to the Court that if the railroad is entitled to a verdict, you wouldn't hesitate to sign that verdict.

If you do find in favor of Mrs. Mohler and the children, then you will have assumed an obligation of determining what is fair and just according to the law in this case.

No person may get on the witness stand and tell you what is fair and just damages. You may hear testimony about damages, but nobody may tell you from the witness stand what it is in number of dollars.

The Court will give you instructions that you should consider and assist you in arriving at that figure if you find in favor of the Mohlers; and the lawyers may argue it; but it is the jury that makes the determination.

MR. CALLAHAN: Your Honor, by way of objection, I think this is going beyond the—

THE COURT: Yes, sustained.

MR. HAYES: I'm winding it up to a question, your Honor.

THE COURT: Very well.

MR. HAYES: My question is this: Do I have your assurance that if the Mohlers are entitled to a verdict, that the verdict is going to be based upon the evidence in this lawsuit in this courtroom, and not upon anything extraneous to this courtroom? You may assure me that?

THE JURORS: Yes.

MR. HAYES: And secondly, that if a verdict for a very substantial sum of money is justified by the law and the evidence, is there any reason why any of you would hesitate to put your signature to that verdict simply because it involved a very substantial sum of money?

THE JURORS: No.

MR. HAYES: There are some people who have a feeling about substantial jury verdicts, and that is their right to have that feeling. It is not their right to sit on a jury if that will affect their judgment so that they could not, even if a verdict is justified by the law and the evidence, they would not want to sign it.

MR. CALLAHAN: Your Honor, once again, I think this is going beyond proper questioning.

THE COURT: Yes. The philosophical approach is—you've just about exhausted that.

MR. HAYES: I'll get away from philosophy.

THE COURT: Very well.

MR. HAYES: Thank you very much. Your Honor, the plaintiff will tender the panel as constituted.

THE COURT: Thank you, Mr. Hayes. Mr. Callahan?

MR. CALLAHAN: Your Honor, we will excuse Mrs. Thomas. Thank you, Mrs. Thomas.[5]

THE COURT: Mrs. Thomas, you may step down. Call another, please.

[5] *See footnote #3 re juror Skye.*

RHONDA MOORE, a member of the panel of veniremen, was examined as to her qualifications.

(The Court then questioned prospective juror Rhonda Moore in the same way as the previous jurors.)

THE COURT: Thank you very much, Ms. Moore. Mr. Callahan you may continue your inquiry

MR. CALLAHAN: Thank you, your Honor.

NATHANIEL BECK, being examined on behalf of the defendant as to his qualifications, testified as follows:

EXAMINATION BY MR. CALLAHAN:

Q Mr. Beck, let me ask you just a few questions. Now you have told us in response to some questions that your family, exclusive of yourself, was involved in this automobile accident and there was a lawsuit about it that was settled to your satisfaction; is that correct?

A Right, sir.

Q Now does that experience, the fact that your wife and your children were parties plaintiff in the lawsuit, does that in any way interfere with your ability to be fair with both sides in this case?

A No, sir.

Q And what I really have in mind is that the question has been asked whether you can start off being fair to both sides; yet as you already know from the facts, the plaintiff's husband suffered an untimely death, and there's a loss there that is the basis for this lawsuit; and the defendant doesn't expect you not to be naturally sympathetic to someone who has been injured or who has suffered a loss.

The question I have, however, is can you, in determining the question of liability in this lawsuit, set aside that natural sympathy and be objective and fair to both sides?

A Yes, sir.

Q So that, if, after the evidence is heard—and by the way, I believe you were asked and, if not, let me ask you now: The plaintiff always goes first. The defendant doesn't put on his witnesses until after the plaintiff is finished.

Would you be able to wait until you've heard what the defendant has to say about this occurrence before making a decision?

A Yes, sir.

Q And if after all the evidence is in, notwithstanding that the plaintiff has suffered a loss, if you found that the defendant was not responsible for that loss, would you be able to find in favor of the defendant?

A Sure.

Q Now I represent a corporation and want to be sure that that fact will not prevent it from receiving a fair trial.

Now if you have any reservations about your ability to be objective and fair about this, we'd appreciate it if you would say so; then we would excuse you, and there's nobody to blame for that.

Do you think you could be fair to both sides in this case?

A No question, yes.

Q Do you understand that anybody can file a lawsuit against anybody else?

A Sure.

Q And the fact that somebody has filed a suit against somebody else doesn't mean that just because the suit was filed, that the person against whom they file it is automatically liable.

A Right.

Q They have to prove it. That's what we're here in court for.

A Right.

ELLEN DRISCOLL, being examined on behalf of the defendant as to her qualifications, testified as follows:

EXAMINATION BY MR. CALLAHAN:

Q MRS. DRISCOLL, if I were to ask you those same questions, would your answers be substantially the same?

A Yes.

Q And there's no reason that you can think of that you could not be fair to both sides in this case? And you understand what I said to Mr. Beck when we say we don't expect you not to be sympathetic for anyone who suffered a loss or an injury, but what we're asking is whether you'd be able to set that natural sympathy aside in looking at the issues presented here?

A Yes.

Q And Ms. Orsi, if I were to ask you the same questions, would your answer be substantially the same?

MS. ORSI: Yes.

Q And, Ms. Moore, if I were to ask you those same questions, would your answers be the same?

A Yes, they would.

Q And you have no reservations about your ability to be a fair juror on this case?

A No.

Q And if the evidence, as it comes in during the course of this trial, is such that you're persuaded that the railroad should prevail, you would not hesitate to bring a verdict in favor of the railroad, even though to do so, you would be finding against the plaintiff?

A No.

Q You could do that?

A Yes, I could.

MR. CALLAHAN: Your Honor, I'll accept this panel on behalf of the defendant.

THE COURT: Thank you, Mr. Callahan. Tender to Mr. Hayes.

EXAMINATION BY MR. HAYES:

Q Now, Ms. Moore, you come from an at least comparatively small family compared to those people, some of the people we've talked to. Does that at all—I guess if one wants to ask whether that has anything to do with the lawsuit, how many people the juror's family has—does it make any difference to you that there are only three kids in your family and not seven or eight? Does that make any difference to you?

A No, it doesn't.

Q Thank you. And, Mrs. Driscoll, does it make any difference to you that there are no children in your family and you have only one brother and one sister?

MRS. DRISCOLL: No.

Q And, Ms. Moore, that's not going to make any difference to you, either; is that right?

MS. MOORE: Right.

Q If—oh, and incidentally, it was said that anybody who filed a lawsuit against anybody else—and I assume that I can pick up somebody in the hall and file a lawsuit against him. It could be done, and I suppose it's the easiest thing in the world to do.

But if that's the easiest thing in the world to do, the second easiest thing in the world to do is for a railroad company to file a paper in court and say, "It's not our fault; and besides, they weren't damaged as much as they say they are."

MR. CALLAHAN: Your Honor, I'm going to object to this.

THE COURT: I think we're getting a bit far—

MR. HAYES: We aren't. It cuts both ways.

THE COURT: The point is that anyone can file a lawsuit, and anyone who is sued has a right to come in and defend themselves, and I believe that covers the point.

MR. HAYES: Now would you assure us that it is not what papers lawyers filed in courts that is going to determine this; it is what the evidence in this case is going to be? Can I get that assurance from all of you?

THE JURORS: Yes.

MR. HAYES: Thank you very much, Ladies and gentlemen. The plaintiff will accept the panel.

THE COURT: Thank you, gentlemen. The Court will administer the oath to the first panel to well and truly try the issue.

(Whereupon, the first panel of four jurors was duly sworn.)

It will be noted that throughout the selection of the jury the attorney for the plaintiff emphasizes the great loss and the number of children in the family of the deceased. The attorney for the defendant seeks to deal with this by emphasizing the obligation to overcome sympathy and to be objective in dealing with the issue of liability, which is entirely separate from the issue of damages. If there is no liability there are no damages. In closing argument the defendant's attorney will revisit the commitments the jurors have made about sympathy and the fact that the defendant is a corporation.

Chapter Four

Opening Statements

Hard are the ways of truth and rough to walk.

— Milton, *Paradise Regained*

If opening statements were not a part of the original trial process, it would have become necessary to invent them. That is because it is often difficult for a jury to understand what is going on in a trial, and how one part of the evidence may relate to another. It is not always possible, even if it may be desirable, to adduce the evidence chronologically. For that reason alone, it is often necessary to give a jury some guidance in advance of the actual testimony so that it is able to get a more comprehensive perspective. The most common word used to explain the purpose of opening statements is "overview." The jury is told that the opening statement will give them an "overview" of the evidence, so that they may better understand it when they hear it from the testimony of the witnesses.

In introducing the attorneys for the purpose of making their opening statements, the Court cautions the jury that what the lawyers say is not evidence. In the course of their opening statements, lawyers usually repeat that admonition and may often add that if anything they say is not subsequently supported by the evidence, the jury is to disregard any such statement and, by implication, to hold it against the lawyer for making a misrepresentation.

It will be noted, further, that these are called opening statements, not opening arguments. Counsel are not permitted to argue either the law or the evidence in their opening statements, and each party is quick to object to any attempt by the other to do so. What they have the right to do is to tell the jury what they think the evidence will be.

In the ordinary case, the opening statement is of somewhat greater advantage to the plaintiff than to the defendant. It is the plaintiff, after all, who instituted the suit and who claims a wrong and an injury. Many times the defendant finds itself in the position of having to admit that much of what the plaintiff claims did in fact happen but that it was through no fault of the defendant. Since he is precluded from arguing the evidence and the law in his opening statement, he may have less of a "case" to give an "overview" of. Nevertheless, the defendant can draw the jury's attention to the weaknesses of the plaintiff's case by discussing what he believes the evidence will show.

The opening statement is the first the jury hears about what the case really involves. Each side can and in many ways does suggest where the actual fault lies.

The jury is also observing the manner in which each attorney articulates his case, the impression he makes as a person, his attitude towards the jury, the Court, his opposing counsel, and even the parties to the lawsuit. Throughout this part of the proceedings each member of the jury is making a number of clear, though tentative, judgments about the case and about each lawyer, any or all of which may be modified or changed entirely by events in the course of the trial.

The following are the opening statements of the plaintiff's and defendant's attorneys in *Mohler*, the same case used to demonstrate the selection of the jury.

> THE COURT: Good morning ladies and gentlemen. To the first two panels, I want you to know we have not been idle. We have been working even though you were in the deliberating room, and we have just completed the selection of the jury.
>
> Now, under our rules, the attorneys, if they so desire, will have an opportunity to make some opening remarks to you.
>
> What they tell you at this time is not evidence. It is simply a statement by them as to what they feel the evidence will show on behalf of their client so that it will give you an opportunity to more reasonably follow the evidence as it unravels before you on the witness stand.

Mr. Hayes, if you are ready, you may proceed, counsel.

MR. HAYES: Thank you, your Honor.

MR. HAYES: May it please the Court, Mr. Callahan.

Good morning, ladies and gentlemen. At this time as the Court has informed you, each lawyer has an opportunity to address the jury in what is called the opening statement, and to tell you what we believe that the evidence in this case will be.

Not always are we able to present evidence in a form which would be the most logical or a kind of chronological sequence of events, because of problems such as the time demands of witnesses. Nevertheless, I will attempt to do so.

The purpose, therefore, of an opening statement is to give you an idea of what each lawyer believes the evidence will be so that you will have some kind of overall picture, and it is the hope that in making such a statement, you will find it to be of assistance in receiving the testimony as it necessarily comes in bits and pieces.

The evidence in a case consists of testimony, as the testimony of witnesses given under oath from the witness stand, and it consists also of documents, papers, et cetera.

Now, I would simply say this, as the Court has indicated to you, what lawyers have to say is not evidence. I would ask you at the conclusion of the case, if you find that I have made any statement which is not consistent with the evidence; if I make a statement now, or at the conclusion of the case, when we are permitted to sum up the case for the jury, I would ask you to disregard any such statement.

I would ask you, of course, to put the railroad to the same test.

Now, there are several places where we can begin by saying that Harold Mohler was born forty-nine years ago in Kankakee, Illinois. We can start with any number of places. I think what I would like to do first of all, before we get into what I believe the evidence will be, is to give you an idea of the procedure that is going to evolve.

As you have been informed, the plaintiff is required to present her evidence first and then the railroad proceeds with its case.

Now, that will be the order that will be generally followed as you will see. I address the jury first followed by the railroad. On behalf of Mrs. Mohler, I will offer evidence first, and then the railroad's case; in the final argument, I will go first and then the railroad will follow, and then I, on behalf of the plaintiff, will have an opportunity of what is called "rebuttal."

Some things may occur during the trial. There is what is called "direct examination." A person who is called as a witness, as her witness or his witness, must be examined under what we call "direct examination." Whereas, the opposing lawyer has the opportunity of what is called "cross-examination," and you will see the differences in those two types of examinations of witnesses.

There is also something that we call an "adverse" witness. Under certain circumstances, a lawyer may call a witness as his witness, but is permitted to interrogate the witness as if under cross-examination.

Now, I believe the evidence will show, and I'm going to start with Harold Mohler who was born in Kankakee, Illinois, and who attended St. Theresa Grammar School in Kankakee, St. Patrick's High School, and after high school he spent four years in the Air Force. After his tour of duty in the Air Force, he worked in a factory. He then got into a restaurant, a bar and grill business in Kankakee. He was in that for awhile, and then he went to work for the New York Central Railroad, oh, I'd say approximately four years before the events that we are going to be talking about.

He and Virginia Mohler had known each other in high school, were high school sweethearts; they married, and when he was assigned to Utah in the Air Force, Virginia accompanied him, and when he was sent overseas, she also accompanied him.

As a matter of fact, one of their children, Carolyn, was born in Germany, and their first child was born in Utah. All the other children, I think, were born in Kankakee. They have lived there all their lives. He went to work on the railroad as a brakeman.

I think you are going to find in railroad parlance there is what is called the "engine crew," and there is what is called the "train crew." The engine crew consists of the Engineer and the Fireman, if there is a Fireman, on a particular train. The train crew consists of a Brakeman and a Conductor, depending upon what the Brakeman does on a given run. There may be a Brakeman who is in the engine or generally rides the engine. He's called the "Headman," and a Brakeman may ride in the Caboose, then he's called the "Hindeman" or "Flagman."

In freight service the work of the train crew involves setting out cars, that is, a train is composed of many cars and on some runs they may be serving industries, various industries along the railroad line, and it will be required that they stop from time to time, going from one terminal to the other terminal to set out cars that they have onto the industry track.

This may range anywhere from a spur track to huge trackage at some industries. They may also pick up cars, that is, stop at the industry and pick up cars that are going to be delivered somewhere else.

You are going to find that there is a difference in the two trips that are involved in this case. There were four men on the train on the December 28th trip, and on the January 19th trip, there were six men, and that has to do with a law in Indiana at that time, a six-man crew law. There was a requirement that there must be a fireman and a crew of six on a train. In Illinois, that was not a requirement.

Now, on December 28, these men—incidentally, this run ran out from Kankakee, their home terminal. The home terminal in this case was Kankakee. All the men on that run worked out of Kankakee and that run went to Elkhart, Indiana, and as far west as Zearing. Now, not always did a train go all the way to Zearing. It might. There is what they call a "turnaround." So there may be, for example, the Streator turnaround. That is, a train could only go to Streator, then it would go back. It would not go on to Zearing.

One of the largest industries served on the west run was Jones and Laughlin Steel in Hennepin, Illinois. I think the evidence will be that the engineer has charge of the power and the engine crew—remember I told you the engine crew is made up of an engineer and fireman, if there is a fireman. The conductor is in overall charge of the movement of the train, and he, of course, is in secondary charge of all of the brakemen, whether they are flagmen, hindemen, or what.

Now on December 28, this run began at Kankakee, Illinois. Now, cars on a train are coupled together by automatic couplers, and the brakes on the train are air brakes, and there is a continuous air brake line throughout the entire length of a train, beginning with the engine or engines, and continuing all the way to the caboose.

Now, if something should happen to break the air hose, the train will automatically go into what is called "emergency braking," and that is what is referred to by railroad men, they call it "big holing." When it goes automatically into emergency braking, it makes a very loud, explosive rush of air sound, and it's called "big holing." That automatically sets the brakes, and the wheels are actually sliding along the track at that time. There may be some control that can be exercised in the engine with respect to how that braking is ultimately accomplished, but there are no controls when that emergency braking goes into effect.

Now, there is such a thing that occurs which is sometimes called a "break-in-two." That means that a train has actually separated into two parts. In this case, I believe the evidence will show that a coupler broke. In the automatic coupling device, there are things that are called "knuckles." They are in the integral part of the coupling device to keep cars coupled to each other. It is something required by federal law, and it broke.

I believe the evidence in this case will be that literally one of the knuckles broke, the train separated into two parts, breaking the air hose, and causing the entire train to go into emergency braking. It may be also that at that time they may have started to slow down for a town called Reddick. The occurrence, the break-in-two, occurred somewhere between, I think it's Union Hill, and Reddick, and it may be they were slowing down, preparing to stop at Reddick, but at any rate, they were moving at various estimated speeds.

At the time the break-in-two occurred, Mr. Mohler was on the caboose. Mr. Mohler was alone in the caboose. This was a four-man crew. This was not a six-man crew. Riding in the engine were the engineer, the head brakeman, and the conductor. What happened was that when this occurred, they finally came to a stop, and they had to replace the knuckle. Now, there is some question as to where they got a replacement knuckle. Somebody says they carry replacement knuckles in the engine. Somebody else says they got a knuckle from an opposing train. That is to say, a train coming the other way. I don't know how likely that is, and you will hear about this in the testimony.

At any rate, they did get a knuckle from somewhere, and what they then do is to put that knuckle on an engine or car. They will run up to where they get the knuckle. For example, if it's on the engine, they will drop the knuckle off, and then they will run up the engine and cars to a point where the last car—where the break occurred, and they will pick up the knuckle, put it on there. Then they will reverse it to where the rest of the separated train is sitting, and then they will take out the broken knuckle, as they did, and replace it with the other knuckle, and then re-couple and reattach the air brake line. Then it takes a long time to get the air pressure up, because all of that air pressure has blasted out in the occurrence.

Now, there were many stops along the trip from Kankakee, which ultimately ended up in Zearing. How many stops were actually made, we don't know. We do believe, and do have from the testimony, that they may have been going to stop at Reddick. They definitely stopped in Hennepin. Hennepin, of course, is one of the biggest stops along the line. There are places at which other railroads cross the New York Central tracks, and those are called "railroad intersections," and there are two or three of those, and at those intersections, there may be towers with which there is radio contact. I believe also that there was radio contact in the engine of this train, and there may or may not have been a radio in the caboose, although it appears that they did not have a radio in the caboose.

One of the responsibilities of the person who is in the caboose, whether it's the hindeman or conductor, whoever is in the caboose, is to drop a flare when they are going to come to a stop. If they are going to stop at Reddick, and the train is slowing down, the man in the caboose knows that the train is going to come to a stop at Reddick, and he will want to drop a fusee out at some distance forward of where they are going to stop, and he must, as a matter of fact, throw out such a fusee, because it serves as a warning to any train that may be coming behind.

Now, this break-in-two occurred, I believe, at something like 4:45 a.m. A fusee is a ten-minute fusee. There is a reason for that. Scheduled trains do not run on freight service closer than ten minutes apart. Now, whether any other train would indeed be coming, I don't know. Sometimes there are extras. Now, there are several ways you can throw a fusee. Some people will sit. If it's a caboose with a kind of a bay window, they will put it on the side. Some people would just drop it out that window. Unless thrown properly, however, that fusee may well roll down the side, and then it might not be easily seen by a train behind it. The function of the fusee at night is that it can be seen for a long distance ahead; any engineer or fireman or anybody keeping a lookout in the engine seeing a red flare knows that he must bring that train to a stop.

I believe the evidence is going to show, and you will understand that Harold Mohler was alone in the caboose and that Harold Mohler is dead. So you will understand that, necessarily, much of it is going to be circumstantial evidence; I think I speak for the Court, but I believe that the jury may consider circumstantial evidence, and the Court may even instruct you that circumstantial evidence is very proper for you to consider in determining the facts in the case.

I believe the evidence will show that Harold Mohler went to the back of the caboose to throw out a fusee on the roadbed between the rails. He was required under railroad rules to make a report if there was any serious injury, and he did make such a report.

So, I believe that you will have the benefit of that report. Also, in any event, the Trainmaster in this case is a Mr. Strickland. The Trainmaster also was required to make a report, and he did make a report, and I believe that that report will be received by you. But in any event, that's what happened, and as that was happening, there was a jolt because the break-in-two occurred. Harold Mohler hit his head against some part of the caboose.

Incidentally, one of the members of the crew is dead. Mr. Tracey was the conductor. He is dead, and Mr. Mohler, of course, is dead.

Now, the next time that Harold Mohler was seen may have been at Streator, Illinois. The engineer says that he talked to him at Streator. The headman works under the conductor, I believe his testimony is that he did not see Mohler until they got to Reddick.

At any rate, that was the end of that trip. I believe the evidence will be that it was believed at that time that he hit his head; he also had blood on, or in, his ear, and in his report, he characterized it as a cut on his ear, and he bruised his head and shoulder.

Now, they stayed over in Zearing and then they made the return trip to Kankakee. Harold Mohler laid off after that for the next day or two, it's somewhat unclear. He did not work, in any event, on the 30th or the 31st or the 1st, and he did work thereafter. There will be evidence as to what he did or did not do between December 28th and January 19th.

So let me jump now to January 19th, the day when they were supposed to take a train back from Elkhart to Kankakee. On the 17th, they had started out from Kankakee going to Elkhart, and it was a long, hard run. They got to Elkhart, and I'm not going to go into all of the details. Eventually, they went to a hotel in Elkhart where they stayed. They didn't get in until 5:00 in the morning or whatever it was, but that day of the 18th, for whatever reason no train or other crews had priority over them to go back, and they laid over in Elkhart that day, staying at the Elkhart Hotel; there will be witnesses to tell what did or did not happen in that layover, which I think was something like twenty-two or twenty-three hours. Harold Mohler was conductor on that trip, and that requires just a little bit of explanation. While he was classified as a brakeman, he was what was called a promoted man, that is to say, he had been promoted, and the way it works, is they bid jobs. He could work as a conductor, if a conductor who was supposed to have the run laid off or didn't take the run for whatever reason. So he was acting as conductor. As a matter of fact, he was a conductor a number of times.

What they have to do is go over to what they call the hump tower, and the conductor has some paperwork to do there, so they drove from the Elkhart Hotel, over to what is called the railroad YMCA. There is a railroad YMCA right near the yards where they have some rooms, and when they are filled, the railroad puts them up at the Elkhart Hotel.

I think they were filled by other railroad men, and this crew stayed at the Elkhart. Harold Mohler went over a little bit early because he had some paperwork to do. Then a brakeman called Norman Phillips came over, and he saw Mohler at the hump tower, and then Phillips went to the caboose. He verified the number of the caboose, and the train track that their train was on, and he went over to the caboose. From that time, there was a six-man crew because they had run into Indiana. Harold Mohler went to the caboose and the last thing that is done before a train pulls out is the conductor signals somebody in the tower, either by loudspeaker, or pressing a button or however, that the conductor is on the caboose, and that means they are ready to go.

So Phillips is on the caboose, and the door opens, he knows it's Mohler, and he said, "Did you tell them we are ready to go, or did you tell them you are on the caboose?" And there was no answer, and then Mohler walked over a few steps, set down his bag, keeled over to his right, and fell down. Phillips went over, turned him over and asked, "Harold, what's wrong?" And he heard Harold gasping for breath as if he were choking on something. He turned him over on his back, put a coat under his head, and then he called to a car inspector who was out there—either called or went up and got him—and told him to get an ambulance over here. They had two-way radios, and then there was a series of a gasp and then silence, and then a gasp, and this happened half a dozen times and at some point somebody tried to get a pulse, either the car inspector or Norman Phillips, and they couldn't find a pulse, and then after the last gasp, then there was silence. A Trainmaster or the Yardmaster came in and looked at Mohler and said, "This man is dead."

Now, there was no color change in Mr. Mohler during this period of time, from the time he walked in, fell, and then died.

Now what about in between? I believe the evidence will show that there were a number of events that occurred that were unusual. You must understand that the railroad men are away from home an awful lot. So there has been an attempt to reconstruct what happened, and we have some evidence that will assist you in reconstructing what happened, so we can tell generally what trips Mr. Mohler was on. First of all, he saw no doctor from the time of the occurrence to the time of his death, although more than one person told him he should. But he didn't.

Secondly, the blood in the ear has been variously described by witnesses as being in the ear or dried blood running down the side of the ear. There also will be testimony by members of the family as to what happened between the 28th and the 19th.

This brings me to the Mohler family. The evidence is going to show a very close knit family. It was a warm, good relationship. Harold Mohler had two passions; one was railroading and the other was his family. Virtually all of the time he didn't spend on the railroad, he spent with his family. They had the best opportunity to observe him, and they are going to tell you about some things that they may not have thought were significant and maybe put them out of their mind, but I believe the evidence is going to show that some significant things occurred between the 28th and the 19th.

First of all, Harold was an outgoing guy. He was not a life-of-the-party guy, but he was always happy, and he was not a person who would just lie around and sleep all day. Some of the things that happened: he would hold his head and complained of headaches, he was seen on several occasions in a staring position, oblivious to what was going on around him, for short periods of time. One time, his daughter, Carolyn, who believes that she was closer to her father than the other children—but the other children probably feel the same way—observed her father in bed having an unusual thrashing episode.

This leads to what I believe the medical evidence is going to show. I believe, ladies and gentlemen, that the evidence is going to show that there were certain behavioral changes that occurred. Not all the time—as a matter of fact, most of the time during that period he appeared to be fine, no problem whatsoever. But there were a number of incidents of behavioral changes, which suggest that there was a degenerative process going on in his brain which, in whole or in part, set in motion what happened on December 28, 1967, and caused his death on January 19, 1968.

You are going to have to listen very carefully to the medical evidence in this case, as you are going to listen to all of the evidence. The railroad is going to offer evidence of two people, evidence supporting their opinions as to what caused Harold Mohler's death. On behalf of the Mohler family, I'm going to offer expert witnesses to give their opinions as to what, in whole or in part, caused Harold Mohler's death. One is a man named Dr. Segarra, who is a board certified[1] neurologist. He is also certified in neuropathology. Then Dr. Donal O'Sullivan who is a pathologist, who then went into internal medicine, and brings together the fields of internal medicine and pathology. The defense is going to offer a Dr. Leestma, who is a pathologist and neuropathologist. They will also offer Dr. John Hughes, who is not board certified, but who practices mostly in the field of electroencephalography and neurology, and has done some work in coroner's cases.

I believe the evidence is also going to include the following: You will be instructed that this case, being a railroad case, is brought under a federal law. As I believe this Court has told you, railroad workers are excluded from Workmen's Compensation. This case is brought under federal law.

MR. CALLAHAN: Your Honor, I object to the discussion of the law. This is an opportunity to say what the evidence will show.

THE COURT: That's correct. You may limit it to your theory of the case without a discussion of the law

MR. HAYES: My theory of the case is this: that there was a violation of the Federal Safety Appliance Act that caused the break-in-two and the injury that resulted, led in whole or in part to the death of Harold Mohler.

Now, you will be instructed as to those elements under the law applicable to this case that you should consider in determining

[1] *A physician who is certified to the public to be a true specialist in a particular medical discipline..*

what damages are fair and just, if you find in favor of the Mohlers. Obviously, if you do not find in favor of the Mohlers, there will be no occasion to discuss the question of damages at all.

I believe the evidence is going to show that Harold Mohler was a good worker, and he worked often. He worked harder trips than the rest. The west run was a pretty hard trip. I believe the evidence is going to show that he was in good health before this occurrence. He had a back sprain at some time in the past on a previous break-in-two when he snapped his neck. He got a cinder in his eye at one time. He had an appendix operation and a tonsil operation, but he was in good health. I should tell you now, also, that after this occurrence in Indiana, he was taken to a funeral home. The body was taken to a funeral home in Indiana, and the body was embalmed. There was no request for an autopsy. The family was in Illinois. In the early morning hours of the 19th, when the family was notified of this, a brother-in-law of the family, a Mr. Heck, who is a pharmacist, said there should be an autopsy performed, and so he arranged for an autopsy to be performed by a pathologist at the local hospital in Kankakee, and that autopsy was performed by Dr. Deland Burns. I believe that the evidence is going to show that there was no evidence from that autopsy of any significant coronary-artery disease or disease of the heart, no symptom of aneurysm of the brain, or brain hemorrhage, or anything of that nature. I believe the evidence will show, also, that there was a moderate amount of mucous retained in the bronchial tree, the only positive finding on the post-mortem examination by Dr. Deland Burns.

Now, this man, had he lived, would be working today. Historically, railroad workers—

MR. CALLAHAN: Your Honor, I object to this. I think this sounds more like a closing argument.

MR. HAYES: I'm going to show that historically—

THE COURT: This is what the evidence will show. He will be permitted to comment.

MR. HAYES: I will make it brief.

At any rate, he would have worked to some time in the future. I don't know whether he would have worked to age sixty-two, sixty-five or seventy or whatever. He was a brakeman, a promoted man, which means that he got the conductor's job often. He would get more money as a conductor, and you were able to bid on more jobs as a conductor. The pay system in the railroad is indescribable. For the operating people, it depends on the number of miles; it depends upon how many engines there are on the train; how many cars there are on the train, and we are going to try to reduce this to simple terms. Frankly, we are going to try to show you, by income tax returns, what Harold Mohler actually made in 1965, '66, '67. And then we will show some comparison from 1968 to today, as to what comparative rates are in effect, and there will be some projections for the future. Suffice it to say, that that is one aspect of the damages.

The second aspect is that under the law applicable to this case, the jury, in determining what is called pecuniary loss, is permitted to determine the value to the children of the loss of moral guidance, superintendence of education, care and that type of thing. In determining what are fair and just damages in this case, you may not consider the grief or sorrow of the widow or children. Nobody is asking you to. I will ask only that if you find that the family is entitled to recover, that that be a fair and just verdict.

Thank you very much for listening to this long explanation, and I'm sure you will give Mr. Callahan the same attention.

THE COURT: Mr. Callahan.

MR. CALLAHAN: May it please the Court, Mr. Hayes.

MR. HAYES: Mr. Callahan.

MR. CALLAHAN: I'm Cornelius Callahan. I represent the defendant, Penn Central Railroad, in this case. I will say again that nothing Mr. Hayes has said, and nothing that I am about to talk about, constitutes evidence. This is an effort on our part to let you know what the case is about so when the evidence comes in, you can understand this case a little better.

You may have seen me taking some notes while Mr. Hayes was talking. The defendant doesn't put on a case such as the plaintiff does. The defendant defends, and what we do often depends largely on what evidence the plaintiff actually puts into the case.

I want to go over briefly the procedure. As you have already seen, the plaintiff goes first in his opening statement. I am now responding. The plaintiff will put on its case, the defendant will then put on its case. The plaintiff has the right to rebut. At the close of the case, the plaintiff again addresses you first, the defendant second, and then the plaintiff will have the final word. So the plaintiff always opens and the defendant always follows, with the plaintiff having the last word, and that's the way the system is set up. The plaintiff, of course, has what is called the burden of proof, which will be discussed in our closing argument in some detail.

Now, the Penn Central is in the business of transporting goods throughout the northeastern United States coming as far west here as Illinois. That is the nature of its business. There has been some discussion as to their past business. Except for some commuting business in New York and Philadelphia, they are not in the commuting business. Basically, all they are involved in is transporting freight. You have heard some companies mentioned, such as Jones and Laughlin and General Motors. The railroads are the people that go to the industries in the United States and take things like coal and steel, and what have you, and transport those commodities in large quantities to various parts of the country. It's not a glamorous business, but it's a necessary business.

What we are dealing with here are two incidents. One has been discussed as the incident of December 28, 1967. I'm not going to go into great detail here because some of these things Mr. Hayes has already discussed. There are some people who were there, who are no longer alive. The evidence is going to come from the witnesses, and I don't want to commit myself as to just what they will say. Although there was a stop on the evening, or the early morning of December 28th, there will be people here to testify about just exactly what caused that.

Let me say that when you use the term "emergency stop" in railroad language, it doesn't mean the same as the term means to those of us who drive automobiles. A railroad train doesn't stop that way. They operate steel wheels on steel rails. They usually have long trains, carrying several hundreds of thousands of tons on them, and they simply don't have the sudden, fast stop capability you have with an automobile. It has what we would think of as an awfully long, slow stop.

So, I think the evidence will be that the train was coming to a stop when this occurrence took place. This stop kind of conditioned everyone on the train to expect that they were coming to a stop in the first place, before the break-in-two, but either way, there was some discussion about it, and there will be somebody here to explain just what did happen.

Basically, there is the air hose connection which has been described to you. There is air pressure in the hose, and the brakes are applied when the air pressure is released. When there is a break or rupture in the air hose, all the air rushes out, causing the brakes to be applied, and the train comes to a stop. I think that's what the evidence is going to show happened in this case. Whether a broken knuckle caused this we are not certain. We will see what the witnesses have to say about that.

In any event, the injuries to Mohler on that night were not significant, and as Mr. Hayes has said, he did not seek medical attention. It seems that he was not interested in seeking it. Once again, we will see what the testimony is. The injury was not significant. It was referred to as a cut or a small cut to the right ear. As to the throwing out of the fusee, I will let the witnesses testify about that. Further, in the caboose of a train, you are supposed to be sitting down, you are not supposed to be up walking around.

The testimony will also show that there was no indication of unconsciousness. That brings us, then, to a period some three weeks or so later. The next thing of consequence that occurred was when he was just beginning work, on the morning of January 19th, Mr. Mohler collapsed and died. As I understand it, the essence of the plaintiff's case is that there is a connection between the injury of December 28, and the death of January 19th. Our view is there is none. I think the evidence will show that the death was sudden and unexpected. There was a coroner's report, I believe. The coroner will testify that he concluded that it was caused by a coronary occlusion, what we normally describe as a heart attack. I think the coroner will be here to testify that there was an autopsy, and that it was inconclusive. They couldn't find the cause of death. Mr. Hayes will have a Dr. Segarra, and a Dr.

O'Sullivan, to testify. I will have doctors Jan Leestma and John Hughes, both of whom are highly competent. The evidence will show that Dr. Hughes is at the University of Illinois, and Dr. Leestma is at Northwestern Memorial Hospital.

The evidence on behalf of the plaintiff will suggest, I believe, that the cause of death was what is called "post-traumatic epilepsy," and I believe that it will be shown that Dr. Hughes is the expert in epilepsy. I believe that he will testify along the following lines.

First, since the injury of December the 28th was insignificant, and was not connected with any unconsciousness, it could not, under any ordinary circumstances, ever set in to motion any kind of post-traumatic epilepsy.

Second, a much greater period of time is required before the subsequent epileptic condition can occur. Third, I believe Dr. Hughes will testify that death from epilepsy is exceedingly rare, and nothing of the circumstantial nature of this death would suggest that he died from that condition.

Dr. Leestma, who is a pathologist, and who is an expert in that field, will testify that probably the most common, and therefore the most likely cause of death, is a coronary occlusion—a heart attack. I believe he will testify that there are three possible reasons that a person could die as a result of a heart attack, which would not be able to be detected by an autopsy.

One reason is that a heart attack is usually caused by a blood clot. A blood clot causes death, but the blood is a very complex mechanism. When the blood clots, certain elements in the blood are activated which dissolve those clots. When a blood clot is formed, and death is caused, these dissolving elements have been set into motion and continue to cause the blood to dissolve the clot, even after death. So the autopsy doesn't show the clot, and the cause of death is ruled inconclusive.

Second, heart attacks can also be caused by constriction of the arteries. But when death takes place, the constriction relaxes and the autopsy does not show that the death was caused by constriction of the arteries.

The third and final reason, though I'm sure there are probably more, is that heart attacks are also caused by a condition referred to as fatty tissue of the blood. If that is a cause of a heart attack, the autopsy once again will not reveal that condition as the cause of death, without extensive tissue tests and other procedures, which I do not believe were done in this case.

Now I think that pretty well completes my observations as to what I believe the evidence will show.

Almost invariably, things develop that may be of consequence in the case to which neither Mr. Hayes nor I have referred. Things that may become significant. This is what we believe the case will show and, in essence, the defendant's position is that there is no connection between the incident of December 28 and the death of January 19.

Thank you very much.

THE COURT: Thank you, gentlemen.

Ladies and gentlemen, we are going to recess now and reconvene at 1:45. You will be instructed daily, throughout these proceedings, that you are not to discuss this case with anybody, not even among yourselves, nor are you to permit anybody to approach you about it, nor seek independent information from any other source.

We will reconvene at 1:45.

CHAPTER FIVE

Putting on the Case

Oh, what a tangled web we weave
When first we practice to deceive!

— Sir Walter Scott

The order of the evidence follows the same precedent established earlier. The plaintiff brought the suit; therefore he has the right and the duty (the burden of proof) to go forward with his case. At the conclusion of the plaintiff's case, when the plaintiff rests his case, the defendant always files a motion asking that the Court enter a verdict in his favor and against the plaintiff—a directed verdict. This motion is made outside the presence of the jury and is based upon an asserted failure of the plaintiff to have sustained his burden of proof. Except in the unusual case, the motion is routinely denied. The defendant then puts in his evidence. The plaintiff also has the right of rebuttal and can, if he chooses and when otherwise appropriate, put on rebuttal evidence when the defendant has rested his case.

Although evidence is commonly put in directly through the witnesses, it may also consist of exhibits, of admissions made by the pleadings, and of stipulations or agreements between the parties. The significant evidence in most cases is that which is adduced from the witnesses. The heart of a case is usually revealed in direct and cross-examination and in the drama which unfolds before the jury. A seasoned trial attorney paints it more artfully.

* * * * * *

After winning a lengthy and complex case brought by one railroad company against another for damages arising out of a major derailment, the attorney explained the process of putting on the plaintiff's case as follows:

> It is one-third the production of a play; one-third a debate; and one-third a fight.

When asked what part legal theory, argument and authority played, he replied:

> The legal side of it is like putting on your uniform before a game. The trial—how the persuasion and counter-persuasion are handled—is far beyond the legal element.

* * * * * *

Motions in Limine

The law's delay . . . .

— Shakespeare, *Hamlet*

In recent years motions *in limine* have come into fashion. A motion *in limine* is one presented at the beginning of a trial, usually before the selection of the jury. The term is defined as: "on or at the threshold; at the very beginning; preliminarily." Such motions are based upon the desire to resolve certain critical issues before jury selection and certainly before opening statements. The concern of the moving party is that the opposing party may try to introduce into evidence improper matters so prejudicial to the moving party that if the jury learned of them, the prejudice could not be overcome and that party could not receive a fair trial. The moving party is asking the Court to rule in advance of any such improper attempt being made.

The following example shows an attempt to use the motion *in limine* as a preemptive strike and demonstrates its limitations as a tool for eliminating prejudicial facts.

* * * * * *

The plaintiff's attorney, representing a woman whose husband had been killed in an accident, made a motion *in limine* requesting the Court to enter an order directing the defendant's attorney not to allude to the fact that she had since remarried. The judge, a peer and friend of both of the attorneys, responded: "Jim, I am not going to enter such an order. Steve, here, knows he may not bring that out directly and I'm sure he won't do so. But I am taking twenty dollars from my wallet, Jim, and placing it in my drawer here. I am not making a bet with you, but if that fact does not somehow come out in the course of the trial, I will give you the twenty dollars. If it does come out, I will return the twenty dollars to my wallet and I will want the two of you to come back in chambers here and give some more serious consideration to settling the case."

The jury was picked and the case proceeded and in due course the widow was called to testify. She was asked if she were the widow of her previous husband, now deceased. She answered "yes" and her new married name was not mentioned. She testified tearfully and at length about the tragic loss of her husband. In the course of the direct examination, she gave her address as 323 Main Street in Peoria, Illinois. The defense counsel noted that this address was different from the one at the time of the accident, 415 Spring Street. On cross-examination he asked the following questions:

Q: Do I understand that at the time of the accident you lived at 415 Spring Street in Peoria, Illinois?

A: Yes.

Q: And you now live at 323 Main Street?

A: Yes.

Q: Who lives there with you?

A: My daughter and my husband.

The Court: Ladies and gentlemen: We will take a brief recess now.

Back in the Judge's chambers: "Okay Jim, I'm putting the twenty dollars back in my wallet. Now let's get down to some serious settlement talk."

The case was settled.

* * * * * *

Although the problem of severe prejudice may be real, there are a number of difficulties with the increased use of the motion *in limine*. The trial process has ways of dealing with improprieties. The stern rebuke of the trial judge can change the outcome of a case. In a way, the motion *in limine* is asking the judge for an "advisory opinion" and trial courts have said for years that they will not issue advisory opinions. "You make your objection, and I will rule on it," is the way most judges handle requests for advisory opinions. In addition, such motions are usually extremely time-consuming and detract from moving the case along once it has reached trial. Finally, if extreme prejudice has occurred, the trial judge has the power, pursuant to motion of the aggrieved party or on his own motion, to declare a mistrial, discharge the jury, and begin the case over again, and to impose appropriate sanctions on the offending party.

Exclusion of Witnesses

Set aside justice, and what are kingdoms but enterprises of robbery.

— St. Augustine, *City of God*

The standard motion made before any testimony is adduced is a motion to exclude from the courtroom all witnesses in the case except when such witnesses are actually testifying. It is made by one or more of the parties to the suit, or by stipulation of the parties, or, on occasion, at the suggestion of the Court. The purpose of the motion is to prevent witnesses from hearing the testimony of other witnesses. It is intended to safeguard against having witnesses influence one another, or worse, having them conform their testimony to the false testimony of others.

As holds true for many of our rules of law, precedents for current practice may be found in the Bible. The wisdom of the motion for exclusion of witnesses is wonderfully demonstrated in the story of the virtue of the very beautiful Suzanna of Babylon, from the Book of Daniel. (Douay version)

Susanna, a married woman, had been charged with adultery by two local judges who claimed to have caught her in the act but who themselves were involved in a scurrilous attempt to seduce her by threatening to make the false charge of adultery if she refused to submit to them. When she rejected them, they made the adultery charge.

At the trial both judges testified to having seen her under a tree in an act of adultery with a young man who ran away when they called out. Although Susanna vehemently denied the charge, the testimony of the two judges was accepted and she was sentenced to death.

On the way to the place of execution Daniel, a young man, called out that he would have no part in the death of this innocent woman. He protested that she was convicted without cross-examination and without clear evidence.

The elders called the two judges back for further examination before Daniel, who demanded that they be separated from one another. He then asked the first judge, "Under what tree did you see them together?" "Under a Mastic tree," he answered. Then Daniel directed that the other judge be brought to testify. "Under what tree did you see them together?" "Under an Oak."

The people and the elders rose up against the two judges and, under the law of Moses, inflicted on them the same penalty they plotted to impose on Susanna; they were put to death. (Dan. 13)

Exhibits

One picture is worth more than a thousand words.

— Chinese Proverb

Exhibits are tangible pieces of evidence, most commonly documents and photographs, but they may also consist of physical items such as weapons, mechanical devices, workmen's tools, bits and pieces of the remains of a failed or destroyed mechanism or structure, and any other such item which may be of probative value. An exhibit is usually identified by a witness who has direct knowledge of it. Exhibits are customarily marked and identified before any testimony is adduced from them. Testimony adduced from an exhibit not subsequently admitted into evidence is subject to being stricken. It is a common precautionary measure for an attorney to offer or re-offer all of his exhibits into evidence before he rests his case to insure that all of his exhibits have been offered and admitted into evidence.

Ours appears to be the age of exhibits, models, photographic enlargements, videos, and ever increasing types of imaginative demonstrative evidence. It has been theorized that it is an outgrowth of the schoolchild's "show and tell" sessions. Be that as it may, you should try to match your opponent's exhibits in kind if not in quantity. Photographic enlargements or blow-ups are currently in use and, as a rule, if your opponent is using them, you should probably have a few of your own to balance things out. You will be remiss if you do not.

The way to introduce a photographic enlargement is to first have the photograph in its original size marked, identified, offered and admitted, and then to request permission of the Court to use an enlargement of the exhibit for the convenience of the jury, the Court, and counsel. For purposes of clarity and record keeping, it is generally advisable not to make the enlarged exhibit a different number; rather, it should be designated as "Exhibit 15 (a)," with the original exhibit previously having been marked "Exhibit 15."

Sometimes exhibits do not work out the way they were conceived.

* * * * * *

A lawyer was assigned the task of defending the architect in a case involving the destruction of a building by fire. In framing the defense, he theorized that because of its design, the room where the fire allegedly started would have had to contain the fire. At considerable expense he had a model built to demonstrate his theory. Not long before the trial there was a dress rehearsal. The room did not contain the fire, the entire exhibit started burning, the fire department had to be called to put it out, and he had to come up with another theory of defense.

* * * * * *

Offers of Proof

Human nature constitutes a part of the evidence in every case.

— Potter, J., *Green v.Harris*, 11 R.I. 5, 17 (1895)

An offer of proof is a procedure by which a witness's testimony which the trial judge has refused to admit into evidence can be made a part of the record for purposes of review on appeal. If the testimony of a particular witness is denied or excluded by the judge, it is necessary for a reviewing court to know what the testimony would have been in order to meaningfully review the trial court's ruling. On the occasions that such testimony is not available, courts of appeal have refused to review such points.

In order to preserve such testimony for appellate review the procedure of an offer of proof is used. This is accomplished by making the offered, but excluded, testimony a part of the record by adducing it on the record outside the presence of the jury. This can be done either by having the jury retire to the jury room or by having the Court, the witness, counsel, and the court reporter step outside the courtroom to the judge's chambers or some other convenient location away from the jury.

The witness is then questioned on direct examination in the same manner he would have been had his testimony not been excluded. At the conclusion of the testimony, the moving or offering party asks that the testimony be permitted to be adduced before the jury. The opposing party renews its objection, and the Court repeats its ruling. But the testimony is now of record and available to the reviewing court on appeal. Although slightly less acceptable, another way of accomplishing the same end is to have the attorney offering the evidence simply summarize the expected testimony on the record rather than take the time to go through numerous questions and answers.

On occasion, the Court will reserve ruling on an offer of proof until he has heard additional evidence, so as to be able to make a more informed judgment.

Objections

In law also the right answer usually depends on putting the right question.

— Frankfurter, J., *Rogers v. Commissioner*, 320 U.S.410, 413(1943)

If the Court allows it, articulate in lay rather than legal terms the reason for your objection:

- "Objection, the question is leading and suggestive."
- "I object to the question, your honor; counsel is attempting to make the witness contradict his answer to the prior question because he is unhappy with that answer."
- "Objection, that question has been asked and answered."

Objection, That Hurts My Case

Restraint must be exercised when objecting to testimony or other evidence which is damaging to your side of the case. If your objection is overruled, you will have emphasized to the jury that you consider the evidence damaging and you will be seen to have been unsuccessful in your attempt to keep it out. You may as well say, "I object, that hurts my case."

Do not fight the inevitable. You are better off letting damaging testimony into the case without an objection than emphasizing it by unsuccessfully making one. Such evidence may be rebutted by other contrary evidence or by an effective closing argument. Your attitude should be casual, "Everyone knew this was coming in."

When an objection to one of the questions you put to a witness is sustained by the judge, you must move along quickly to another question or series of questions. Do not appear daunted or troubled by the ruling. Sometimes you can overcome any negative impact by beginning your next question, "Well, in any event, you are sure that …" and then restating the witness's unequivocal response to a prior question or some other fact that you are sure the witness will agree with. Your attitude in general should be, "Well, it's too bad the judge doesn't want a full inquiry but we will have to move along because I can prove my case in a number of other ways anyway."

If the area of inquiry is crucial to your case, you might best proceed by addressing the Court: "Well, your Honor, let me see if I can lay a bit more of a foundation." You can then attempt to make the objectionable question acceptable by laying a more thorough foundation. If the Court persists in sustaining the objection, you are then relegated to making an offer of proof to protect your record on appeal.

Adverse Rulings

During a trial there will be a number of rulings by the trial judge which you think are wrong, perhaps woefully wrong. That is what happens in the course of trials and you must be able to move on. You have a case to try and you cannot waste time wringing your hands and anguishing about unfair treatment.

Maybe it was a bad call. It happens all the time in sports. Maybe the judge is prejudiced against you or your client. Another possibility, although often the last one considered, is that you were wrong and the

Court's ruling was proper. In any event, you still have a case to try. You can still win it with the jury so move on.

You should be attuned to any procedure which seems contrary to the proper and accepted way in which that procedure is customarily carried out. Thus, you object not necessarily because something damaging has already occurred but because the change in the manner of the proceedings suggests that the stage is being set for such an event. The ability to perceive such a variation in proceedings comes only from experience, of course, but it can be described in lay terms as a sudden feeling that you are being "set up" in an effort to adduce evidence which ordinarily would not be admissible. See, for example, the objection interposed during the direct examination of Joseph M. Segarra on page 107 when the questioning begins to go from a hypothetical question to questions eliciting direct testimony from the witness.

Motions During Trial

A jury trial is a fight and not an afternoon tea.

— Riddell, J., *Dale v. Toronto R. W. Co.*,
34 Ont. L.R. 104, 108 (1915)

In the course of a trial, it is necessary for the attorneys to make a number of motions. A motion is merely a request or suggestion that the Court rule or act in a certain way. Many motions are uncontested, and are often for the benefit of all concerned:

- "Your Honor, I move that all witnesses be excluded from the courtroom except when testifying."
- "Your Honor, could I request that the document be marked before the witness is asked any questions about it?"
- "In view of the lateness of the hour, your Honor, could I move that we adjourn until tomorrow morning, and that the witness be directed to return to the stand at that time?"

Motions considered important should be in writing. The fact that a motion is written can often demonstrate to the trial judge that the moving party considers the matter to be significant. Moreover, it gives the reviewing court something more substantial than a simple oral statement in the midst of what may be a long, complicated and tedious transcript of proceedings.

For the defendant, two motions must be in writing, and must be made in the course of a case tried by a jury. These are the motions for a directed verdict made first at the close of the plaintiff's case and then at the close of all the evidence. It is the denial of these motions, together with the rulings on the post-trial motion, which forms the basis for a subsequent appeal on behalf of the defendant.

MOTION FOR A DIRECTED VERDICT

> Now, at the close of the plaintiff's case, the plaintiff having rested, comes the defendant and moves the Court to direct a verdict in its favor, and against the plaintiff.

Again at the close of all the evidence, after the defendant has put in its evidence, the defendant makes a very similar motion.

MOTION FOR A DIRECTED VERDICT

> Now, at the close of all the evidence, both parties having rested, comes the defendant and moves the Court to direct a verdict in its favor, and against the plaintiff.

Chapter Six

Cross-Examination and Impeachment

Thy adverse party is thy advocate.

— Shakespeare, Sonnets XXXV

Cross-examination is the single most important aspect of a trial. It is not too much to say that it is cross-examination, more than any other element of a trial, that brings out the truth. Without cross-examination, a trial would become a process similar to rival advertising campaigns in the merchandising of commercial products or, even worse, like political campaigns, more concerned with hiding rather than revealing the truth.

Since witnesses do not take the stand without having carefully gone over their testimony, they may be fully prepared to maintain and defend testimony which is wholly false. It is extremely rare to catch a witness in a lie. Nevertheless, the jury is watching closely and may perceive the deception even if the witness is never actually demonstrated to be testifying falsely. Sometimes even a well-rehearsed witness will seem to be struggling as if to come up for air. And, of course, the right to comment on the witness's testimony in final argument can bring the jury's attention back again and again to what was believed to be false testimony.

> CLERK: "Raise your right hand: Do you swear to tell the truth, the whole truth and nothing but the truth, so help you God?"
>
> WITNESS: "I do."

Despite the profundity of that oath sworn to by every witness before testifying, many witnesses lie under oath. Some lie to enrich themselves, or to aid someone else who is seeking to be enriched. Others lie out of antagonism towards or affection for another person, corporation or institution. And still others lie for causes which they consider to be greater than the truth. It is in these situations that cross-examination becomes an instrument of justice.

The technique of cross-examination may be explained by comparing it to a certain play in the game of football. Let us assume that the wide receiver has caught a downfield pass and that there is only one defensive back between him and the end zone. For purposes of this description, the wide receiver—the runner—is the witness and the defensive back—the tackler—is the cross-examiner.

The runner has numerous options. He can run in any direction, change direction, change pace or otherwise do whatever he can to mislead or deceive the defensive back. The tackler moves to counter each move of the runner, reducing the amount of space the runner has in which to maneuver. In the same sense the cross-examiner adjusts his questions in response to each answer of the witness. The witness can deny, hedge, fudge, obfuscate and lie. His ability to sustain his false testimony is tested by a penetrating cross-examination. That questioning is guided by the cross-examiner's view of what the real truth is or by a determination to get to the truth no matter what that truth may be.

There are two sides to cross-examination: when your opponent is cross-examining your witness and when you are cross-examining your opponent's witness. We will deal first with your witness being cross-examined by your opponent. To put this in perspective the following brief insight is offered.

* * * * * *

A defense attorney and his associate were walking back from court discussing the way their case was going. The plaintiff had rested his case the day before and that day had been spent putting on a number of defense witnesses, each of whom had been damaged on cross-examination. The associate made the observation:

"Everything was going great until we started putting our case on."

* * * * * *

Preparing Your Witness

In preparing your witness for his testimony you must be sensitive to his exposure to effective cross-examination. If there are negative elements to his testimony, it is often the wiser choice to bring that testimony out on your own direct examination. This is usually better than giving your opponent the opportunity to bring out the testimony dramatically on his cross-examination and make it look as if you were trying to hide something from the jury. And, if your witness can be shown to have a reason to be partisan in some way or another, that should be brought out on your examination.

A recent development in preparing witnesses for testifying is the use of videos to demonstrate to a witness how he appears when testifying. They are used to develop better demeanor and communication skills in the witness by giving him an opportunity to see for himself what he needs to do in order to come across as an honest, straightforward and believable witness.

There are two approaches to preparing witnesses for cross-examination. The more common method is to take the place of the cross-examining attorney and to ask the questions in the accusatory, high-pitched and contentious manner in which many attorneys cross-examine in an attempt to frighten, confuse and intimidate witnesses. Most attorneys feel that this dress rehearsal best prepares the witness for the real thing in court.

The second approach, although apparently superficial, is often more effective than the more time-consuming conventional method. That is, after discussing his testimony in general, to simply say to the witness, "You were present, you know what happened; the attorney cross-examining you was not present and has no direct knowledge of what happened. You were there; he wasn't. Therefore, simply continue to tell the truth on cross-examination. There is nothing that can be asked of you which you will not be able to answer. Any improper question, of course, I will object to."

To be sure, this method lends itself most readily to a suit involving a single incident in which the witness was directly involved. In more complex cases, such as business or commercial litigation, the witness needs more preparation because he will be cross-examined on a much broader amount of material and over a greater time period.

In either type of litigation, it is important that the witness understand your theory of the case. That is, he should understand not what may be a complex legalistic theory of the case, but rather a broad common sense perspective of your side of the case. You should articulate your theory of the case to your witness in equitable or theme language.

All of your witnesses should understand the basic reason or reasons why yours is the fair and just side of the case. This is necessary because each witness will almost certainly be asked questions for which he was not specifically prepared. Unless he has some broad perspective on your view of the case, he may find himself unable to adequately respond to those questions.

Rehabilitating Your Witness

On occasion your witness will be damaged or compromised by an effective cross-examination. This places you in the position of quickly having to decide whether to attempt to rehabilitate him. Any delay will suggest insecurity and add to the already damaging effect that the cross-examination has produced. Will you be able to explain away in your closing argument the apparently damaging effects of the cross-examination? Do you have other witnesses whose testimony can help?

Those questions must be weighed against the extent to which you believe you can rehabilitate the witness. One of the simplest and most effective ways to at least *appear* to rehabilitate a witness is to repeat the questions that will cause him to re-state the clear, firm and unequivocally beneficial portions of his testimony which were not compromised on cross-examination.

On occasion a trap can be set to catch your opponent on his cross-examination of your witness.

* * * * * *

A doctor was to testify as a medical expert for the railroad in a case involving crushing injuries to the foot of a railroad switchman caused while he was involved in coupling freight cars. In addition to the question of the extent of the disability of the injured man, there was a serous question as to whether the injury could have been caused in the manner to which he testified.

It happened that the doctor had worked as a railroad switchman himself while he attended medical school some thirty years before the time of the trial. The railroad lawyer intended to examine him as an expert witness using both his medical expertise and his practical railroad switching experience in connection with the nature of the injury received and how it was caused.

Anticipating that the doctor would be vulnerable on cross-examination about being involved in switching operations from so long ago, the railroad lawyer arranged for him to be taken to a railroad yard a week or so before the trial to observe several switching operations using the same kinds of railroad cars which were involved in the accident.

The testimony of the doctor went as expected on direct examination and no mention was made of the doctor's recent visit to the railroad yard. When the plaintiff's attorney was concluding his cross-examination, the following exchange took place:

Q: When did you attend medical school, doctor?

A: From 1961 to 1965.

Q: Well, doctor, that was more than thirty years ago was it not?

A: Yes, it was.

Q: And yet, you come in here and testify about things that you may have done that long ago—thirty years ago—and expect this jury to accept that testimony as evidence of switching operations in 1996?

A: Well I observed those switching operations last Thursday.

Q: You what!?

A: Last Thursday the railroad arranged for me to go to one of its railroad yards and watch switching operations of the same kind of railroad cars involved in this accident.

Q: No further questions.

* * * * * *

Cross-examining Your Opponent's Witness

Turning now to that part of the trial in which you are cross-examining your opponent's witness, certain elementary but important things must be understood. It is necessary to listen to the witness on his direct examination. Hear him the way the jury hears him and see him the way the jury sees him. As previously explained, do not follow his testimony by reading his deposition as he testifies. Rather, watch and listen to him the way the jury does, as if you are hearing his testimony for the first time. (It is, of course, the one time that he testifies in open court).

When you conduct your cross-examination, many of the questions you ask are those that the jurors too are curious about and interested in. When you ask such questions you are establishing a bond with those jurors who feel you are asking the very same questions that they would ask if they were in your position. And this is so even if the questions you ask are only nominal inquiries relating to clarification and completeness and do not in any way go to the heart of the case.

There are two ways to approach the cross-examination of a witness who has given testimony damaging to your case. First, you find an approach which you believe will discredit the witness before the jury. Second, you choose not to cross-examine—at least not on the substance of his testimony. Rather, you elect to rebut the damaging testimony with contrary evidence and in your closing argument you urge the jury to disbelieve or disregard the witness's testimony.

Whether or not to follow the first alternative is a matter of judgment. If the testimony is subject to being contradicted by other witnesses or can be dealt with effectively in closing argument, the best alternative is not to cross-examine on the substance of the witness's testimony. The compelling reason for restraint is that ineffective cross-examination simply causes the witness to repeat and emphasize the damaging testimony. You should exercise the right to remain silent.

* * * * * *

Consider the words of the legendary Mayor Richard J. Daley of Chicago who one Sunday had gone fishing in Lake Michigan to promote its newly-stocked Coho Salmon. At the time, shortly after Jimmy Carter had been elected President of the United States, *Playboy* magazine had just published an interview with the new President in which he had unwisely discussed such subjects as lusting after women. Returning with a catch of salmon late in the afternoon Mayor Daley was immediately surrounded by the media. They soon asked him what he thought about Carter's *Playboy* interview. Holding up the salmon, Daley answered: "See these fish? If they had kept their mouths shut, they'd still be in the lake."

* * * * * *

Innovative approaches to cross-examination often can yield just the desired result. Take the case of a railroad worker who was injured when a boxcar door fell on him. At trial he testified that he had suffered a severe back injury which incapacitated him from future railroad work. In the course of his cross-examination, the attorney for the railroad suddenly produced a yardstick while stating to the plaintiff that he was unclear from the plaintiff's testimony on direct examination as to just how high the boxcar door was and how many feet it fell before striking him. He asked the plaintiff to take the yardstick over against the wall and demonstrate to the jury just how high the door was.

The judge permitted this over the vehement objections of the plaintiff's attorney. When the plaintiff stooped and raised and stretched himself to make the measurements, the actual condition of his back was made far more apparent to the jury than any conventional cross-examination—or defense medical testimony—ever could have shown.

Some things are not taught in law school.

* * * * * *

An impressive bit of cross-examination is attributed to Weymouth Kirkland, the founder of the law firm of Kirkland & Ellis. A man alleged that he suffered a severe injury to his shoulder resulting in the "freezing" of the shoulder. He claimed that the injury limited the movement of his arm so that he was able to raise it only to about the level of his shoulder. This was demonstrated to the jury on direct examination.

On cross-examination, Kirkland asked the witness to again show the jury the limitation in the movement of his arm as a result of the accident. The plaintiff was delighted to comply with the request. Then Kirkland directed: "Now, show the jury how high you could raise it *before* you were injured." Whereupon the man raised his arm to its full height above his shoulder!

* * * * * *

A police officer had testified in an intersection collision case that his analysis of the accident indicated that it was caused by the bus running the stop light. The attorney for the bus company recognized that any attempt to persuade the officer to change his testimony would be unsuccessful. Nevertheless, he did not want to concede the matter by asking him no questions at all. So, on cross-examination he asked this single question:

Q: Officer Donovan, have you ever made a mistake?[1]

* * * * * *

The plaintiff's expert medical witness, a distinguished and highly accredited physician and a member of a great number of medical societies, had done an excellent job in testifying, leaving no room for effective attack. On cross-examination, the attorney for the defendant stated to the doctor that he had made notes of the number of American and international medical societies to which the doctor belonged. He read from his list and asked the doctor if he had stated he was a member of those organizations. The doctor affirmed that he had. The attorney then read the names of a number of other organizations that the doctor had mentioned and the doctor again affirmed that he was a member of those organizations too. He then asked the doctor if he had named all the organizations to which the doctor belonged. The doctor responded "no" and added a few the attorney had not mentioned. Expressing incredulity, the attorney asked his final question:

"You mean you pay dues to all those organizations?"

The jury chuckled; the attorney returned to his table and took his seat.

* * * * * *

[1] *The beauty of this question is that it can be used with great effectiveness in closing argument. You summarize all the testimony that supports your view of the cause of the accident. Then, without questioning the officer's veracity, you refer to his concession that he had made mistakes and urge the jury that this was such a case.*

A man who had been served with a subpoena to appear to testify at trial as an adverse witness failed to respond to the subpoena. So a body attachment was issued and the Sheriff brought the man into court in shackles—and he was put on the stand in that condition. The first substantive question was the following:

Q: "You don't have anything to hide, do you?"

* * * * * *

The following story of cross-examination, apocryphal no doubt, demonstrates how with the witness's persistence and dogged determination the truth will come out.

After testifying about his extensive injuries received when he was struck by a vehicle while crossing a country highway, the very first question put to the plaintiff on cross-examination was the following:

Q: Isn't it true that just after the accident you stated that you were feeling fine?

A: Well sir, I got up that mornin', got my dog Blue, good dog Blue, got my mule and my rifle and started out to go ahuntin'—

Q: Objection, just answer the question.

A: Well sir, I got up that mornin', got my dog Blue, good dog Blue, got my mule and my rifle and started out to go ahuntin'—

Q: Objection. Your honor, would you direct the witness to answer the question.

THE COURT: The witness is directed to answer the question.

A: Well sir, I got up that mornin', got my dog Blue, good dog Blue, got my mule and my rifle and started out to go ahuntin'—

Q: Objection. Your honor the witness is not answering the question.

THE COURT: Answer the question.

A: Well sir, I got up that mornin', got my dog Blue, good dog

Blue, got my mule and my rifle and started out to go ahuntin'—

Q: Objection. Your honor the witness is still not answering the question.

THE COURT: Ah, let him answer it his way. Go ahead.

A: Well sir, I got up that mornin', got my dog Blue, good dog Blue, got my mule and my rifle and started out to go ahuntin'. We cut across yonder and were crossin' the highway when this vehicle comes out of nowheres like a bat out of hell and crashes into my dog Blue, good dog Blue, and my mule and me and spreads us all over the highway. I'm alayin' there sick, sore, lame and disabled and the next thing I knows the Sheriff pulls up. He gets out of his vehicle and walks over to my dog Blue, good dog Blue, and takes a look at him and says, "This dog's a goner." He takes out his big ol' revolver and "bam," that's the end of Blue. Then he goes over to my mule, takes a look at him and says, "This ol' mule has had it" and "bam," he shoots him too. Then the Sheriff walks over and looks at me and says, "How you feelin'?" and I says, *"I'm feelin' fine!"*

* * * * * *

As previously discussed, there are many times when there is nothing to be gained by cross-examining a witness. This is true even when the witness has given damaging testimony. If your questioning causes him to repeat what he has already testified to, then your cross-examination has served only to reinforce the damaging testimony. You have hurt your case. The point is that you often best serve your interests by remaining silent. When in doubt, it is best to remain silent. Act as if the testimony was of no great significance. ("Let's get on to some real witnesses.")

Always end your cross-examination on a high note. Have a question or two which will insure answers that are beneficial to your case. Assume, for example, that an opposing witness did not come to the scene until after the occurrence. Your can conclude your cross-examination with these questions:

Q: But do I understand, sir, that you did not come on the scene until some time after the occurrence?

Q: You did not actually witness the accident?

* * * * * *

The story is told of an attractive lady of a certain age who had stood up very well to a withering cross-examination. Finally, frustrated, but knowing that the woman was considerably older than she looked, the lawyer inquired maliciously:

Q: How old are you?

A: Why, … I don't know.

Q: You don't know?!

A: No, I have never seen either my birth certificate or my baptismal certificate.

Q: But, surely, your mother must have told you how old you were at some time?

A: Yes, of course she did but (turning to the judge) that would be hearsay, wouldn't it?

THE COURT: Indeed it would, madam. You need not answer that question and unless counsel has another question, you may step down.

* * * * * *

Levels of the Game

From time to time one sees a dramatic and unexpected turn of events in the midst of a trial. When this is happening a feeling of electricity flows through the courtroom. The often bored and disinterested jury comes alive and follows everything with acute perception and comprehension.

After the plaintiff rested, the first witness put on by the defense was a "private investigator," a specialist in surveillance. The witness identified certain photographs which he had secretly taken which showed the plaintiff involved in physical activities that appeared to contradict testimony as to the severity of his injuries and the extent of his disabilities. When the witness's direct testimony was completed things looked grim indeed for the plaintiff.

The plaintiff's attorney, the resourceful Philip H. Corboy, began his cross-examination quietly and simply enough, asking the witness a number of questions to complete and clarify his testimony. The witness was asked to further explain the work which he had been hired to do. This careful but undramatic cross-examination developed that the witness had followed and photographed the plaintiff over a considerable period of time.

Then Corboy inquired if the witness had taken other photographs of the plaintiff. Yes, he had.

Q:"Well, let's take a look at them, shall we?"

Those other photographs were produced, examined by Corboy, and in due course were marked as *plaintiff's* exhibits. What was developed was that while the photographs produced by the defense did suggest that the plaintiff was exaggerating the extent of his injury, the numerous photographs brought out by Corboy's cross-examination—those not produced by the defense—tended to strongly confirm the disability! The tables had been turned. What began as a devastating attack had suddenly become an even more devastating counter attack. And the jury picked up on every bit of it.

Every offense invites a counter offense. And time and time again the most powerful weapon can be effectively and unexpectedly used against the party who brings it into play.

Impeachment

Behold, my desire is … that mine adversary had written a book.

—Job

An integral element of cross-examination is impeachment. A witness may be impeached by demonstrating that on some prior occasion he made a statement or acted in a manner contrary to or inconsistent with the way he has just testified. In the most common situation, the witness has given a statement or testimony at his deposition contrary to his immediate testimony at trial. As an example, assume a trial involves an automobile accident and the witness testifies in court that the speed of his automobile just prior to the accident was twenty-five miles per hour whereas his deposition states otherwise, impeachment is carried out as follows:

Q: Mr. Witness, do you recall your deposition being taken in this case on November 16, 1995 in my offices?

A: Yes.

Q: And you and I and your attorney were present?

A: Yes.

Q: And you recall also that you were sworn to tell the truth and that a court reporter was present taking down all the questions and answers?

A: Yes.

Q: And, Mr. Witness, was this question asked and did you give this answer:

"Question: 'How fast was your car going just prior to the accident.' Answer: 'Sixty miles per hour.' Was that question asked and did you give that answer?"

A: Yes.

As can be seen from the foregoing, the examining attorney reads that question and answer or, on occasion, those questions and answers which are impeaching. If the questions and answers are not in fact impeaching, the opposing counsel will object and make a motion to strike the examination relating to it, and ask the Court to instruct the jury to disregard the testimony. "I object, your Honor. That is not impeaching. I move to strike that examination and ask that the jury be instructed to disregard it." If the Court deems that the testimony is or appears to be impeaching, the objection will be overruled and the witness will be directed to answer the question.

If, as occasionally happens in the course of impeachment, the witness takes the position that his memory of the event is better at trial than it was at his deposition, he is subject to the following line of questioning.

Q: Is it your position then, Mr. Witness, that a person's memory of an occurrence is better two years after the occurrence than three months after?

The witness finds himself in a no-win situation.

* * * * * *

The witness had been impeached by admitting that a statement he made shortly after the accident was contrary to his testimony at trial. Attempting to rehabilitate the witness, his attorney asked the following question:

Q: Were you under oath when you made that statement?

A: No, I was not.

On recross-examination the opposing attorney asked this single question:

Q: Do you only tell the truth when you are under oath?

* * * * * *

On both cross-examination and impeachment it is not necessary, and may be counter effective, to make your strongest points at the outset. It is best to deal first with the basic points you wish to cover and only then to proceed to your most telling points. Moreover, if you are in a position to impeach a witness, and yet you know there is much in his testimony that supports your view of the case, you should extract the beneficial testimony first, because once he has been effectively impeached he is no longer a credible witness.

Like most abilities, the ability to be an effective cross-examiner does not come naturally. It must be learned. It should be understood, too, that effective cross-examination is not always dramatic and does not have to be. It is the jury's reading of the witness that is important. The jury sees, often far more clearly than either the cross-examiner or the witness, what the real truth is and the attempts to manipulate it. Have faith in the jury. It is on the side of the truth. You do your job and you can count on the jury to do the same.

CHAPTER SEVEN

Expert Witnesses

Expert opinion is only an ordinary guess in evening clothes.

— Bok, J., *Kerstetter v. Commonwealth*, 404 Pa. 168, 173 (1961)

The ordinary witness can testify only to his direct observation or knowledge of the facts of a case. An expert witness is one with special knowledge by way of education or experience who can give his opinion in response to questions involving certain facts of a case. The opposing attorney is given wide latitude in his cross-examination of the expert, and may vary the facts that the expert assumes when giving his opinion on direct examination.

Because the testimony of the expert witness can often determine the outcome of a case, he must expect to undergo the most vigorous attack on his analysis, his integrity and his interest in the outcome of the case. From time to time, one sees an expert witness brought into a case who has the impression that he is there merely to set things straight from the viewpoint of his expertise. Nothing could be further from the truth. In fact, he is entering a battlefield and he will be treated as a combatant by the opposing party from the moment that he steps into the courtroom.

Many attorneys spend inordinate amounts of time developing expertise in those areas for which they have retained experts. Contrary to common assumption, the lawyer does not have to become enormously informed on all aspects of the expert's subject matter. The lawyer needs some informed knowledge, of course, but basically he must merely be aware of the conclusions to which his expert witness can testify. He needs to know the bottom line and can leave it to his expert to explain how he reaches his conclusions, and to defend those conclusions on cross-examination.

With some assistance from his own expert, the same approach can be taken in cross-examining opposing experts. You rely on your expert to assist you in approaching the cross-examination of the opposing expert. You attack the opposing expert's conclusions and the basis for those conclusions.

Traditionally, the expert witness testifies by way of a hypothetical question; a combination of assumed or proved facts and circumstances is stated in such form as to constitute a coherent and specific situation or state of facts upon which the opinion of the expert is asked. The facts and circumstances, of course, mirror those of the evidence in the case. One of the principal reasons for the hypothetical question form is that often certain "facts" may be in dispute, or otherwise not credible to the jury. Hypothetical inquiry permits expert testimony but does not substitute the opinion of the expert for the ultimate finding of the jury. Whether the facts of the hypothetical question support the opinion of the expert is for the jury to determine.

In a number of jurisdictions the procedure has been changed and the expert may testify as to his opinion of the relevant facts of a case without resorting to the hypothetical question approach. The burden is then on the cross-examining attorney to test the opinion by varying the facts and delving into the underlying premises upon which the expert's opinion is based.

Avoid Extensive Objections

Under most circumstances, the substance of the testimony of an expert witness will go into evidence. It must be recognized, therefore, that the injection of repeated objections may not succeed in restricting or limiting the admission of the testimony. Furthermore, the jury, seeing the extensive objections, may attach a greater significance to the testimony than is merited. Consider both points when deciding the extent to which to interpose objections. This does not imply that you do not object to clearly improper questions.

Perhaps the better approach is to demonstrate the weaknesses of the testimony by effective cross-examination rather than repeated objections. Thus you make your point more powerfully to the jury and avoid the cost of appearing to be an obstructionist.

At trial many cases develop into a "battle of the experts." This is what happened in the *Mohler* case. Four expert witnesses, two presented by each party, gave their testimony: for the plaintiff, Joseph M. Segarra, a medical expert and Walter Johnson, an economist; for the defendant, two medical experts, Jan E. Leestma, a pathologist, and John R. Hughes, an expert in epileptic seizures. Their testimony is set out in the following pages.

Broadly speaking, the plaintiff uses the expert medical witness, Joseph M. Segarra, to demonstrate that the death of Harold Mohler was the result of his injury on December 28, 1967, when the break-in-two occurred. By using Dr. Segarra, the plaintiff is trying to persuade the jury that the injury was in fact the cause of the death on January 19, 1968. The defense, on the other hand, tries to discredit the theory that there was a connection between the injury and the death and asserts instead that the death resulted from a simple heart attack.

The plaintiff puts on economist Walter Johnson to develop through a learned and credible witness the great economic loss suffered by the surviving family of Harold Mohler. On cross-examination of Dr. Johnson, the defense attempts to show, through the earning power of money, that a significantly lesser amount of money would still bring substantial income to the surviving family.

The defense puts on pathologist Jan E. Leestma to demonstrate that the most likely cause of death of Harold Mohler was a heart attack. The plaintiff seeks to discredit Dr. Leestma's testimony by a penetrating cross-examination.

The final expert witness for the defense is John R. Hughes, a highly qualified expert in epileptic seizures. Although attacked in every possible way on cross-examination, Dr. Hughes, a very experienced witness, handles himself so well that the attorney putting him on asks not a single question on redirect examination.

Plaintiff's Expert Witnesses

JOSEPH M. SEGARRA, called as a witness herein, having been first duly sworn, was examined and testified as follows:

DIRECT EXAMINATION BY MR. HAYES:

Q Doctor, will you be kind enough to keep your voice up and just talk right to these people.

A Very good. I will.

Q Will you state your name, please?

A My name is Joseph M. Segarra.

Q Doctor, where were you born, sir?

A I was born in Spain.

Q And where did you attend medical school?

A I went to medical school in Barcelona, Spain and then I did post-graduate training in Madrid, and then Paris, France, and finally Boston.

Q At what institution did you do your undergraduate training?

A At the University of Barcelona.

Q And the medical school was?

A Medical school, the University of Barcelona Medical School.

Q Okay, and did you receive what would be the equivalent of an M.D. in the United States?

A There, I got the M.D., and then I went to the University of Madrid. I received a doctorate; it's a little more than the M.D., so to speak.

And then I went to Paris to train in neurology. And after this, I got a scholarship through the Rockefeller Foundation, and I went to Harvard. I did research there.

Then I started residency training at Tuft's University, where I was Chief Resident. And after that, I became the Chief of Neuropathology at the Boston Veterans Administration with BU University.

Q BU is Boston University?

A Boston University Medical School. And I stayed there for twenty-some years. And, you know, I went up the academic ladder little by little, and that's where I am now.

Q What is your practice now, sir?

A Well, it's mixed. I have a private practice, and in addition, I lecture around at conferences of the VA.

Q Now, Doctor, each of us has a copy of your curriculum vitae. I see "Boursier Etranger." I don't know if I am pronouncing it correctly.

A No, you are not pronouncing it very correctly.

Q Pardon me?

A You are not pronouncing it correctly.

Q I'm sorry.

A That's all right.

Q I don't even speak English too well sometimes. Will you tell us what that is, sir, from '47 to '48?

A It's a scholarship the French government used to give to foreign students.

Q Okay. And then I see another one at the National Center for Scientific Research in France.

A Yes.

Q '48 to '50.

A That was a regular job as a researcher in a government agency of the French government. The first one was a scholarship given through the French embassies abroad.

And then after a year or two in Paris on this scholarship I got a regular job as a researcher in the Centre Nationale Scientific, and stayed there one more year.

Q Then there was the assistantship at the Hospital of Paris?

A Well, the title that I got at the end of these years was assistant *etranger*. That means foreign assistant.

Q And did that involve your receiving a diploma from the Sorbonne?

A Yes. They give you a very nice piece of paper.

Q And then in Barcelona from 1950 to 1952, what was your association with the Barcelona Neurological Institute?

A Yes, I was a physician there. There are different titles in Spanish, you know, intern or things of this sort, but basically it was like a resident.

Q And were you in charge of neuropathology at this institution?

A Yes, I was in charge of neuropathology there before coming to this country.

Q Now, then, at Harvard University, you were a research fellow in neurology?

A Yes.

Q And thereafter, you were an assistant resident in neurology at Boston City Hospital?

A That's correct.

Q Where you worked with Denny Brown?

A Denny Brown.

Q Who is Denny Brown?

A Denny Brown is the granddaddy of American neurology, although he was English originally. But he is probably the greatest figure in neurology in America.

Q Now, what academic appointments have you had in this country?

A Well, I was a lecturer or something at Harvard. Then I was and I am still, assistant professor at Tufts, and I am associate professor in neurology at Boston University.

Q Have you contributed to the medical literature?

A A little bit. I'm guilty of that. Yes.

Q Well, how many of your articles have been published in recognized journals?

A Well, I don't have the exact number, but I suppose twenty or thirty, possibly a little bit more than thirty. And I published a monograph or two.

Q And have you lectured at the World Congress of Neuropathology?

A Yes. Yes. I presented papers.

Q What field have your papers been, sir?

A Well, neurology, obviously. I have been interested in the problems of consciousness, when people look like a mummy, but are they conscious, do they feel what's going on or not, a little bit in the realm of like the Quinlan case, or the other day it was in the newspaper, also, a little girl wakes up after three years in a coma, this kind of problems I have been interested in. And I think I made a modest contribution to this problem.

Q Have some of your articles and lectures involved epilepsy ?

A Yes. I also lecture almost every year on the problems of epilepsy, the different modalities and the pathology that goes with it.

Q Now, of what specialty organizations are you a member, Doctor?

A Well, I am a member of the Royal Society of Medicine in London. I am a member of the American Academy of Neurology. I am a member of the Massachusetts Medical Society. I don't know, I probably am a member of something else. I can't think of it.

Q Doctor, have you worked in encephalography?

A Yes, I also worked on EEGs.

Q Electroencephalography?

A Yes.

Q Doctor, are there what are called National Certifying Boards in this country?

A Yes, of course.

Q Why don't you tell the jury what the American Boards are?

A Well, the American Boards are really private institutions run by the AMA, the American Medical Association, to ensure to the public that whoever is certified or said to be a specialist really has gone through a program of training and exams so he is a real specialist. So, in a certain way, it's like a quality control seal on doctors.

Q Are you a member of an American Board?

A Yes. I am certified in neurology and the Board of Neurology and Psychiatry, and I am certified in the sub-specialty of neuropathology. That is a part of the Board of Pathology.

Q So that you have been Board certified by the American Board of Neurology and Psychiatry?

A Yes.

Q And that certifies in either neurology or psychiatry or both, is that right?

A In either, not both.

Q Not both?

A You have to take two different Boards.

Q And you are certified in?

A In neurology.

Q And the American Board of Pathology, you are—

A Certified in Neuropathology.

Q Now, Doctor, what is neuropathology?

A Neuropathology is this part of medical knowledge that has to do with the changes in the brain, in the nerves and a little bit in the muscles of neurological diseases. In other words, when somebody is sick in the nervous system, the part that shows what is sick and the mechanism of the sickness is what goes by the name of neuropathology.

I don't know if I put it too well, but that more or less is the idea.

Q And, Doctor, what is neurology?

A Neurology is the part of medical knowledge that has to do

with clinical knowledge of diseases of the nervous system, the brain, the spinal cord, the nerves and so on.

Q Doctor, in connection with your practice, your training, your studies, have you had occasion to perform autopsies of a neurological nature?

A Well, yes. As Chief of Neuropathology at the Boston VA for twenty-three or twenty-four years, I certainly did my share of autopsies of the brain and the spinal cord.

Q Doctor, will you tell us something about, Doctor, of what—I know that this could take lectures for years, but can you give us—

A I will restrain myself, I assure you.

Q Doctor, if you will, tell us just something about the brain and diseases.

A No, you have to ask me something more specific. What would you like me to—

Q I think what I will do then, Doctor, is I will ask you—I have told you that there would be what is called a hypothetical question put to you, and perhaps I will put the question to you, and then after you give us your opinions, we can kind of zero in on things that are relevant to this case. Would that be a better way of approaching it?

A Fine.

Q Okay. Doctor, and incidentally, have you had occasion to testify on my behalf in the past, sir?

A Yes.

Q And have I consulted with you with respect to the case of Harold Mohler?

A Yes, you have.

Q And, Doctor, I want you to assume that on—

MR. CALLAHAN: Mr. Hayes, do you have a prepared hypothetical question?

MR. HAYES: No, I have a—as far as the findings of the autopsy, I have the actual transcript of Dr. Burns' testimony. This is going to be a question as to what Dr. Burns' testimony was.

I will be reading from the transcript prepared for me by the court reporter of the testimony he gave the other day, and the other is my notes of what the evidence in the case has been.

THE COURT: Please proceed, gentlemen.

MR. HAYES: Thank you.

MR. CALLAHAN: I am going to object to his reading from the transcript. If he wants to read from his notes or something—what I am trying to do is make it simpler so I can see what the question is that he is going to ask.

THE COURT: If you have a hypothetical question that you wish to propound to the witness, please do so. I know of no requirement which requires him to provide you with a copy of the transcript, counsel.

Proceed.

MR. HAYES: I should also like to point out, your Honor—

MR. CALLAHAN: Your Honor, I am going to object.

THE COURT: I don't believe any further discussion is necessary. Please proceed.

MR. HAYES: Thank you, your Honor.

Q Doctor, I want you to assume that on December 28, 1967, a man who was about six feet one inches in height, and who weighed about 160 pounds, was riding as a brakeman in the caboose of a railroad train, that at some point in time before, while he was working, he was standing and was about to go to the rear door of the caboose to throw out a fusee, which was a part of his duties.

The train went into an emergency braking, and the man's head was slammed against the back of the wall of the caboose. That occurred at approximately 4:45 a.m. There were three other members of the crew on the train, but they were all riding in the engine. None of those men saw the caboose brakeman, I will call him, at any time until perhaps two or three hours or so later when he was seen in a town called Streator, at which time he went to the engine of the train and asked the engineer what happened at Reddick. Reddick is the town on the railroad line where the stop occurred. The engineer replied, "We went into emergency."

Then the man told the engineer that he had hit his head. The engineer noted a cut on the top of his ear with a small amount of blood. Several hours later the train reached a town called Zearing, which was the end of the line. At Zearing, the man met with the other members of the crew and had a conversation with one of them. That man noted that he had a large amount of blood which appeared to be dried or drying, and he would say perhaps a tablespoon or teaspoon in his right ear.

During that day or that evening that man was described by the person who also saw the blood in the ear and with whom he bunked that evening at a local hotel, a Holiday Inn, as being just not quite the way he was, just something unusual about him. At a town called Hennepin, which was one of the places on the line where there is a lot of work to be done in switching cars, setting out and picking up cars, the brakeman did not participate in the work done at that stop. Then the next day, it also appeared to another fellow employee that he seemed tired and kind of just not himself at that time.

Now, he got home and told his wife about the accident, and she noted that he had blood in the right ear, and thereafter he went to bed. And between that time and January 19, 1968, members of the family observed episodes of what they concluded was unusual behavior for the man.

While he had been an outgoing person, and lively, he was observed on a couple of episodes of one time standing as if like a statue and staring straight ahead. It was observed for a period of time believed by the man's daughter to be perhaps ten seconds, and after that she didn't observe him any longer. She turned away. And another episode involved the daughter seeing her father in bed. He was thrashing about, rolling from side to side, his arms flailing and his head turned. He was moaning and not making any intelligible sounds.

He did not respond to any questioning of his daughter when she asked him, and she kept calling his name and kept asking him what is wrong. And this went on for some period of time. Part of this episode was also observed by his wife, who said that it was very unusual, she felt afraid, and felt that something was wrong. But shortly thereafter, the daughter came out of the bedroom and said to her mother, "He is sleeping now."

There was an episode or a couple of episodes where he held his head and said that he had a headache. His mother observed at one time, when he went over to her house to assist her in putting down some stripping, that as he got up, he put his hands to his head and said, "My head, ever since the damned accident." And then the last time that he was seen alive by a member of the family was, I believe, on January 17th, when his wife was going to go to a neighbor's house, and he said that he was going to go to bed. He was lying in bed. As he was lying in bed with his head against the pillow, he was observed by his wife to be staring straight ahead as if in a trance, with a vacant look, an unusual look about his face. She characterized it as "an unnatural look."

She said a couple of things. She told him she was going to Ruth's, "Do you want anything," and there was no response. She then went across to the neighbor's house, and a short while later, her husband called her at the neighbor's house and said, "They have called me for work." She went back immediately to the house to take him to work, and he seemed fine with no problems.

And while this man had been a pretty good father, he didn't strike the kids, didn't hit the kids, except when they were young children, when he spanked them, but on one time his eldest daughter, for something that was rather trivial, he either struck her or shoved her across the room. And this was the only time that he wife had ever seen him act like that with the children. And yet a little while later an incident occurred at dinner that somebody would have a right to be upset about but he wasn't. And the episode with the daughter occurred, and then after that, he went to bed again and went right to sleep. Later on he appeared normal.

On January 17th, he was called to work, and he went on a trip to Elkhart, Indiana. They arrived at Elkhart, Indiana, in the early morning hours, I think it was about 4:15. And then he went to the hotel, and during that day all along the trip, he was fine. A man who saw much of him during that trip, a friend of his, didn't observe anything unusual about him. That day they laid around in town, and they played pool, played cards, and he had no problems at all. During that trip he was the conductor, and his friend was one of the brakemen. There were three brakemen on the trip.

Then at about 2:00 in the morning, they went over to a small hotel, different from where they were staying. It was located in the railroad yard and was called the Railroad YMCA. They had coffee and then he and the friend departed there, and he reported to a tower where, as conductor, he was supposed to prepare lists of trains and cars and things of that nature. The friend went to the caboose, but then returned to confirm that this was the right caboose, the right train that they were going to be on. And about an hour later, the man had completed his work, and then went to the caboose.

Now, the friend was sitting in the caboose, and he heard the man, the conductor, come in. He said, "Have you told them you're on the caboose?" This is a phrase in railroading which means that the train is ready to go. He didn't answer, but walked several feet, put down his bag and keeled over onto his right side. The friend turned him onto his back, and the man started gasping and choking. He took the man's coat and put it under his head. The gasping and choking continued for a period of some three to five minutes. And at some point, the man's eyes rolled back. And somewhere near the end of the episode, they tried to take the pulse and couldn't get a pulse. And at that moment, a trainmaster walked in, and he felt the man and he said, "This man is dead."

Now, the man had been in good health throughout his life. He had an appendectomy. He had strained his back once, and he was in the hospital for a few days for that. That was back in 1960. In 1963, he hired on the railroad. A railroad doctor examined him. He completed a questionnaire as to his physical history, and he—you have seen the questionnaire, have you?

A Yes

Q He was examined by a physician—

MR. CALLAHAN: Excuse me, your Honor. I am not sure that that has been admitted or whether you—

THE COURT: What's the number of that document, sir?

MR. HAYES: That is No. 18, your Honor.

THE COURT: It's been received in evidence.

MR. CALLAHAN: Thank you.

MR. HAYES: And may the jury also know that the other document that was the subject of discussion was also received?

THE COURT: Exhibit 20, both received in evidence.

MR. HAYES: Thank you.

Q So that in 1963, he had an examination, which included a checklist of all of the things about the body, vision, hearing, blood pressure, colored vision, et cetera, et cetera, et cetera. At that time a physical examination was performed, and it was fine. And then in December of 1966, December 27, 1966, almost a year to the day before the accident, the man was examined by a railroad surgeon and found to be in good health. He was described by his family and friends as being in good health and an outgoing type of person. And there is some other evidence of his activities during those last days of his life.

Q Doctor, have you seen this book called Group Exhibit No. 20?

A Yes.

Q Have you looked—did we look over it together, sir?

A Yes.

Q And did you observe particularly the notations made by this man after the 29th of December?

A Yes, I noted the change.

Q Okay. There was a change in the way in which the man noted his—what he was doing?

MR. CALLAHAN: Just a minute. I think we have gone from a hypothetical to direct testimony. I think I'd like to get some idea where we are going here.

THE COURT: It's based on hypothesis, of course.

MR. HAYES: I'm asking him to assume that these things were observed in the hypothetical person's records.

MR. CALLAHAN: I'm going to object to that because there is no testimony to any such changes in—the first reference I heard is when it came out here with this doctor and Mr. Hayes.

MR. HAYES: I offered the document into evidence, and you said you had no objection. It was received in evidence. If it's in evidence, it's in evidence.

MR. CALLAHAN: It's in evidence, but I am objecting to him taking a hypothetical question and turning it into direct examination. That's improper. If he wants to put a hypothetical question, put it.

THE COURT: Anything else?

(No response.)

Objection is overruled. Proceed.

MR. HAYES: Q I want you to assume that what you observed about the notations in this book were the notations of the hypothetical man that we are talking about in this question.

Doctor, after the death the body was taken by someone to a mortuary in Elkhart, Indiana, where the body was embalmed. Then later on, the body was picked up by a funeral home located in the town where the man lived, and his body was taken to that funeral home, where an autopsy was performed by a pathologist certified in general pathology.

The examination included examination of the extremities as well as the torso and head. It was noted that there was an incision in the right paramedian and paraumbilical portion of the abdominal wall, and an appendectomy scar was noted. The remainder of the examination, external examination of the body also indicated to the doctor that there had been the incision which he spoke about indicated that the body had been embalmed. The remainder of the external examination was within normal limits. There were no abnormal pigments, no abnormal growths or tumors present on the external body. Then he opened the body in the routine fashion. The body cavities were opened. The organs were examined individually.

The abdominal cavity was found to contain adhesions on the right lower portion of the body deep to or adjacent to an ancient, well-healed scar, being the appendectomy scar. And it was observed that the appendix was absent. The remaining portion of the abdominal viscera as they lay in the body appeared to be essentially intact. The chest cavity or thoracic cavity was examined next. They were essentially intact, excepting that the body had been embalmed and the embalming work involved the use of trocar, which inflicted a great deal of tearing and ripping and penetration of the viscera by the instrument. Excepting for those injuries, which were obviously caused after death, the abdominal portion of the examination appeared to be normal.

The thoracic cavity was examined in a similar manner, and the extent of that examination was within normal limits. The thoracic cavity was free of fluid, adhesions or displacements of the organs which would indicate any pre-mortem abnormality. The organs of the upper half of the body were removed and dissected individually. The heart was described as of normal size. The cavities contained some post-mortem blood clots, which are blood clots that form after death. The heart was also penetrated by the trocar and so also sustained post-mortem damage. The heart was a normal weight of 370 grams. The surfaces of the heart were normal. The cavities were opened, and they were found to be normal. The heart was measured, including the valves that separate the various chambers, and they were all within normal dimensions. The thickness of the muscle was normal on both sides of the heart, right and left.

The heart cavities were of normal dimensions and consistency. The coronary arteries, which are the arteries that carry blood into the heart muscle, were dissected and were found to be widely patent throughout, and there was no evidence of occlusion of the coronary arteries. In one small area, there was a shallow thickening of the wall of the artery, which was an intimal plaque, a shallow flattening of the inner surface of the artery. This was not associated with any demonstrable disease or closure of the coronary arteries. The aorta was dissected and found to have some early minor changes of arteriosclerosis consistent in a person of that age, but not indicative of the kinds of changes that would be associated with the cause of death. The vena cava was dissected at that point, and it was found to be intact, free of signs of any pre-mortem disease.

The lungs were dissected. They weighed approximately 500 grams apiece. The damage from the embalming process was noted. The examination of the lungs was essentially normal with one exception, and that is of clear mucus material in both of the air tubes of both the right and left lungs, primarily on the right. The main branches of the air tubes were widely patent.

The spleen was examined, and it was found to weigh 100 grams, and on cross-sectioning it was normal in every respect. The pancreas was examined and sectioned, was found to weigh 100 grams, and then cross-section showed entirely normal structures. The liver weighed 1300 grams which is normal weight. Dissection of the various portions of the liver, of the arteries, the veins, the biliary system were again normal.

The gastrointestinal tract was examined. The stomach, small intestine and colon were examined and found to be within normal limits. The stomach contained a small amount of undigested food and mucus. There was no sign of bleeding or of any other disease process that could be related to the cause of death. The adrenal glands were examined. They were found to be within normal limits, and on gross examination showed normal characteristics. The kidneys were examined in conjunction with the urinary bladder and genitalia. The kidneys were normal and were, for all intents and purposes, normal structure.

Next examined were the organs of the neck, the larynx, the voicebox, the upper esophagus and trachea. Again, they were examined, and, again, no abnormalities were found. The thyroid gland was examined and found to be normal.

Examination was then carried on about the head. The examination of the head involved incision down to bone over the top and then reflecting the layers of the scalp forward and back. And the tissues of the scalp were examined for evidence of injury, recent or old, and none was found. The top of the skull was then removed with appropriate devices, the surfaces of the brain examined. The brain surfaces were normal in every respect. There was no evidence of hemorrhage either old or recent. The general conformation of the brain in terms of dimensions and organization of the surface were again normal. The brain was then removed from the cavity of the head, and was turned over, examined on the bottom side. The blood vessels that lead to it from the brain were found to be essentially normal. The brain itself was then sectioned in increments like slicing something and were sectioned across, and examination of all of the surfaces was performed in an effort to determine any abnormalities of the brain. None were found. The surfaces or the membrane that lines the skull, the inner side of the skull, was reflected in an effort to find evidence for hemorrhage on the base of the skull or evidence for a basilar skull fracture, and none was found.

And that was essentially the autopsy. He noted that all the serosal surfaces were normal and glistening. Pleural surfaces were normal and glistening. The mediastinum was in the midline. All of the epicardial, pericardial and endocardial surfaces were smooth and glistening.

There was not anything that was found relating to the entire arterial system or coronary system. The lungs were all normal, with the exception of the presence of a moderate amount of clear mucoid secretion obstructing as we have described. Those largely obstructed the secondary bronchus to the right lower lobe, and it obstructed the smaller branches in the right middle and upper middle lobes. And with that exception, the lungs and any associated structures were normal.

Now, Doctor, the exterior of the tissue below the part where the corona of the skull was removed, those were not reflected exteriorly. But the examination of the dish-like skull that remained was examined internally with stripping of the dura, as I indicated.

Now, Doctor, first of all, I'd like to know, based upon that evidence, sir, and all the things that I have asked you to assume with respect to that document and everything else, first of all, Doctor, can you come to any absolute statement as to the cause of death?

A. An absolute, no. Nobody can.

Q. Are there any absolutes in medicine on anything?

A. Except death.

Q. Pardon me?

A. Except death.

Q. Doctor, do you have an opinion, based upon a reasonable degree of certainty, as to the probable cause of death of this man?

A. Yes, I do.

Q. And what is your opinion, sir?

MR. CALLAHAN: For the record, may I show an objection to the hypothetical question at this time, your Honor?

THE COURT: Yes, sir. Objection is overruled.

THE WITNESS: Well, the way I construe the sequence of events leading to this unfortunate man's death is, first, the head blow of whatever intensity created a period of confusion, and this led subsequently, as is well known that happens, to small episodes of epilepsy. The facts that you mentioned of staring in space, in my opinion, were so-called minor epilepsy. They are not exactly petty mal. Petty mal refers to something else, but it's minor epilepsy.

The thrashing that he did also indicates in this direction. And I think that what happened most likely is that in the final event, during one of these small episodes that he had been having during this three weeks between the accident and his death, that he had one of those episodes which led to laryngospasm when he was seen choking, and this in turn led to lack of oxygen or blood supply, oxygenated blood supply, and death as a result.

MR. HAYES: Q Doctor, you have mentioned epilepsy resulting from trauma. Now, this pathologist examined the brain as carefully as he examined all of the rest of the organs, and he made a lot of slices of the brain, and he examined those surfaces. What is the significance of the fact that no evidence of injuries to the brain—

A I see what you are leading at.

THE COURT: Can we have the completion of the question for the record, please?

THE WITNESS: I'm sorry.

MR. HAYES: There was no evidence of injury anywhere in the brain or, indeed, anywhere else in the body except that caused by the trocar work.

THE WITNESS: You see, the lesions that lead to epileptic attacks can be very subtle, so subtle that they are not seen when looking at the brain in the so-called gross examination.

No hemorrhages are seen, no strokes, no lesions that you can recognize with the naked eye. And it is only when you go into a microscopic examination of sometimes fairly sophisticated that you can see the small changes that explains the occurrence of seizures.

Q Now, does that occur over time, Doctor?

A Those changes?

Q Yes, sir.

A Yes, they can. Those changes that explain attacks of epilepsy are of two kinds. The more acute ones, the more immediate ones, that explains the immediate attacks that can happen, and then comes scar process, a scar formation, and the scar formation is a little bit like the arthritis of an old person, good days where the person hardly feels the joints and then bad days for some reason where the scar, instead of being quiet, begins discharging electrical impulses to the rest of the brain, and then you have an attack.

Q Doctor, in your opinion, what are the mechanisms of this, the opinion that you have expressed with respect to the death of the man? What in your opinion is it that happened to the brain?

A Well, what happened to the brain is two things, basically. One is that the nerve cells that are the creators of this electrical activity are damaged either directly by the blow or more often than not by blanching. There is not enough blood for a moment, the brain being compressed, just like blanching of the skin if you put your thumb (indicating). And this blanching modifies the nerve cells. They become sick, if you want, and they begin to discharge a diastolic provocation, and by infecting the other nerve cells with this abnormal discharge, finally all of the nerve cells begin discharging. And this disorganized discharge is what constitutes an epileptic attack.

Q Now, Doctor, are there fibers in the brain that are, or can be, disturbed in head injury?

A Yes. That's another thing that can happen.You see, when you have a head blow, the brain is shook inside, and part of it scratches, as it were, the irregular surface of the bone. That's one thing that happens.

But the other—this is a very interesting mechanism—is that the brain is twisted within itself, and as a result of this twisting, the brain may look like Jell-O, but it is not uniform. There are fibers that go from the back to the front and fibers that go across and fibers that go sideways. And as you twist the brain, on displacing it from the blow, then certain fibers resist, but others don't, and there is a breakup, a breakup of fibers.

It is microscopic. You don't see it. If you look at the brain, nothing shows, okay, but it's there if you stain the brain with proper stains and so on.

Q Is that a rather sophisticated technique of staining?

A Yes. Those are not the run-of-the-mill hematoxylin; this is the most used stain for general pathology.

But with special stains for the brain, you can pick up subtle lesions that otherwise can pass undetected.

Q Do you know who has done a lot of work on this?

A Well, yes. Yes, I do, as part of being a neuropathologist. The best work is by an American neuropathologist named Courville. He wrote beautifully on these problems. And then there is this English lady neuropathologist, Sabina Stritch, who was probably the first one to put on the map those fiber breakings that can be so subtle as to manifest themselves, not by a paralysis, you know, weak arm, weak leg, okay, but by changes in personality, by, say, "Oh, Uncle Willie is not the same that he was before," this kind of subtle changes, that slowness, you know, of reacting sometimes are due to those changes that Sabina Stritch, this English neuropathologist, had first pointed out.

Q Doctor, have you explained the basis of your opinions and the bases for your opinions?

A Yes. Well, I don't know exactly what you are asking me.

Q Well, okay. I want to now talk about this epilepsy that you mentioned. You mentioned that epilepsy can occur as a result of an injury, in the scarring, certain things happen?

A Yes.

Q You have also mentioned that you have a particular interest in and have done a lot of work in consciousness. What forms do epileptic or epileptic form seizures take or what forms may they take?

A All right. Basically, to make it short, okay, I don't want to give you a lot of expert double-talk. You will get lost. But basically, there's four forms.

One is the grand mal generalized seizure. The generalized grand mal seizure where the patient shakes all over, usually shouting before passing out. That's well known. It's the kind you see on the street sometimes. All of a sudden, a big cry, big shake. That's one form.

The other is the petty mal attack. That occurs generally in children, and is this kind of staring spell (indicating), just a little bit out to lunch for a few seconds, and then the resuming of what one is doing.

The third form is the so-called temporal lobe epilepsy. This is the discharges in the temporal lobe, and these are the ones that fascinate the newspapers most because those are the ones that can be manifested by attacks of uncontrollable rage, you know. Remember the case of this fellow in a Texan University that went up in a tower and began shooting everybody. And he was found to have a small tumor in the temporal lobe, and those are the ones of the person with a knife going around crazy and knifing anybody in front of him, this kind of events that sometimes are very traumatic, and they are associated with change in personality, the person becomes suspicious, paranoid, very difficult, very sticky, you know.

And then the other kind is the focal epilepsy; in other words, small spots in the cortex, in the surface of the brain where a discharge will begin and the patient begins with a twisting of the finger, sometimes going on to the whole hand and then the whole arm, et cetera. Okay. And those are basically the main types of epilepsy.

Q You mentioned the second form of epilepsy which is found usually in children and is manifested by staring.

Now, you also mentioned this staring episodes in the case of the hypothetical person we are talking about.

A Clinically, this is a distinction, how should I say, for the experts. Clinically, it's very similar between the so-called minor epilepsy—this is, this is a small attack—from a focal and the petty mal.

The petty mal is an entity in itself, and I would like not to get confused.

They may resemble in the sense that it's the same staring spells. They resemble each other, but they are not exactly the same in terms of mechanism, but this is a distinction, you know, for the experts in terms of drugs to use. The EEG changes, they differ from one to the other and so on.

Q Doctor, one of the persons that was sitting watching the testimony was a little confused about a point. I think perhaps the jury may be too. I want to see if we can clear it up. You talked about four general forms of epilepsy, and one was the grand mal, petty mal. There was another. Another was minor epilepsy, and then temporal lobe epilepsy. What are we talking about in this case? Is that the distinction you were making between petty mal and minor epilepsy?

A Yes. In this case, the proper label is minor epilepsy.

Q And the question that I forgot to ask you is what did you consider to be significant in the hypothetical man's book after the 29th of December?

A The idea is that this is a well-organized, well scheduled book. And then all of a sudden, exactly on the date right after the day of the accident, the book becomes disorganized.

The way of putting the date, and the job number, and things like this become very jumbled and changed, and to me, that means a change in behavior, a change in what technically is called cognitive abilities; in other words, a change in the way the mind of this gentleman was functioning.

Q Thank you very much.

CROSS-EXAMINATION BY MR. CALLAHAN:

Q Could I see that exhibit please. Now, Doctor, what did you consider to be the date that the occurrence involving the blow to the head was?

A The date is in the record. I don't remember now.

MR. HAYES: December 28th.

THE WITNESS: 28th. 28th.

MR. CALLAHAN: Q Well, then, he worked the 29th, of course?

A Yes.

Q And that appears to be in the same manner, does it not?

A Yes.

Q And, of course, these entries here begin a new year, we are into 1968, from December to January?

A Yes.

Q Do you make any kind of diagnosis, any medical diagnosis based upon people's handwriting?

A No, of course not. I never make a diagnosis in general based on one little detail. The importance is the constellation; in other words, the many factors together, then you make a judgment. That's the way clinicians operate.

Q Now you described neuropathology to us. I don't know whether you used the phrase, but is it restricted to the head and to the spinal column generally?

A No. The peripheral nerves are also part of the neuropathologist's bailiwick, if you want.

Q What kind of nerves?

A The peripheral nerves, you know, the wire-like structures that go to the fingers, the legs and so on.

Q Throughout the body?

A Throughout the body, yes.

Q Now, do I understand that you are currently at Veterans' Hospital in Boston?

A No, not now.

Q That was when you were giving us your history. You were there at one point, is that correct?

A Yes. I am still running lectures and conferences at the Bedford VA Hospital.

Q You did indicate that you have a private practice?

A Yes.

Q What kind of people do neuropathologists treat?

A Neuropathologists don't treat anybody.

Q When you say a private practice, what are you referring to?

A In clinical neurology; in other words, live people.

Q All right.And what problems do you treat, then in clinical neurology?

A In clinical neurology, all the problems, all the diseases and the conditions of the type of problems of neurology, headaches, fainting spells, brain tumors, strokes, paralysis of all sorts, et cetera, et cetera, multiple sclerosis.

Q Now, if this hypothetical man had sought medical attention after the occurrence, was there some treatment for this condition?

A Yes.

Q And could he then have been treated in such a way that this untimely death would not have occurred?

A Yes.

Q And would you, as a clinical neurologist, treat a man of this kind?

A I would treat him. Now, if the treatment was successful or not, I don't know. That's something else again.

Q Well, I don't think there is anything in the hypothetical question—as a matter of fact, I think I can say that the evidence is that the man did not seek any medical attention.

A Yes.

Q And my question to you is had he, could this condition have been diagnosed and treated?

MR. HAYES: May I ask the question, Mr. Callahan, to define what type of medial treatment, being a general practitioner or one would have to be fortunate enough to find himself in the hands of a very competent neurologist?

THE WITNESS: I don't follow your argument. What is the question?

MR. CALLAHAN: Excuse me, Doctor,it is not an argument. It's a question.

THE WITNESS: I mean the question.

MR. CALLAHAN: Q Now, if this man, immediately after, let's say, on December 29th, went to a competent physician.

A Yes.

Q Related the incident—the very things you heard here.

A Yes.

Q Put in a few staring spells and what have you.

A Yes.

Q And the doctor was competent, or at least competent enough, as many general practitioners are, to refer him to somebody like you, a neurologist, say, somebody more expert in the field that's indicated. Would that expert be able to diagnose this condition and to have treated it?

A Potentially, yes, within the capabilities of a neurologist.

Q I am assuming that a capable neurologist. I mean, you have diagnosed this condition without seeing this man, is that correct. You never saw this hypothetical man?

A No.

Q You didn't perform the autopsy?

A No.

Q So, you have no direct knowledge of anything that occurred?

A That's correct.

Q And yet, you are making a diagnosis for this jury on those grounds. Now, my question to you is if a competent doctor saw him while he was still alive, and ran some tests on him, could he have diagnosed him?

A Yes.

Q And could he have been treated then, and this untimely death would not have occurred, is that correct?

MR. HAYES: Your Honor, I object to this. I don't see the relevance of what might have happened had he gone to a doctor.

THE COURT: Step up, gentlemen.

(Whereupon, a sidebar discussion was had between Court and counsel outside the hearing of the jury.)

THE COURT: I have called this hearing, gentlemen, more or less to pursue an academic point as well as give some thought to your objection, Mr. Hayes.

Does this not go again to the issue of contributory negligence for the failure to mitigate one's damages, which is not in the defense here?

MR. CALLAHAN: Well, damages are an issue that's separate from liability, and the allegation of damages is there.

THE COURT: That's what I'm inquiring about. Is that a defense?

MR. CALLAHAN: It's not a defense.

THE COURT: I'm making the inquiry because I don't know the answer.

MR. CALLAHAN: It's not a defense on the question of liability. It's a defense on the question of damages.

THE COURT: Is that available?

MR. CALLAHAN: Yes.

MR. HAYES: If the violation of the Act to cause the death and resulting in the death in whole or in part, the defendant is liable, not unliable in terms of—

THE COURT: What I'm suggesting is would it not be inappropriate for me at the appropriate time to instruct the jury on a person's duty to mitigate his damages? I couldn't give that instruction under the Safety Appliance Act.

MR. CALLAHAN: Certainly I intend to submit it. I have prepared it. I am not going to ask any more questions—

THE COURT: If I can do that, the evidence can be admissible. If it's not a defense, then the objections are well taken. That's what I'm trying to determine.

MR. CALLAHAN: Right now it's in, and I am not going into it any more.

MR. HAYES: Once we get the decision on the call, I may have a motion—

MR. CALLAHAN: The one person that the jury sees talking is Mr. Hayes.

THE COURT: Gentlemen, I can't keep sending the jury out of the box for every hearing.

Okay.

* * * * * *

(Whereupon, the following proceedings were had in open court in the presence of the jury:)

MR. CALLAHAN:Q Now, doctor,I don't believe in the hypothetical question that you were told what speed the train was traveling at. Do you recall that?

A Say that again. I didn't catch it.

Q Going into the early part of the hypothetical question, Mr. Hayes was relating to you that this man was riding on a caboose, and the caboose of a train was moving along the line of a railroad. There was a stop. The train went into an emergency stop.

The man's head was slammed against the wall. Did you assume a speed of the train? Do you know how fast the train was going?

A No.

Q All right. Would it make any difference if you did know how fast the train was going?

A I don't think I can answer that. It seems to me, and I am talking now in general terms, not as an expert on anything, that I wouldn't know if the man—I am talking in general terms—slipped, and the train was moving slow, made him slip and hit his head harder, I think we would be in a territory of pure speculation. It seems to me.

Q Seems that way to me too. That's why I am asking the question. Does it make any difference about how soft or how hard the blow was to the head?

A Oh, I see. That's different. To this particular answer, the following, it is often a surprising discrepancy between the mildness of a blow to the head and the catastrophic consequences of it. The literature has many examples of this. People that have a piece of shrapnel go through their head, and they go to the station, they get patched up, and nothing happens.

And on the other hand, people with a very minor bump in the head, the kind that is usually dismissed as not significant, sets a train of catastrophe one after the other for reasons that nobody knows exactly. Seizure can occur, anoxia can occur, that piles on, and the end result can be very disheartening.

Q Well, let me ask this question: Do I understand you to say it doesn't make any difference whether it's a hard or soft blow?

A That's right. It doesn't make any difference. What counts is the result.

Q Bumping one's head is not an uncommon thing, we all do it from childhood on?

A That's correct.

Q I bear a scar here, which may be noticeable to you.

A But perhaps the consequences weren't catastrophic.

Q Perhaps they were, and perhaps they were not.

THE COURT: By catastrophic, you mean it led to his becoming a lawyer?

MR. CALLAHAN: I was heading for medicine.

(Laughter.)

Q Every time a person strikes his head, should he consider himself a candidate for post-traumatic epilepsy?

A Here is where clinical judgment comes. Everybody, somebody sprains his back, that doesn't mean that there is a herniated disc, surgery and pain for the rest of his life, as sometimes happens. So, any medicine is constant examples of very serious diseases that, again, with a little symptom that looks unimportant, but subsequent events prove to be important.

Therefore, what I am trying to convey is that it's true that bumps on the head occur in the millions and nothing happens, but it is equally true that equally mild bumps in the head, for reasons that nobody has been able to exactly point out, lead to one complication after the other.

Q All right. I take it that as a pathologist, you have conducted a number of autopsies?

A Many.

Q And you have become familiar, I imagine, with some of the causes of sudden death?

A Yes, a little bit. Yes.

Q And could you, for the benefit of the jury, tell us what, in the order of sudden, unexpected death, what ranks highest, next and so on?

MR. HAYES: May I ask whether this is based upon sudden deaths that are investigated, those with or without post-mortem examination, or does it include the people who suddenly die, and therefore, somebody says, "Well, he had a heart attack."

I'd like to know the basis of what the class, what group of people the doctor is being asked to describe, major causes of sudden, unexplained death.

MR. CALLAHAN: Your Honor, may I respond to that very quickly? Mr. Hayes can go into that on redirect. I think I am entitled to ask my questions the way I want.

MR. HAYES: It seems to me to be irrelevant, your Honor, that most people may, and most sudden, unexplained deaths are ultimately explained or at least give it a cause as whatever it is.

I suspect it would be a heart attack, but I suggest it's irrelevant to an inquiry as to the cause of death in this man that most people die of this or are said to have died of this or that or lung cancer or whatever.

That is the basis of my objection.

THE COURT: Objection is overruled. I will permit the inquiry.

MR. CALLAHAN: Thank you.

THE WITNESS: I can really talk with a modicum of authority on deaths, fast deaths, if you want, that are of neurological mechanism.

Q I am not restricting the question to a neurological—

A I know that, but I can't answer—let me put it another way.

One type of sudden death, for instance, is crib death, children that are found dead in their cribs, that I have an idea what this is.

The consensus nowadays is that this is something which happens in older persons, too. They can't breathe automatically. They have to have a certain degree of consciousness to breathe, and, therefore, when they fall asleep, they stop breathing, and it's this stopping breathing that in children leads to sudden death.

Q Well, doctor, really, I am referring to—

A This—obviously, that doesn't refer to what you are leading at. Okay.

Q You mean infants, not children?

A In infants. In older persons, sudden death can be the result of epileptic seizures, leading to anoxia, choking on one's own secretions, and ultimately paralyzing the heart.

All deaths are ultimately paralyzing the heart. Okay. So, this is another mechanism of the sudden death.

Q I think you have explained that. I am asking you about some other mechanism of sudden death in adults, and I wonder if you as a pathologist and a physician and a neurologist, can tell us what some of these other common deaths are?

A Now, there is another mechanism of sudden death. It is a heart attack.

Q Yes.

A I have seen a couple of odd mechanisms, but I am sure they are irrelevant, too, to the case in point.

Q Well, could some other examples be, for example, in addition to heart attacks, a pulmonary embolism can cause sudden death?

A Yes. There is another one now that you—we are into the subject, a sudden death has also occurred by reflex stimulation of the coverings of the brain. For instance, there are cases where a lumbar puncture, that this procedure we do all the time, the mere fact of punching the skin of the coverings of the spinal cord, people have a sudden reflex inhibition of the heart and die that way.

There are other sudden deaths from putting a needle in the pleura for diagnostic purposes, and just the putting the needle is enough to stop the heart and provoke death that way.

There's a couple of reports of cases in which the epileptic, the only manifestation of an epileptic seizure was a change in the heart rhythms, arrhythmia of the heart, as the only manifestation of an epileptic discharge. And this was a very nice report, was done while doing the brain wave; all of a sudden would appear the spikes indicating a seizure coming, and the heart would change its rhythm.

Q Let me give you some other possible examples. We have covered heart attack, pulmonary embolism. Cirrhosis of the liver can cause a quick death on occasion, can't it?

A Really? I don't know.

Q Choking, of course, is a common example?

A Yes.

Q Shock can sometimes cause death suddenly?

A Yes.

Q And you have already described a reflex brain activity as sometimes being a cause.

A Yes.

Q Now, doctor, when the episodes of the hypothetical man was being put to you, the questioner, Mr. Hayes, was referring to episodes of unusual behavior, and one was staring straight ahead. Another was the daughter seeing the man in bed thrashing about, the phrase I thought I heard used there was for some time, for some period of time. Does the time of this activity, is that of any consequence to you as a neurologist?

A No.

Q So, it could just be a second?

A Yes, it could be a few seconds or several minutes.

Q And when someone says to you "some time," you just make a decision yourself as to how much time it is, or is it the activity that's being observed rather than the time that it continues?

A No. I usually—I inquire about how long it went on, because this, in a certain way, gives you an idea; it is a criteria of the severity of the attack.

Q All right. Now, there's also a phrase that at one point this man had an unnatural look about his face. Is that of any consequence to you?

A Yes, that this kind of sudden change of the facial expression, this all of a sudden the face going blank for a short period of time is very significant.

Q Well, I think that was just, as I understood it, an unnatural look about his face. Now, do you interpret an unnatural look to be a blank stare of some kind?

A No.

MR. HAYES: Excuse me. Your Honor, the testimony was an unusual look about the face, unnatural look, as I recall the testimony, and the eyes were just staring.

THE COURT: Whatever was included in the hypothesis that was presented to the witness, and if the witness is depending upon his recollection of those factors, he may respond.

MR. CALLAHAN: Q So, when you hear the phrase an unnatural look about his face, are you assuming an episode of staring?

A Yes.

Q Now, I don't know that a time was given to you in the hypothetical question for the time of death between the time the man fell and, of course, he was not pronounced dead until some time later, but he appeared dead in a period which is variously described, if I am correct, from three to five minutes. Is that time episode of consequence to you?

A Yes. I think that this was the time where the laryngospasm and the lack of oxygen was—the anoxia was building up.

Q All right. Now, in your example, you alluded in an answer to the Texas man who became the sniper and later on they found that he had a tumor in the temporal lobe. That was just an explanation, you are not suggesting there was a tumor or anything of that kind?

A No, no.

Q Now, the symptoms that you have been given in the hypothetical question were descriptions of laymen, lay persons?

A Yes.

Q I take it you would prefer, if you could have them, symptoms related by medical experts.

A No. Actually, I like lay words rather than long words, which usually mean the same thing, but they confuse the real appraisal of facts.

Q All right. And these are symptoms which are given by persons, some of them persons who at times were as young as thirteen years old, and the occurrence took place about twelve or thirteen years ago. Does that present any difficulty to you in arriving at your conclusion?

MR. HAYES: Excuse me. I hope you don't—I think there is something that may be a little confusing. They were thirteen years old at the time.

MR. CALLAHAN: Right.

MR. HAYES: Okay.

THE WITNESS: I have to make my judgment according to the data given to me.

MR. CALLAHAN: Q Well, what I mean is you are answering a hypothetical question. The question I have is, is it difficult for you to rely upon information that was used to formulate the hypothetical question when that information was originally derived from the observations of children as young as thirteen and the period of time between that observation and today is about twelve years?

A You are bringing here another problem that is the reliability of the witness, which, you know, is not up to me really to question or to—this is a side problem you shouldn't address yourself to me. I can only tell you what medically is reasonable and very probable.

Q What I am saying, doctor, is that you are willing to give us an opinion?

A Yes.

Q And I am saying, does it trouble you that some of the information which forms the basis of your opinion is so remote?

A Let me answer this by saying that in general, I don't base an opinion on one little detail. It's the constellation of different pieces of a puzzle that fit together. If I had only one small fraction of all the sequence of events, I would then have more doubts in my mind, but there is a pattern here that it fits together.

Q All right. Now, I think you have already told us that it is not of consequence whether or not there was any unconsciousness associated with the original occurrence.

A With the original blow to the head?

Q Right.

A That's correct. The unconsciousness, yes, is neither here nor there. It is within limits, not in an absolute sense.

Q Now, you have already told us too, I think, that you testified for Mr. Hayes in other cases, is that correct?

A Yes, that's correct.

Q And have you lived in the Boston area ever since you came to the United States?

A Yes.

Q And when you testified for him, was it coming here to Chicago to do so?

A Was my reason for coming?

Q No, no. When you did testify, you told us you testified for Mr. Hayes in other cases, did you testify here in Chicago?

A Yes.

Q As a matter of fact, in this building?

A As a matter of fact, I think, in this room.

Q Well, there's a lot of rooms that look like this.

A They may look similar. I don't know.

THE COURT: If it was here, it was on my day off.

(Laughter.)

MR. CALLAHAN: Q Now, you do not practice in the Chicago area?

A No.

Q Do you know whether or not there are neurologists in the Chicago area?

A Sure.

Q And probably neuropathologists?

A Yes.

Q Could you tell us when you were first consulted to testify in this case?

A Well, one of my residents, a fellow whom I trained, came to practice here in Chicago, and, in fact, he is still practicing here in Chicago, and he is one who put me in touch with Mr. Hayes to—just like I am doing now, basically to make a judgment on a neurological case and say what I think.

Q Okay. One of the other things that were put to you was that this man was examined by a railroad surgeon on December 22, 1966 and found in good health. You, of course, do not know the extent of any such examination?

A No.

Q Now, would it be of any consequence for you to know that the person who performed the autopsy in this case—

THE COURT: You are speaking of the hypothetical situation, counsel?

CALLAHAN: Yes. Performed the autopsy referred to in the hypothetical question, testified from a summary that was not dated, that did not show who the autopsy was performed on by name, and it did not show where it was performed. Does that make any difference in your reliance upon those elements relating to the autopsy that were in the hypothetical question?

A No.

MR. HAYES: Your Honor, the fact of the matter is that the hypothetical question asks the doctor to assume that the doctor performing the autopsy was telling the truth.

THE COURT: Is there anything before me that I can rule on?

MR. HAYES: I object to the question.

THE COURT: The objection is sustained.

MR. HAYES: Thank you.

THE COURT: Proceed, counsel.

MR. CALLAHAN: Q Now, I think that it was involved in the hypothetical question, but let me ask, is it of any consequence that the trocar in this hypothetical autopsy entered the heart and probably dislodged any occlusion that might have been formed there?

MR. HAYES: I object to that. Your Honor, that was not the testimony of Dr. Burns, and that was a hypothesis postulated by Mr. Callahan. It was not the doctor's testimony.

THE COURT: I don't recall it in the hypothesis presented to this witness, and I don't recall that testimony either.

Would you like to recess so I can review it?

MR. CALLAHAN: Well, I think I am, of course, going from my notes, but I—

MR. HAYES: If you object to my looking at the testimony of Dr.—

MR. CALLAHAN: But you went ahead and did it.

THE COURT: Gentlemen, I don't believe any colloquy is called for.

Give me a few moments to review my notes. Perhaps I can locate the area.

All right, gentlemen, would you step up on a sidebar, please?

(Whereupon, a sidebar discussion was had between the Court and counsel out of the hearing of the jury and the reporter.)

MR. CALLAHAN: Your Honor, let me withdraw the question.

THE COURT: Very well.

MR. CALLAHAN: Q Let me just ask you this, doctor: Is it possible that a death by heart attack could occur And the clot, after the death, but before an autopsy was performed would have been dissolved?

A That's unlikely. It seems to me, however—

THE COURT: Did you say it's—

THE WITNESS: Unlikely. However, I must qualify that, that I am not a general pathologist, and I would like not to get involved, so to speak.

MR. CALLAHAN: Q Well, you have told us that you do perform and have performed many autopsies?

A Of the brain.

Q You have done none of the body, is that right?

A When I was in training, but that was long ago. I don't hold myself to be an expert in general pathology.

Q I understand that, and the same would be true about heart disease?

A That's correct.

Q All right. One other thing, is it important to you as a neuropathologist to have samples of tissue and things of that kind in making a determination as to the cause of death and the condition of the body and what have you at the time of death?

A You mean in the rest of the body?

Q Well—

A Or the brain?

Q Often when autopsies are performed, the person—performing it takes certain tissue samples, does he not?

A Yes.

Q And as a matter of fact, there is general name for those. Histology, I think, is the term?

A Yes.

Q Could you explain that to us?

A Well, what that involves is taking pieces of the different organs of the body, and this is done of the brain also making it into convenient cubes, usually, and then you pickle those pieces, so to speak, and you embed them in paraffin, which make it like a hard slab. And this hard slab in the tissue, that is called a block, is then sliced with a microtome, which makes very thin pieces, and these are stained with different stains, mounted in a piece of glass, in a slide, and looked under the microscope.

Q And those are the kinds of things that can be taken from the body to make a more specific examination to more precisely determine the cause of death?

A Yes.

Q Particularly in a case where there appears to be no certainty as to cause of death from the preliminary autopsy?

A Yes.

Q So that as a neurologist, if you were attempting to make a determination as to the cause of death, you would like to have some of those samples, would you not?

A Yes.

Q It would make it easier to make a determination which you are attempting to make?

A That's correct.

MR. CALLAHAN: I have nothing further.

REDIRECT EXAMINATION BY MR. HAYES:

Q Doctor, you used the term laryngospasm. I don't think I asked you to define that term. What is laryngospasm?

A It's a spasm of the gullet, if you want, or the voicebox. That prevents normal breathing. Like in children in the old diphtheria cases, you know, whether there would crop up in the upper trachea, and the child would choke.

Q Now, you referred, in answer to the question of Mr. Callahan, I believe, about the substance of the brain being kind of like Jell-O.

What is the substance of the brain like?

A Well, well, the brain is 90 percent water, surprisingly enough, and the rest is nerve cells, fibers, and then some sort of spidery tissue called glia, which means glue, because it holds the brain together. But the consistency is very soft.

Q And how does the brain sit in the skull?

A It doesn't sit. It floats in a cushion of water. So, it is actually held up by negative pressure on a cushion of water. That's what protects the brain.

Q Okay. Now, counsel asked you about your having testified at my request, and that has been twice, has it doctor?

A Yes, twice.

Q And you mentioned to him that I was introduced to you by a neurologist who was formerly a student of yours and a friend of mine.

A Yes.

Q And did I learn from him that you studied under the great Denny Brown?

A Yes, that's right. He told you.

MR. HAYES: Thank you very much, doctor.

MR. CALLAHAN: Excuse me, I have one or two questions which I neglected to ask the doctor, and I wondered if I could before he is excused?

THE COURT: Yes, sir.

RECROSS-EXAMINATION BY MR. CALLAHAN:

Q Doctor, you very clearly said that in your opinion there is a connection between the occurrence and the death.

A Yes.

Q Could you explain to us how death came in this case?

A Death, in my opinion, came through the process of a minor attack of epilepsy leading to a disturbance in the respiratory mechanism, which, in turn, produced anoxia, a lack of oxygen, and this lack of oxygen, as is well known, can paralyze the heart.

Q All right. The respiratory center is located someplace in the brain, is that correct?

A There are several respiratory centers.

Q And do you think, then, that the blow to the head in some way or another affected the respiratory part of it?

A Yes.

Q Or it created epilepsy, and so that came up later, which way?

A The respiratory center is under the influence of the cortex, the upper part of the brain. The best demonstration that this is the case is that you can breathe in and out voluntarily. I breathe in (indicating); you do this, and this is the origin for this voluntary breathing, is in the cortex, in the surface of the brain. But in addition, there are two or three centers down in the brain stem that are the ones that function automatically. And the lowest one, for instance, is the respiratory center for gasping breathing (indicating), this that you see in people about to die, and so on and so forth.

Q All right, but what you are saying is that this condition, this was a petty mal effect or attack or episode?

A A minor attack.

Q A minor. All right. And in the minor attack, somehow or other the respiratory center was affected, the man stopped breathing, and that was the cause of death?

A Well, yes. Yes. What I said is that the minor attack led to a certain constriction of the windpipes, of the passage of air, and that led to anoxia, and that ultimately led to death.

Q Is it uncommon for post-traumatic epilepsy, which you have talked about, to develop so soon after it occurs?

A It can occur—there are two kinds of post-traumatic epilepsy. One is the early, and that can occur a day after, two days, up to a week, at least. And that's the early post-traumatic. And then there is the late post-traumatic, and this—can go from a week to four, five years or so.

Q All right. Is one more common than the other, the early or the late?

A The early—and there are some cases that have both, have early and late. Those are in the minority. The figures, I don't have the figures in my head.

Q Let me ask these few questions to which we have alluded, but I didn't ask you. Do you consider staring into space as an epileptic episode?

A Yes.

Q Do you consider thrashing about in sleep is an epileptic episode?

MR. HAYES: Object. There is not evidence that he was asleep, but in bed.

THE WITNESS: Let me put it this way: I don't think that every thrashing is epileptic, but in this context, in this clinical situation, with this particular constellation of events, this, I think, is significant.

Q Is death from a petty mal attack common?

MR. HAYES: I object to the use of the word petty mal. The doctor has distinguished petty-mal from minor epilepsy.

THE WITNESS: From minor epilepsy is not terribly common, but is known to occur.

Q All right, and what about death from other types of epilepsy?

A From other types of epilepsy, yes.

Q My question isn't does it ever happen. I am asking is it common.

A Common?

Q Yes.

A No, it's not very common.

Q Now, finally, I want to ask you just one more question or two about blows to the head. Up in your area of the country a week or two ago today, there was a famous boxing match.

MR. HAYES: Your Honor, I have to object. Counsel said that he had wanted to ask a couple of questions that hadn't been asked on direct examination, but it seems to me—on cross-examination, that we are going into another—

THE COURT: Counsel, I long ago learned that when an attorney says he has one or two questions, he doesn't mean that he has one or two questions.

Proceed.

MR. CALLAHAN: Thank you.

Q There was a rather well-known boxing event up in Montreal, as a matter of fact. Now, it occurred to me when you were testifying about blows to the head, that probably, certainly most likely the occupation to get repeated blows to the head of varying intensity is boxing. And yet, I don't know that I have any reason to think that boxers are more inclined toward epilepsy than any other part of the populace.

A That's not true. Certainly, there is a tremendous amount of neurological complications in boxers. The thing that happens is that nobody examines boxers with care. One is the so-called encephalopathy of boxers, which manifests itself by loss of memory.

Q Well, doctor, I am not disputing that boxers suffer a lot of problems and damage. I am merely raising the question as to whether boxers are more likely than people in other occupations to become epileptic, to suffer from post-traumatic epilepsy.

A These, I would have to, you know, check the figures for that. There are many factors here, and is that most of the blows in boxing, and I don't want to engage obviously, in a discussion of the neuropathology of boxing, but if people knew, probably boxing would be outlawed, but most of the blows you see are more in the jaw, with a displacement of the brain stem system, that is, the part of the brain that contains consciousness.

That's why there is the passing out rather than a sudden deceleration, as we say in the business, when the head would be traveling at a certain speed and meets an irreversible object. Do you see the difference?

Q That, to me, is the description of the boxer who is weaving to avoid a punch and gets one, his head is going this way and the immovable object—

A Well, I don't—

THE COURT: I think we are getting into a rather academic—

THE WITNESS: Yes, very technical.

MR. CALLAHAN: Q In any event, do you know of any studies that have demonstrated that boxers are more inclined to suffer from post-traumatic epilepsy than people in other occupations?

A No, I can't quote a specific paper, no.

MR. CALLAHAN: I have nothing further.

THE COURT: Mr. Hayes.

MR. HAYES: No questions.

THE COURT: You may step down, sir.

(Witness excused.)

[The defendant filed a motion to strike the testimony of Dr. Segarra on the grounds that, on its face, it was incompetent. The motion asserted that the witness had no care or concern about where the evidence on which he relied to form his opinion came from, who it came from, the competence of the persons who testified to it, the witnesses age, the duration of time involved in various events, the speed of the train at the time of the sudden stop, and so forth. The motion went on to argue that, under these circumstances, the testimony simply was not competent. It could not properly be accepted or used as a basis for an expert opinion because of the deficiencies and uncertainties as to so many of the facts upon which it was based, and also because of the cavalier attitude of the witness. The Court denied the motion ruling that the testimony of Dr. Segarra was a matter of credibility for the jury, rather than one of admissibility for the Court.]

Explanation and Summary of Economist's Testimony

In death and serious injury cases, the plaintiff's attorney customarily uses an economist as an expert witness to compute, project and verify the economic loss suffered as a result of the death or injury. The economist goes over the entire financial picture including lost wages, supplemental benefits and every other aspect of the loss. When the case involves the untimely death of a young wage earner, the future wage loss becomes very substantial.

In this case the loss from the date of the accident to the time of the trial was shown to be $247,000. The projected future loss for a retirement at age seventy was shown to be $1,053,818. Thus the total loss was $1,300,818.

This testimony was adduced from Walter Johnson, a professor of Economics at Sangamon State University in Springfield, Illinois. Mr. Johnson testified that he holds a B.A. in Economics from Washington State University and an M.A. and Ph.D. in Economics from the University of Oklahoma.

It is difficult on cross-examination to effectively attack the testimony of an experienced, competent economist. Although there is certainly an effort to maximize the loss, an effective cross-examination may result in simply reducing the total loss from $1,300,000 to, say, $950,000. The defense is still faced with a very significant loss figure and, of course, the principal thrust of the defendant's case is that the death was caused by a heart attack which was in no way the fault of the railroad.

In the event the jury should find the liability issue in favor of the plaintiff, however, then it seems the better course to use the earning power of money approach to demonstrate to the jury how much income can be generated over time by investing a certain amount of money. This is designed to prompt a jury to recognize that a significantly lesser award would still provide the survivors with a substantial income and to suggest that the plaintiff in fact is overreaching on the issue of damages.

The cross-examination follows:

CROSS-EXAMINATION BY MR. CALLAHAN:

Q Dr. Johnson, I don't know whether you used the phrase, but when you talk about investing money and receiving interest on it, you are talking, in a general way, about the earning power of money?

A That is correct.

Q You used a figure of 7 percent, and you explained that is what some current U.S. Savings Bonds actually earn; is that true?

A Currently, yes.

Q Now, if you were to invest in bonds of a well known financial institution such as, say, Sears Roebuck and Company, or Peoples Gas, or Commonwealth Edison, something like that, what kind of an interest can you get on investments of that kind?

A Generally those will pay a higher rate because of the security factor.

Q Well, I have today's Wall Street Journal. Could you look at that and find out?

A I have not seen this morning's, no.

Q You know where to find that, don't you?

A In the journal?

Q Yes. I will hand you my copy.

A They have gone to the two section. I will have to look. Do you want a specific?

Q Well, I just want some idea, some well known institutional bonds and what they are paying, what kind of interest they are earning.

A Some institutional bonds now, according to the paper, are paying 10-plus percent.

Q And are some paying as much as eleven or twelve?

A That is correct.

Q These are well known institutions, I take it? This would be common knowledge?

A Right, such as Georgia Pacific or AT&T.

Q That is a considerable amount higher than the 7 percent which you used in your figures, is that correct?

A That is correct.

Q Now, in making your computations, in recognizing that certain amounts of monies that might be paid in the future would be subject to tax, you worked those into your calculations, did you not?

A Yes, I did.

Q There is a form of investment which is tax free, is there not?

A Municipal bonds.

Q And what do they pay?

A Generally somewhat lower than the going rate. I have not looked at the quotes today. I looked at them on Friday, and they ranged from 6 percent all the way up to 8 percent.

Q Let's use the figure of 7 percent, just because that is convenient, and in between 6 and 8, which you gave me.

Let us deal only with the figure of the retirement at age seventy. And to make it simple, let's use only the one million dollars. Now, if that one million is invested in tax free municipal bonds, what will be the return on that investment at the end of one year?

A The return will depend upon the maturation date.

Q Let me rephrase the question. If I invest, or a person invests, a million dollars at 7 percent, what do they get at the end of the year?

A Leaving the whole million dollars in there for the year, that would be $70,000 at the end of the year.

Q Now, if a person does that for a period of ten years, they will have earned, in interest, from that investment, $700,000, is that correct?

A No, that is not correct.

Q Well, if you invest a million dollars each year at 7 percent and you get $70,000 in one year, don't you end up, after ten years with $700,000?

A If you are investing only a million each year.

Q That is what I am talking about.

A Under your assumption, it would be the same as investing 10 million this year.

Q I am talking about one million each year, I am sorry if I didn't state it clearly. I am talking about the same million dollars, as a matter of fact.

A And you take the interest out?

Q Right.

A Each year?

Q Right.

A So that at the beginning of the next year you'll only have the one million in there?

Q Exactly.

A Then you will return $70,000 each year.

Q So at the end of ten years, the investor will have received $700,000?

A That is correct.

Q And the million dollars would still be in there?

A That is correct.

Q And if this goes on for a period of twenty years, the investor will have received $1,400,000; is that correct?

A That is correct.

Q And the one million is still in there?

A And the one million is still in there.

Q And if it goes on for thirty years, the investor will have received $2,100,000?

A Under those assumptions, that is correct.

Q And if you add the one million dollars that you invested in the first place, you still have that, if you add that to that figure, you get a figure of $3,100,000; is that correct?

A That is correct.

Q And if you add the extra two year's life expectancy, which we have been told is thirty-two years, that is $70,000 each year, and the total figure would be $3,240,000; is that right?

A If I follow your example, yes.

Q At the end of thirty years, you agreed it was $3,100,000?

A Right.

Q And if I just add two more years, it would be $70,000 each year, and that would be another $140,000. My figures say that equals $3,240,000.

A Yes.

MR. CALLAHAN: I have nothing further.

REDIRECT EXAMINATION BY MR. HAYES:

Q First of all, corporate bonds, do corporate bonds have maturation dates?

A Yes.

Q And if I were to invest a million dollars in a corporate bond paying—what are the maturation dates? Do they show the maturation dates of some of those corporation bonds?

A Some of them do, yes.

Q Maybe twenty or thirty years in the future?

A That is correct.

Q And so if I invest a million dollars in a corporate bond paying 10 percent, I can't collect that money until twenty or thirty years?

MR. CALLAHAN: I'm going to object to the leading nature of these questions.

THE COURT: As to form, sustained.

MR. HAYES: Q Will I be able to collect $700,000 a year or a hundred thousand dollars a year or $50,000 a year on those corporate bonds?

A Not in some instances, no.

Q Not in any instance of a long term bond?

A Of a long term.

Q Now, are corporate bonds callable?

A Many of them.

THE COURT: Are they what, sir?

MR. HAYES: Callable.

THE COURT: Would you define that?

THE WITNESS: That means the interest rates can change in favor of the corporation, that they could call the bonds back in and pay you at that point and reissue at a more favorable interest rate to them, which is to say that they might be paying 10 percent now, but if the interest rate were to drop to 5 percent, they could call it back, and if you wanted to reinvest your investment, potentially it would drop down to that rate.

MR. HAYES: And are banks some of the people that issue these corporate bonds?

A Banks handle them.

MR. CALLAHAN: Let me show an objection to the extent that my cross-examination, your Honor, was directed to the municipal tax free, municipal bonds.

MR. HAYES: I thought I heard AT&T and all those, too.

MR. CALLAHAN: We were just discussing the interest rates at that time.

THE COURT: I believe the witness was examined in reference to commercial bonds and investments in commercial bonds. Overruled. You may inquire.

MR. HAYES: I am sorry. What was the question pending?

MR. CALLAHAN. I think he had answered that there wasn't.

THE COURT: May we have the question, sir?

MR. HAYES: Never mind, I recall what it was.

Q Can you give us some examples of some corporations that were really great or thought to be great investments, and went down the tube?

A Corporations?

Q Sure.

A Well, I think J.C. Penney is an example now of one that is in trouble and has some issues out. There are a number of them that have done it; that is correct.

Q And now let's talk about municipal bonds. Do municipal bonds bear a maturation date?

A Yes, they do.

Q And so one cannot say, with respect to investing in municipal bonds - can one say, with respect to investing in municipal bonds, that maybe pay 7 percent today, that one could invest a million, get back $70,000, and invest a million, get back $70,000?

A Decidedly not.

Q And are municipal bonds callable?

A In most instances, they are.

Q And, historically, have municipal bonds been lower, in some instances, substantially lower than they are today?

A Yes, they have.

Q Now, are municipal bonds totally tax free?

A No, they are not.

Q What tax are they subject to?

A To the State of Illinois tax of 2-1/2 percent.

Q Okay, and tell me, Professor, what municipal bonds would you suggest somebody invest in? Let's say, ten years ago, were New York bonds considered pretty good?

A Ten years ago, yes, New York bonds were probably considered good.

Q How was Cleveland considered ten years ago?

A Also considered good.

Q How was Chicago considered two years ago?

A They were considered as a Double A rating, which is the highest rating.

Q What are they now?

A They are an A rating.

Q Do you know what they are going to be tomorrow?

A No, I don't.

MR. HAYES: Thank you.

RE CROSS-EXAMINATION BY MR. CALLAHAN:

Q Dr. Johnson, do I understand that you are using the figure of 7 percent for the calculation that you told us about?

A Yes, I did.

Q And are you now saying, in response to Mr. Hayes' question, that that is probably not a reliable figure?

A No, I am not saying that.

Q You have no doubts about that, do you?

A About the reliability of the figure?

Q Yes.

A What I said was, that the figure is based on a moving average, and that that is the reason that I used that figure.

Q So you are not retracting from the percent figure that you used in your figures?

A No, I am not.

MR. CALLAHAN: All right, I have nothing further.

Defendant's Expert Witnesses

JAN E. LEESTMA, called as a witness herein, having been first duly sworn, was examined and testified as follows:

DIRECT EXAMINATION BY MR. CALLAHAN:

Q Would you state your name, please?

A Yes, Jan, J-a-n, E. Leestma, l-e-e-s-t-m-a.

Q What is your profession or occupation, sir?

A I am a physician.

Q And where do you live?

A I live and work in Chicago.

Q Could you tell us, Doctor, what medical school you are a graduate of?

A Yes. I am on the faculty of Northwestern University School of Medicine.

Q And what medical school did you graduate from?

A I graduated from the University of Michigan in 1964.

Q And after that, Doctor, did you go through a period of internship or some further study?

A Yes, I did.

After medical school, I pursued a study of pathology, and that was at the University of Colorado Medical Center in Denver. Following that, I chose to sub-specialize or super-specialize, as the case may be, in neuropathology, and I went to the Albert Einstein College of Medicine in New York.

Q Doctor, let me interrupt you and ask you if you could explain to us what neuropathology encompasses?

A All right, neuropathology is the study of diseases of the nervous system, in its broadest possible form; that is, what causes the diseases, how they progress, how they regress, as the case may be.

This study does not generally include the direct treatment of patients or the prescription of drugs for neurological diseases.

Q You were telling us of some further study in New York.

A That's correct.

Q Would you tell us what that was, Doctor?

A I spent approximately one year at the Albert Einstein College of Medicine, in a fellowship on studying neuropathology. I suppose you could say my studies continued on, in spite of the fact I was in the military service. I spent three years at the Armed Forces Institute of Pathology, at the Walter Reed Army Medical Center in Washington.

Q What years were those, Doctor?

A Those were from 1968 to 1971. I was in the military service for three years.

Q And then did you go through some further training or practice?

A No. At that point I suppose you could say I concluded my training. The distinction between practice and training becomes a little blurred after a while. I then joined the faculty of Northwestern in 1971.

Q All right. And that's Northwestern University Medical School?

A That's correct.

Q And, Doctor, there's been some discussion here about board certification.

Could you, first of all, tell us what that is?

A The American Board of Pathology is a group which, many years ago, got together to certify the training, and the fact that training had been accomplished in people who had gone on in pathology as a specialty.

The American Board has number of examinations that it oversees within the field of pathology, and these are basically in the obvious areas of pathology; anatomic pathology, which would be autopsy pathology, interpretation of surgical materials and so forth; clinical pathology, which would have to do with examination for competency in running a clinical laboratory, the blood bank, that sort of thing, in a hospital.

There are other parts of the Board. Neuropathology would be one of them that conducts the examination for competence in that area and a few other of the sub-specialty areas of pathology.

And this examination, or this licensing procedure, if you will, involves several days of examinations of a practical nature, a written and, in the past sometimes, an oral examination.

If at the end of that time, the Board feels that your training is appropriate and you have done well enough on the exam, they issue you a diploma for having successfully completed that field of study.

Q Thanks, Doctor. I don't know whether you told us or not in your testimony. Are you certified, sir?

A Yes, I am certified in anatomic and neuropathology.

Q Now, incidentally, Doctor, in prior testimony, there's been a reference to the Whitman case that took place in Texas a few years ago.

Did you have occasion to do an examination or testing in that case?

A Yes, I did.

Q And what, in general, was that case involved with, if you can tell us?

A That was a case of a young man who went up to a tower in the center of Austin, Texas, and over several hours' time, proceeded to snipe away at whatever moved on the street below.

As I recall, some seventeen or eighteen people lost their lives. And, I believe some thirty or forty more were wounded, in connection with that incident.

Q Did you have occasion to examine some specimens, and things of that kind, in that case?

A I did, yes.

Q All right. And, Doctor, what subject or subjects do you teach at Northwestern University Medical School?

A I more or less confine myself to neuropathology; that is, the teaching of medical students, my fellow physicians, residency training, that sort of thing. I also do some teaching in general pathology to the medical students in their second year of study.

Q Are you called upon, from time to time, to consult and assist in making examinations, in terms of your specialty?

A Yes.

Q And would that be in the Chicago area?

A Yes.

Q And could you give us some examples of cases in which you may have been consulted?

MR HAYES: I would object to that, your Honor. That doesn't add to anything. I think it gets into ancillary issues.

THE COURT: As to the number or specifics?

MR. CALLAHAN: I thought a case that might be familiar to the jury. If counsel objects, I will withdraw the question.

THE COURT: The objection will be sustained on relevancy.

MR. CALLAHAN: I take it, Doctor, that you have published some articles in your field?

A Yes, I have, a collection of about forty papers by now and some chapters of textbooks and a book or two along the way, yes.

Q Now, Dr. Leestma, do you presently serve on the Cook County Board of Medical Examiners?

A Yes. I have an appointment with the Office of the Medical Examiner of Cook County, as an assistant.

Q And what is the function of that body?

A Well, the function of that office is to determine the cause and manner of death in which foul play is suggested, or in which the cause of death is not known. A person is not attended by a physician at the time of death, and at any time in which there's some question about, outside of a medical institution, the manner in which an individual met their death, and I function as a consultant to that office for questions of diseases of the nervous system.

Q Thank you, Doctor.

When you are attempting to make a determination of the cause of death, within the description you just gave us, what kinds of things are taken into consideration by you in making such a determination?

MR. HAYES: Your Honor, what may be taken into consideration in determining death under those circumstances, may be irrelevant to the present inquiry.

THE COURT: Overruled. He may answer.

THE WITNESS: Very well. The process of investigation that goes on has several parts. Certainly, one part of this would be the bringing of the body of the deceased into the facility, where an examination of the body is made externally as well as internally.

An autopsy is performed. Studies to look for drugs and so forth in the blood is commonly a part of that. When necessary, X-rays are made, that sort of thing.

In addition, a considerable amount of information is collected, regarding the history of this individual, the circumstances under which the death occurred, was it observed, the facts relevant to the circumstances of death in regard to where the person was found, did anyone observe the death, were there any other bits of information around.

Usually, these data are not collected by the forensic pathologist himself, but by an investigator who goes to the scene, interviews people, collects whatever physical evidence is there, and that forms part of the information which is presented to the pathologist, which he looks at and performs appropriate studies, based on what he sees in that information.

Q Could you tell us, in a general way, what it is that you do in performing an autopsy?

A We had begun to outline that a little bit.

Before the body is brought into the hospital or the morgue facility, the clothing is usually removed and an external inspection of the body is performed for any marks, any distinguishing features, incisions, whatever it may be.

There an internal examination proceeds, in which usually a Y-shaped incision is made, usually from shoulder to shoulder and down the middle of the body, in which most of the organs are removed.

These are further examined, dissected, weighed, X-rayed, analyzed in various ways, such that the functioning of these organs and what might be inside them is visible for examination.

Unless it is specifically prohibited by the autopsy permit or, in the case of a Medical Examiner's case, that isn't a consideration, the brain is usually removed by an incision from ear to ear, and the brain is removed after sawing the skull.

It is usually not examined extensively at the time. It is usually fixed in formaldehyde or pickled, if you will, for a week or so.

This facilitates the examination so that the consistency of the brain alive is somewhat jelly-like; after treatment with formaldehyde it becomes a little firmer and easier to examine and it is examined in much the same way as other organs are.

Q When you say, "examined in much the same way," first of all, did I understand you examine appearance, weight, tissue samples, paraffin blocks, things of that kind? Is that customarily done in order to assist you in your determination?

A Yes, they are. When we are in the process of dissecting the organs, representative pieces are taken and set aside for preparation of microscopic slides.

Q From time to time, does an autopsy examination, after these tests and various things are done, still remain inconclusive as to the cause of a man's death?

A Yes.

Q And is that an uncommon occurrence?

A I wouldn't say it's rare. It's not uncommon. It occurs regularly enough that I think most pathologists have experience with that.

Q Does the pathologist, in addition to what you just described to us, rely upon any other kinds of information to assist him in making determinations as to the cause of death?

A Yes.

Q And what would that be, Doctor?

A These would be the clinical history, medical history, whatever records exist concerning the patient in life.

Oftentimes, these provide a key to what has happened. Oftentimes, the lack of findings at an autopsy is, in a sense, a positive finding, because this narrows certain possibilities.

That may not seem too logical, the lack of findings at an autopsy would be an important finding in and of itself, but in fact this can be the case, and supported by other information, this can and is used to come up with the information that we do this thing for in the first place.

Q Would any complaints the deceased may have made prior to his death be pertinent?

A Yes, they would be pertinent.

Q And any other statements as to his condition?

A Yes.

Q And as to pain or suffering, or anything else of that kind?

A That's correct.

Q All right.

Now, Doctor, at this point I would like to put a hypothetical question to you and at the conclusion of that I'm going to ask you if you have an opinion, and then I'll ask you some questions about that.

Assume, Doctor, a man thirty-six years old, weighing 160 pounds, who, upon reporting for work on January the 19th, 1968—and assume, further, that the man is a railroad man who has been employed by the railroad for some time, and that he's reporting to work at about four o'clock or so in the morning of January the 19th; and assume further, Doctor, that his place to report and his place to begin work that day, is a caboose of a train, and assume, Doctor, that the man climbs into the caboose of the train, and almost immediately upon getting in there, he collapses, falls on his right side, and then, or shortly thereafter, he dies.

Thereafter, there is a statement made by someone locally who says he is dead. The coroner is called and the coroner pronounces the man dead sometime later.

Now, Doctor, based upon those hypothetical facts which I've given you, do you have an opinion based upon a reasonable amount of medical certainty, as to the cause of the man's death?

A Yes, I do.

Q And what is that opinion, Doctor?

A Well, in my opinion—

MR. HAYES: I would object to this, your Honor. It doesn't include all of the facts in evidence.

THE COURT: He may ask his opinion. Overruled.

A In my opinion, the man most likely expired from a sudden stoppage of the heart, or cardiac arrhythmia perhaps.

That is a fatal disturbance of the rhythm of the heart.

Q And let me incidentally add, Doctor, which I failed to do, that an autopsy was subsequently performed, which was an autopsy, I assume, along the lines which you have described, except that no tissues were taken or, if they were, they were not available for anybody to use and, so, for all practical purposes, the entire autopsy was just what you may have referred to as the gross autopsy; but there were no tissue, nor paraffin tests; and that, among other things, the autopsy found that the heart, upon being weighted, weighed three hundred seventy grams.

Now, adding those facts to the hypothetical question, does that change your opinion, Doctor?

A No, it doesn't. In fact, it tends to support it.

Q All right. Now, would you explain the basis upon which you make that statement?

A Yes.

Beginning with the barest of facts that you gave me in the hypothetical question, when a relatively healthy young individual expires, dies within minutes, examination in many cases of this type in the medical literature, and in my own experience has shown the most likely mechanism of death to be mediated by the heart.

There are certain other causes which can result in sudden death, but, in terms of an analysis of many thousands of cases of this sort—and not in my hands necessarily, but by others—when an autopsy is done, or based upon other additional information in life, history, what have you, the cause of very sudden demise is generally conceded to be something in the heart, whether or not you demonstrate it at autopsy.

Following down that list, most other causes of death in the absence of course of a bullet wound or something traumatic like that, take an additional period of time. That is, many minutes to hours, and this would include fulminate bleeding from the gastrointestinal tract, a perforated ulcer perhaps, hemorrhages in the brain.

Things like this, in spite of there being a very obvious and catastrophic illness, often take many hours to fully bring about the death of the patient and so, on that fact alone, I'm saying that the most likely cause is something in the heart.

Now, you've given me some additional facts; that is, that an autopsy was done, and the heart in this individual of 160 pounds was reported to be 370 grams. For a person of that age and weight, that heart would be considered outside the bounds of normal. It would be heavier than normal.

Q What's the significance of that, Doctor?

A An individual with a heart that is heavier than normal indicates that that heart has increased in size to meet some demand, that—just as if you use your arm muscles a lot to lift weights or something, they're going to get bigger.

This can indicate that the patient had high blood pressure, but there may have been an underlying problem in the heart. Sometimes, and not frequently, people with coronary artery disease or other primary diseases in the heart will have an enlarged heart.

Q Now, is it possible that someone dies of a heart attack, and the fact that that was the cause of death is not able to be determined by an autopsy?

A Yes, I've heard of that and I've experienced it myself.

Q And could you tell us the way or ways in which this could have occurred?

MR. HAYES: Your Honor, this is speculation, guess, and conjecture.

THE COURT: Overruled. He may answer.

THE WITNESS: Very well.

There have been cases, and I've observed one of these cases firsthand, in which an individual presented to an Emergency Room with acute left-sided chest pain, sweating, all of the symptoms that almost anyone would recognize as that of an acute coronary, or heart attack. Electrocardiogram leads were put on, and it was quite evident that the man was having an attack at that time and he proceeded to die in a few minutes, in spite of whatever efforts could be arranged to try and bring him back.

The autopsy on that man, which I performed—and there are many other cases listed exactly like this in the medical literature—did not reveal any significant abnormality in the heart: this in the face of every good bit of medical evidence that the man had just sustained a heart attack.

This—to be frank with you, this astounded me. I was in training at the time, and I then proceeded to investigate what had been written about this.

As it turns out, in somewhat less than fifty percent of such cases exactly like this, the autopsy will not reveal a blood clot in a coronary artery, and some cases report, or some series of the similar cases report this finding in as little as 25 percent of such cases.

The fact of the matter is that the death in this instance occurred so rapidly that the effects on the heart muscle could not have evolved. It stopped, it altered the rhythm or whatever, but the evidence of death of muscle cells in the heart didn't have time to evolve.

MR. CALLAHAN: Now, are there ways in which the blood itself has some effect upon any kind of a clot in the blood, that might be involved in a heart attack?

A Yes.

Q And what does blood of an ordinary person do, in connection with acting on blood clots?

A The blood contains many factors, in addition to those which produce clots. There are many things within the blood which serve to break up clots which form, and in that way, there's both mechanisms existing side by side, those to make the blood solidify and those to keep that from happening, and, in fact, dissolve a blood clot that may occur somewhere.

Q Can a blood clot cause a heart attack, and yet dissolve before a subsequent autopsy examination?

A Yes.

Q And can heart attacks be caused by constriction of blood vessels in the heart or in the heart area, Doctor?

A This is a phenomenon—

MR. HAYES: Your Honor, may I have a continuing objection to what can be?

THE COURT: As to this last question, the objection is sustained.

MR. CALLAHAN: All right.

Q Are there other ways, Doctor, in which heart attacks occur which are not ordinarily detectable or may not be detectable by subsequent autopsy?

MR. HAYES: Same objection.

THE COURT: Same ruling. Sustained.

MR. CALLAHAN: Q Are you familiar, Doctor, with a condition known as fatty blood? I'm using a lay term. Excuse me for doing that, but are you familiar with a condition known by that name?

A Yes. There are conditions that I'm sure you could apply that term to.

Q And what would that condition involve, from a medical point of view?

A Well—

MR. HAYES: Excuse me. Are we now asking the Doctor to speculate upon what conditions a lay person might call fatty blood?

MR. CALLAHAN: No. I apologize for using that term, because I don't know the medical term, and I'm asking the Doctor to testify—

THE COURT: Can you tell us what fatty blood is, Doctor?

THE WITNESS: Sure.

THE COURT: Tell us.

THE WITNESS: The blood normally contains a modest amount of fat in everyone. There are some individuals in which this fat concentration of blood is excessive, and may constitute twenty or even thirty percent of the actual blood volume.

MR. CALLAHAN: Doctor, can that be a contributing cause, or a sole cause of a heart attack?

A Yes.

Q And how would that mechanism work?

A There are a number of mechanisms that are possible in someone's blood who should have the red blood cells carry the oxygen around, but they're displaced by fatty material. This immediately dilutes the effect of the blood. Furthermore, there are times during the day, and depending on the diet of an individual, when this fat concentration may become quite excessive, such that—

MR. HAYES: Your Honor, may I interrupt? Are we going to have any evidence of fatty blood in this case?

MR. CALLAHAN: Well, your Honor, we have the pathologist's report that cannot explain the cause of death. Through this expert witness, I am suggesting various ways in which death can occur, and yet it cannot be determined upon subsequent pathological examination.

THE COURT: I'll permit the inquiry.

THE WITNESS: There are times in which the concentration of fat in the blood may be such that adequate oxygen cannot be transported, and in certain blood vessels, as the heart pumps, they may get a shot of virtually 100 percent fat or a globule of fat, which somehow is segregated from the rest of the blood. This would be very damaging, as this bogus of fat could in fact obstruct a blood vessel for a period of time sufficient to produce damage to the heart.

MR. CALLAHAN: And could it cause death?

A Yes.

Q Now, Doctor, let me give you some other hypothetical facts which I did not include in my first one or two questions.

Assume that this individual on December 28th, 1967, which would be three weeks or so before the date of death I gave you, of January the 19th, was at work in the caboose of a train which was underway, and assume that that train, while beginning to come to a scheduled stop, was caused to go into what is called emergency, which caused it to stop a little faster than it might have, but still in a continuing slow-down manner. Assume, further, that after the train stopped, he later on was observed by the engineer of the train to have a small cut over the ear, but he did not observe anything else unusual about him.

He was caused to be slammed against the back of the caboose, resulting in a cut ear and a bruised arm and head. Assume further that that was not accompanied by any period of unconsciousness, that the man continued to work till the end of that shift—that was on December 28th—and that he also worked on December the 29th, that he did not work on the 30th, the 31st or the 1st of January, 1968, but thereafter, he continued to work regularly on January the 2nd, the 3rd, the 4th, the 5th, the 6th, the 7th, the 8th, the 9th, the 11th, the 12th, the 13th, the 14th, the 16th, the 17th, the 18th, and then, as you already know, he was going to work on the 19th, when death occurred; and assume further that in that intervening period that he was observed, from time to time, by members of his family or relatives, in episodes in which he appeared to be staring in space for a period as long as ten seconds; that on another occasion, he was observed by his daughter and also by his wife to have been thrashing about in bed, and that he went to a New Year's Eve party and was observed to be "not acting like himself." And now, if you make those additional assumptions, Doctor, do they in any way change the opinion you've given us as to the cause of death?

A No.

Q Now, are you familiar, Doctor, with a condition known as post-traumatic epilepsy?

A Yes.

Q Is there anything in the entire hypothetical question, assuming all the facts I have given you, that suggest that this individual might or could be suffering from epilepsy, as a result of the beginning of the occurrence on December 28th, 1967?

A No.

Q Would you explain that, Doctor?

A Yes.

Based upon the experience I have with the condition of post-traumatic epilepsy, there are basically two phases of this. There's, so called, early epilepsy and late epilepsy.

The early epilepsy activity, or seizure activity, begins characteristically within hours or days of a very severe head injury, the magnitude of which usually places the individual in a medical care institution.

They are usually unconscious for a prolonged period of time. There is usually evidence of bleeding somewhere in the head, not on the head but in the head, skull fractures, things of this sort. Generally, these people who develop seizures as a result of trauma in this early period—this is, a week or so—are in very serious condition.

There then follows a period in which, after a significant head injury of the type I've just described, epilepsy is less common. At about, oh, four, five, six weeks, and so forth after that, for periods even up to years have been reported, epilepsy may again occur. More than likely, the individuals who develop epilepsy, as a result of trauma, also have had it early. Probably, what is happening at that point is that it's a different set of circumstances. Scarring and repair is taking place, which somehow makes brain cells unstable, and they go into seizure activity.

Q Now, let me add one other possible fact, which I omitted, and that is, assume further, that upon returning home from work after the occurrence of December 28th, the man is observed by his wife to have a small amount of dried blood in his right ear. Would that change your opinion in any way?

A No.

Q Now, Doctor, if there was evidence as to statements or symptoms given by the man—referring now to January the 19th, 1968—immediately before he fell to the floor and died, would those be of any consequence to you in making a determination, or in adding to a determination you've already made, as to the probable cause of death?

A Yes. That, as I mentioned before, would be an important part of the supporting or ancillary information that would go into the examination.

Q And are those things that are customarily used by you, in making such determination?

A Yes.

Q And do they become of particular significance, Doctor, if your autopsy is unable to determine the specific cause of death?

A Yes.

Q And do you, in making a determination, on occasion refer

specifically to such information as been developed in that fashion?

A I do.

Q Now, let me just give you a couple of additional facts for the hypothetical question, Doctor.

Would you also assume that, in the pathologist's examination, he observed no bruises or cuts to the body, that he found the ears and auditory canals normal and clear, and that he found that there was no reason to ascribe trauma as the primary or secondary cause of death?

Now, Doctor, with those additional facts, is your opinion still the same?

MR. HAYES: Well, I would object to the latter. That may have been the testimony of Dr. Burns. I thought he was describing what the pathologist did, but I'll withdraw the objection, in the interest of moving the matter along.

THE COURT: Carry on.

THE WITNESS: That additional information would not cause me to change my opinion.

MR. CALLAHAN: All right. Thank you, Doctor. That's all I have.

THE COURT: You may inquire.

CROSS-EXAMINATION BY MR. HAYES:

Q Doctor, what is a clinician?

A A clinician is usually considered to be a physician who is engaged in the treatment of patients directly, directly prescribing medicine, doing surgery, that sort of thing.

Q And are you a clinician, sir?

A No.

Q You are not a clinician?

A Not under those definitions, no.

Q Neurologists are people who practice neurology, seeing people and treating people, real people. They are clinicians, are they not?

A That's correct.

Q And there is a certifying, a series of certifying Boards in this country, is there not, sir?

A There are.

Q As a matter of fact, it is an organization through the A.M.A., of many of the organizations, like the American College of Surgeons, the American College of Physicians, and other organizations which certify people in particular specialties; is that not right?

A Close, but many of these organizations, while having connections with the American Medical Association and the other professional societies, are independent certifying agencies, and are not under the aegis of these other organizations.

Q I'm talking, Doctor—

A But they do—

Q I'm talking, Doctor, about the—

MR. CALLAHAN: I'm sorry, but I think counsel interrupted the witness.

MR. HAYES: I'm sorry. I thought he finished.

THE COURT: Have you completed your response?

THE WITNESS: Yes.

THE COURT: The witness indicates he has completed his response. Proceed.

MR. HAYES: I'm talking about those boards which may be found in the publication, the three-volume publication by Marquis of the Directory of Medical Specialists.

A Yes. I'm not quite sure of the question. The boards are listed in publications of that sort.

Q Now, one of those boards is the American Board of Neurology, is it not?

A Yes.

Q You are not certified in neurology, are you?

A I am not.

Q You are certified, as I understand it, by the American Board of Pathology, in anatomical pathology and neuropathology?

A That's correct.

Q You are not board-certified in clinical pathology?

A No.

Q There is a board within the American Board of Pathology which certifies physicians in clinical pathology; is that not right, sir?

A That is correct.

Q And Doctor, in what specialty would you expect to find people who make a study of blood?

A It could be in two different areas.

Q Well, let me ask you if, in the American Board of Pathology, if there is not a board within the board, a sub-board, sub-specialty, called hematology?

A There is a sub-specialty of that. I'm not certain as to whether that has become a bona fide board examination or certification at this time. I know it will be before long. It's certainly been talked about.

Q Well, it either has been—you say you think it will be?

A I think in time.

Q But it may be already?

A It may have—

Q Pardon me?

A It may have been passed recently. In all probability, there will be such a board before very long. Hemopathology is another name for it.

Q Let me ask you something about a blow to the head. Can a blow to the head cause what is commonly called cerebral concussion?

A A blow to the head may do that, yes.

Q Yes. And may a blow to the head cause something known as retrograde amnesia?

A Yes, it may, but it would have to be other than a simple blow. I think we ought to be putting in some quantifiers here, measures of how severe it is, but if you include all blows, great and small, within that, I'd have to agree with you, yes.

Q Well, let me ask you, what type of blow, in your opinion, would be necessary in order to cause retrograde amnesia?

A Usually, this requires a fairly substantial blow to the head, which, if not producing unconsciousness, is very close to that.

Q And retrograde amnesia is a condition in which there is amnesia for events preceding an occurrence; is that correct?

A Yes.

MR. CALLAHAN: Your Honor, this certainly doesn't seem to have anything to do with the events of this occurrence, or in my direct examination. This is the first I've heard of retrograde amnesia from anyone.

THE COURT: Yes. I believe that's my personal knowledge of retrograde amnesia as well. Is there some relevance of this?

MR. HAYES: Well, if I may be permitted to pursue this for a moment, your Honor.

THE COURT: Very well.

MR. HAYES: A person is playing, let's say, in a football game, and he gets tackled and whacked on the head and may fall down, may not fall down, is confusional and he says, "What happened?" and he doesn't know what happened, is that retrograde amnesia?

A I suppose under those definitions, yes. I've read about these things in news publications, I'm sure, as everyone has, yes.

Q Okay. That retrograde amnesia simply means not knowing the cause or the usual asking "What happened," and it may be for seconds, it may be for minutes or hours or longer; is that correct, sir?

A It may be, yes.

Q Now, how severe a head blow—you say a head blow that would require unconsciousness, or did you modify unconsciousness?

A I said or close to it.

Q Or close to it?

A Yes.

Q Okay. Like confusional, "What happened?"

A Resulting with a blow on the head, you mean, or—

Q Yes, sir.

A Blows to the head may certainly result in confusion, and that might be indicative of a good lump on the head, yes.

Q Now, in the hypothetical question, you were told that the man was slammed against the back of the caboose, and got a bruised head and arm and a cut on the ear, and you were told nothing else about that incident, or the activities that followed. You were told, however, about, in the piecemeal fashion in which you were asked the questions

MR. CALLAHAN: Well, your Honor, I'm going to object. If counsel wants to put a question, fine, but he's criticizing me.

THE COURT: The objection as to the form of the question is sustained.

MR. HAYES: Well, Doctor, what I'm asking is that in giving a hypothetical question, you answered a question, and you were given a few more facts, and you said that wouldn't change your opinion, and you were given a few more facts, and that wouldn't change your opinion, and you were given a few more facts, and you said that wouldn't change your opinion.

MR. CALLAHAN: Your Honor, I object. If he wants to ask a question—

MR. HAYES: I'm not criticizing. I'm not criticizing the manner in which it is done, your Honor. I'm leading into it.

THE COURT: Overruled. Proceed.

MR. HAYES: Q Doctor, when the question was first asked, you said that it was due to what? What was the, in your opinion, the mechanism of death?

A I said it was probably a stoppage or arrhythmia of the heart.

Q Well, Doctor, whatever we die from, the heart stops, doesn't it?

A Eventually, that's true.

Q And the inquiry here, Doctor, is, you know, why did the man die? And you've been given some facts from which you stuck unwaveringly to the conclusion given initially, based upon the mere fact of death, that it was due to, I assume you mean primary cardiac causes?

A Yes.

Q The sudden arrhythmia of the heart. Is it a fact, Doctor, that what you're saying is that sudden death occurs, or may occur, from cardiac physiology, the heart becomes altered, one cannot stay in life without a heart, and death follows fairly rapidly?

A (Nodding.)

Q Now, is that a description of a cardiac—I mean of a sudden death?

A That's a fairly good description of what I've said, yes.

Q But what the inquiry is, is why the heart stopped, what caused it to stop; correct, sir?

A It may not necessarily be. It would be nice if we had that information, but the fact that everything seemed to be going along fine, and suddenly the heart stops, I think is a meaning significant in and of itself.

Q Doctor, in your opinion, is sudden news of death or sudden shocking experience, can that produce sudden, unexplained death in the absence of known cardiac disease?

A It has been reported as such, yes. It can occur.

Q Okay. So that there is an example of something unrelated to cardiac disease or know cardiac disease which causes death. Let me ask you this: Can choking precipitate cardiac arrhythmia, by simply producing a deficiency of oxygen, and then arrhythmia of the heart?

A It may, yes.

Q And Doctor, is it not a fact that there is neural reflex, neural brain activity which is mediated through the respiratory system, and can lead to this final event of the heart stopping, and a person dying?

A There are nervous connections, or neural connections, between all of the visceral functions of the body and the brain, and they can certainly mediate sudden death.

Q Now, Doctor, you mentioned that early epilepsy—you mentioned the concept called early epilepsy, and you recall being asked questions about epilepsy at the time of your deposition, do you not, Doctor?

A I do.

Q And at that time, you said that the head injury would not produce epilepsy, epileptic seizures for, oh, at least a month that, in your opinion—

A I don't recall specifically saying only that. I do remember saying, as I said here today, that epileptic seizures may occur some weeks or months, or even years, after a bit of trauma, yes.

Q Now, Doctor, I thought I heard you testify here today, that you now concede that there can be an entity which would in a head injury produces epileptic seizure, within hours or days.

A I don't have to concede it. I said that, yes. It's true.

Q You characterize it as a severe head injury, though.

A Yes.

Q What do you mean by a severe head injury?

A Well, it usually constitutes someone having been made unconscious for an extended period of time. They would usually, or they may, have a skull fracture. These are people who are usually in a medical care facility or on their way there, something which is quite obvious to everyone, that the individual involved is seriously injured.

Q Doctor, is it true that epileptic seizures can be manifested in anything ranging from momentary alteration of the state of consciousness, to full-blown grand mal seizures?

A I would prefer to avoid this particular area, since I am not a clinician, I am not a physician who knows all the ins and outs and variants of epilepsy. I can certainly be informed, or am informed about some basic aspects of epilepsy, but I wouldn't want to be drawn into a discussion in which I would hold myself out as an expert in this area, which I don't.

MR. HAYES: Well, Doctor, what I was reading was a—

MR. CALLAHAN: Excuse me. Let me, by way of objection, say that the defense expects to produce a Dr. John Hughes, who will be fully qualified to answer these questions, counsel.

MR. HAYES: May I continue with my examination, your Honor?

THE COURT: Proceed, please.

MR. HAYES: What I was reading was a statement from your deposition, Doctor. You expressed no reluctance, at the time of your deposition, to answer those questions, did you?

A I don't recall precisely what the level of questioning was concerning epilepsy. I recall you asked me a few questions, and I felt reasonably comfortable in answering them, at that time.

Q Did you express to me, at that time, that you didn't think that you were an expert in the subject, and therefore, shouldn't be getting involved in it?

A No, I didn't. You didn't ask me questions which I felt approached that borderline my competence.

Q Well, Doctor, let's get the deposition. Page 29.

"Doctor—well, isn't it true that epileptic seizures can be manifested in anything from a momentary alteration of the state of consciousness to full-blown grand mal seizures?"

"Answer: `That is true!'"

A Yes.

Q You were asked the question. Did you make that answer?

A Yes.

Q Now, let me ask you this, Doctor: Is it true that episodes of blank staring, that that may represent epileptic activity? Is that correct, sir?

A Without regard to age, and I believe I put that qualifier in there in that answer, blank staring spells may be a manifestation of epileptic seizures, yes, that's true.

Q And Doctor, is—can thrashing about represent epileptic activity, sir?

A It may or may not.

Q Well, obviously, if I go like this (indicating), you know that I'm not epileptic, right?

A I would gather not, no.

Q Well, but you don't know that I'm not, do you?

A I don't know whether you are epileptic or not, but what you were describing there—

Q Because to an epileptic—

A —wasn't an epileptic seizure.

MR. CALLAHAN: Just a minute. Counsel is interrupting the witness, and I would object to it.

THE COURT: The witness may complete this response.

THE WITNESS: Yes, the thrashing about, as you've just described, would not, in my opinion, be a manifestation of an epileptic seizure.

MR. HAYES: Shaking, thrashing about or shaking may represent epileptic seizures; is that correct, sir?

A It may or may not.

Q Well, okay. Then it may—if it may or may not, then it may; is that correct, sir?

A Well, it seems to me you're negating part of my answer. It can represent a seizure and it cannot. It isn't specific for it.

Q An episode was reported to you, in a deposition, about the thrashing about in the bed, and did you answer, or is it your testimony now, sir, that that thrashing about in bed, that you would concede that the episodes reported by the family of the thrashing in bed could be epileptic attacks?

A They could be, yes. I don't think they are, but they could be.

Q Now, you were asked questions at the deposition about the relationship between these episodes afterward, and the occurrence of December 28, 1967, and essentially, the facts given, all the facts and series of facts given here, were given there, and you opined at the time of your deposition that it was your opinion that this was not epileptic attacks.

A Yes. I believe I made that statement.

Q What was it that gave you trouble in saying that these were not epileptic attacks?

A Okay. The diverse nature of the symptoms which were reported, staring spells, thrashing in bed, within the context of my experience with epilepsy and my reading about it, would not be classical seizures at all.

The fact of staring into space, as you mention, can certainly be a manifestation of petit mal epilepsy, which is usually confined to childhood.

I'm unfamiliar with any classic seizure activity, which is manifested in the symptoms which were related to me, or the observations which were related to me in the materials I had to examine and the hypothetical questions which were put to me. They just don't sound or appear to be epilepsy, according to my experience and definition.

Q Question, on Page 37 of your deposition—

MR. CALLAHAN: Just a minute, Mr. Hayes.

MR. HAYES: I'm going to ask a question whether he was asked these questions and whether he made these answers.

MR. CALLAHAN: Well, you're suggesting that there's something inconsistent with that answer. You may—

MR. HAYES: There certainly is. May I proceed, your Honor?

THE COURT: Proceed.

MR. HAYES: Did I—do you recall my mentioning, just as I've been here, that you do not believe that the attacks, like these epileptic attacks, were, in your opinion, epileptic attacks in this case?

A I said I didn't think they were.

Q Right. And your statement at Page 37, "There is a temporal sequence here which gives me trouble. It may be a part of that sequence, but the fact is that this man died, correct me if I'm wrong, about three weeks or so after the accident." "Yes, sir."

"Answer: 'That is not usually the time period after a traumatic event, and by 'traumatic event,' I mean something fairly significant, in which there was loss of consciousness, possibly a skull fracture, and possibly medical treatment and recognition of a major head injury. Usually, three weeks is not the period of time after which epilepsy appears. This is often many months later. The time is a little too close in this instance!'"

Did you make that answer to this question?

A Yes, I did.

MR. CALLAHAN: Your Honor, that is not impeaching. That's exactly what he's testified to here today.

MR. HAYES: Quite the contrary. The Doctor has said now that there is early epilepsy, but he said this would have to be a severe injury, such as a skull fracture, and everybody knows what's wrong, and medical attention, and a seizure can come, and that can come within hours or a day or so following the occurrence.

MR. CALLAHAN: Your Honor—

THE WITNESS: I did.

MR. CALLAHAN:—there's a pending objection, or there seems to be, and instead of awaiting a ruling on my objection, Mr. Hayes makes a speech here.

THE COURT: I believe he was responding. Objection is overruled. You may answer.

THE WITNESS: Yes, I testified to that. In fact, perhaps the reason—

MR. HAYES: Excuse me. The witness—the question is whether those questions were asked and whether the answer was made.

MR. CALLAHAN: That is not the question. I object to that. That was not the question that was put to this witness. Counsel read some testimony. There was no question read that I'm aware of.

MR. HAYES: Okay. So there's no question.

Q Were you asked—

MR. CALLAHAN: Objection. There was a question put to the witness, but it wasn't preceded by any question of counsel.

THE COURT: May I have the last question put to the witness before the recital by counsel of the deposition comments?

(Record read.)

THE COURT: Objection sustained.

MR. HAYES: On the basis that I called it a question and, it was merely an answer?

THE COURT: On the basis that there was no foundation laid for the proposed impeachment.

MR. CALLAHAN: Well, one point, your Honor, that I thought he wanted to ask was, what was in the answer that was impeaching.

MR. HAYES: Well, the distinction is not to be found in the time period. At the time of the deposition, he said—

THE COURT: There was no foundation laid for the proposed impeachment, counsel.

MR. CALLAHAN: Thank you, your Honor.

THE COURT: This is a witness—

MR. HAYES: Oh, I'm sorry.

Q Well, you recall that it was—that deposition was taken on May 21, 1980?

A I don't recall precisely, but that's about right.

Q At my office, sir?

A Yes.

Q And I questioned you?

A Yes, you did.

Q And Mr. Callahan accompanied you to the deposition?

A He did.

Q And he was present during the deposition?

A That's correct.

Q And you were sworn under oath?

A I was.

Q And you testified under oath?

A I did.

MR. HAYES: I would now, your Honor, ask to be permitted now to ask the question, whether he was asked the question and made the answer.

THE COURT: Proceed.

MR. HAYES: Thank you, your Honor.

Q What I read you, did you make those answers to those questions at the time of the deposition, at the time and place stated?

MR. CALLAHAN: Well, your Honor, it's been so long now, it's

not clear what he read. I don't yet remember him reading a question. As far as I know, he just read an answer.

THE COURT: Proceed in proper form, counsel.

MR. HAYES: "But you do not believe that attacks like epileptic attacks are part of that syndrome; is that correct?

Answer: There is a temporal sequence here which gives me trouble. It may be a part of that sequence, but the fact is that this man died, correct me if I'm wrong, about three weeks or so after the accident."

Statement by Hayes: "Yes, sir."

Answer: That is not usually the time period after a traumatic event, and by 'traumatic event,' I mean something fairly significant in which there was loss of consciousness, possibly a skull fracture and medical treatment, and recognition of a major head injury. Usually, three weeks is not the period of time after which epilepsy appears. That is often many months later. The time is a little too close, in this instance."

Were you asked those questions, and did you make those answers?

A I did. I did, yes.

Q Well now, you will now concede that there is at least some type of head injury which can produce epileptic seizures within hours, or a day, or a couple of days?

A I testified to that a few minutes ago.

Q Yes, sir.

A And attempted to lay this out, that there are two peaks in time—

Q Excuse me, Doctor.

MR. CALLAHAN: Now, just a minute. I think it's fair to let the witness answer the question, before he's interrupted and another question is put to him.

MR. HAYES: Your Honor—

MR. CALLAHAN: Now, I object.

MR. HAYES: I object to the answer, on the ground that it is not responsive to the question.

THE COURT Gentlemen. Would you please read the last question and answer back, Miss?

(Record read.)

THE COURT: Counsel is correct. The witness will be permitted to hear the question, and make his response to the question before another question is put. The objection is sustained as being not responsive. The answer will be stricken. Put the question to the witness.

Q Now, Doctor, would you say, Doctor—are you saying that it is impossible that there is a relationship between the occurrence of December 28, 1967, and the man's death on July 19, or January 19th, 1968?

A By an impossibility, I presume you mean the slightest chance. I'm not saying that. I said in my opinion, this didn't happen.

Q Well, using "possible" in the term—in terms of logical alternatives, would you concede that it is possible that the man had a seizure, causing him to choke on his own mucus, and that led to anoxia, which led to cardiac standstill and cardiac arrhythmia?

A That's not logical, in my opinion.

Q At Page 43:

"Question: Isn't it possible, Doctor, that the man had a seizure, causing him to choke on his own mucus, and that led to anoxia, which led to cardiac standstill and cardiac dysrhythmia?

Answer: Again, we are in the same framework of using `possible' in terms of logical alternatives. I would have to concede that is possible. I don't know what that is—I don't know that that is what happened. I don't think that it is."

MR. CALLAHAN: Well, your Honor, That is not impeaching, and I would object to it.

THE COURT: Overruled. It may stand. May we have the response from the witness, please?

MR. HAYES: Were you asked those questions, and did you make those answers at the time of the deposition in my office on May 21, 1980?

A Yes, I did.

Q Doctor, are you familiar with Dr. Oppenheimer?

A There are many doctors Oppenheimer. Would you identify which one it is?

Q I believe it's J.R. Oppenheimer. He's from Oxford.

A Yes.

Q Or D.R. I'm sorry.

A I'm aware of who he is, yes.

Q And did he determine a method, or at least report on a method where a brain, on gross examination by a pathologist, after being cut into sections, reveals no evidence of any injury to the brain, but upon a special type of staining, that in cases of head injuries with more than a few hours survival, microscopic examinations of the brain reveal lesions that are not apparent on naked eye inspection?

A I'm not familiar with that article, per se. I perhaps have read it. I don't know. I'd have to look at it to—

Q Would you agree that the statement is true?

A I don't doubt that Dr. Oppenheimer published an article of this sort. Whether I agree with his conclusions or not, I haven't had a chance to examine the evidence, so I don't know. I'm aware of this issue in the medical literature, but—

Q Well, let me ask you a question, then. Do you agree that in cases of head injury where the patient survives with more than a few—for more than a few hours, that microscopic examination of the brain may reveal lesions, which were not apparent on naked eye inspection?

A Yes, that's possible.

Q And Doctor, is it also possible that anoxic cell changes are frequently seen in such cases where the injury has been complicated by respiratory troubles?

A That's a fair statement, yes.

Q And that the microscopic lesions are attributable to accelerations within the brain substance at the time of injury?

A That would be controversial. I'm sure that's Dr. Oppenheimer's opinion, but there's an equal body of literature that disputes that and raises questions about it. I haven't made up my mind about that.

Q Well, Doctor, do you have any opinion about shearing of nerve fibers, as a cause of brain damage due to head injury, especially in acceleration injuries?

A It undoubtedly occurs. We see evidence of it all the time.

Q Now, Doctor, I want to get to this situation of the early epileptic seizure or convulsion, requiring this major type of head injury which you've postulated.

Doctor, are you familiar with the American Journal of Neurology, Neurosurgery and Psychiatry?

A No, not the American Journal. There is a journal called the Journal of Neurology—

Q I'm sorry. It is from our friends in England. You're familiar with that journal?

A Yes, I am.

Q Is it an authoritative journal, sir?

A It's a journal in good standing, yes.

Q And do you know of Small and Woolf, through any of your reading in literature?

A Again, I would have to be appraised of initials or where these people are from. They don't immediately leap to mind.

Q Doctor, does your opinion about the major type of injury necessary to produce early seizure, does that postulate an older person?

A No, not necessarily.

Q A younger person or a middle-aged person?

A Not necessarily, no.

Q So it is a, I take it, not an age dependent thing but a severity of injury dependent thing?

A My experience, this can occur at all age groups. There may be some more likelihood in one group or another, but it's not exclusive to any one age group.

Q Doctor, I want to read you a case report. The patient—

MR. CALLAHAN: Your Honor—

MR. HAYES: —a boy age—

MR. CALLAHAN: Just a minute. We have no idea what it is counsel is reading from. He hasn't produced any of these documents, which I think were requested of him before this.

THE COURT: Sustained. I don't know what it is, either. Whatever it is you have, would you have it marked as an exhibit, please.

MR. HAYES: Yes, sir.

(Whereupon, Plaintiff's Exhibit No. 27, was marked for identification.)

MR. CALLAHAN: Your Honor, that looks like a several-page document. I wonder if—

THE COURT: All right. We'll take a recess.

MR. HAYES: Your Honor, will the Court instruct the witness, please.

THE COURT: Yes. You're instructed not to discuss your testimony with anybody or permit anybody to discuss it with you. Anybody is all inclusive.

(Whereupon, the following proceedings were had in open court, in the presence and hearing of the jury.)

THE COURT: Proceed, counsel.

MR. HAYES: Q Doctor, you have read the report of a case history reported by Woolf and the other person?

A Small. Yes.

Q Woolf and Small. And Doctor, does it report the case of an injury, a head injury to a child playing soccer?

A I believe the game is cricket.

Q Or some game. Cricket. I'm sorry.

A Yes, it does.

Q And how is the injury described, sir, the head injury?

A May I read from the report finding?

Q Yes, sir.

THE WITNESS: "On the evening of July 7, he was fielding whilst playing cricket with two other boys when his attention was momentarily diverted by someone calling to him. At that moment, he was struck by the ball which was of cork full on the forehead. The ball had come directly from the bat without hitting the ground. He fell over backwards but picked himself up and went on playing as though unaffected, and …" Well, that's a description of the accident.

Q Okay. And then he spent a normal night, didn't he? Wasn't that the case report?

A Yes, apparently so. He behaved normally throughout the remainder of that day, and I believe was normal until around supper time, six o'clock or so.

Q And till about twenty-four hours later; it that correct, sir?

A Let me be sure of that. I don't think it was twenty-four hours later. I think it was the same day, 6:15 p.m. They don't mention any other dates here, so it's a little confusing, but

Q Excuse me, sir. He—

A Oh, "passed a normal night," yes. Correct.

Q Okay. He passed a normal night. The next day he went to school?

A Correct.

Q He behaved normally at school; then he returned home, carried out a shopping errand, and seemed in every way normal units 6:15 p.m.; correct, sir?

A Yes.

Q And then his mother noticed that he appeared to be unconscious. A fever—

MR. CALLAHAN: Your Honor, if we're going to use the witness for this testimony, it would seem appropriate for the witness to testify.

THE COURT: Proceed.

MR. HAYES: Doctor, is it true that the boy then had not only epileptic seizure, but a convulsive epileptic seizure?

A Well, the two would be synonymous. He had a convulsion, yes.

Q Thank you very much, Doctor.

Now, Doctor, just a couple of more questions. You mentioned something about the size of the heart being outside of normal limits on the—as reported by the pathologist who did the autopsy on the man in this case.

A Yes.

Q Doctor, you had that, all of the information in the report of pathology at the time of your deposition on May 21, 1980, didn't you?

A I did.

Q And you had read it, had you not?

A I had.

Q And is it not true that at that time, sir, you were asked if there was any pathology or abnormality demonstrated in that autopsy report?

A I was.

Q And did you answer that there was no pathology or abnormality demonstrated in the autopsy report?

A That is the answer I gave at that time, yes.

Q Okay. Now, Doctor, is there such a thing known as—I mean are some people's hearts larger than other people's?

A Yes.

Q And Doctor, the heart of a person who is an active person, is that larger than the heart of a person who is sedentary?

A It may not be.

Q Well, is it usually, sir?

A No.

Q Is there such a thing known as athlete's heart?

A Well, that may be a different matter. Yes, there is something known as that, yes.

Q People who exercise and do hard work have larger hearts because of the work that is placed on the heart, and that has an effect upon the muscle, and the heart is largely muscle; isn't that correct, sir?

A The heart is largely muscle, but the hearts may not necessarily be enlarged. They may be. The athlete's heart business has to do more with the physiology of the heart more than anything else.

Q Okay.

A Not necessarily size—

Q Let's not talk about an athlete. I'll withdraw that.

MR. CALLAHAN: Your Honor, excuse me. Counsel again has interrupted the witness, and I think it's improper.

MR. HAYES: Have you finished your answer?

THE COURT: You may complete your answer, if you wish.

THE WITNESS: I would like to say a few more words. The athlete's heart—

MR. HAYES: Excuse me. I'm going to withdraw athlete's heart. We're not talking about that.

MR. CALLAHAN: Your Honor, the question was put. The witness was answering the question.

THE COURT: The witness may answer the question.

THE WITNESS: The additional part of the athlete's heart business is these people have a decreased pulse rate. The fact is their heart is more efficient than most people, but I wouldn't want to imply that their hearts are necessarily enlarged as a result of this activity.

MR. HAYES: Doctor, and lastly, would you consider it a logical hypothesis that a person may have a seizure and remain unbreathing for up to a minute or more?

A That can occur, yes.

Q And usually, people in such circumstances regain breathing, do they not?

A In most instances, they do.

Q And would you accept as a logical hypothesis that in some cases, there are individuals that do not start breathing again, normal breathing, after a seizure?

A That has been alleged in the literature. I personally have not observed that.

MR. HAYES: Thank you very much, Doctor. I have no further questions.

REDIRECT EXAMINATION BY MR. CALLAHAN:

Q Doctor, have you ever, referring to the game of cricket, have you ever seen that game played?

A I have.

Q And do you have any idea of the size of a cricket ball?

A Roughly, it's approximately the same of a baseball. I believe it's slightly larger.

Q Does the article, that you referred to there, say that the boy was struck by the ball and it had not touched the ground before it struck him?

A That's what it reports.

Q All right. From your observation of—incidentally, have you ever had occasion to watch cricket played?

A As a child, I lived in Buffalo, New York, and for some reason, there were quite a population, mostly of Jamaicans, that played cricket in the park every Sunday, for these indeterminate periods that this game goes on, and we would go there and watch the game on several occasions.

Q All right. Then, in view of the fact that the—and incidentally, did we refer to this as a child or young man, or is there some indication of the age of the person?

A Yes. It's stated he's thirteen years old.

Q Is it of any significance to you that he was struck in the forehead, as I understand it to be described, without the ball ever having struck the ground before striking him?

A The ball was probably moving at a pretty good clip, and I think the reason they mention this is that it didn't touch anything else, and was not slowed down. It looks to me like knowing how fast this ball goes, that he was hit reasonably well, and they said "hit full on the forehead," so—

Q So that would be significant?

A Yes.

Q Does the article relate to any other such death?

A I don't recall so. I believe this is presented as a single case report and is describing, I think, by the tenor of it, a rather uncommon occurrence.

Q All right. Now Doctor, do I understand that you do place significance on the fact that the heart of this 160-pound man weighed 370 grams?

MR. HAYES: I object to that as leading and suggestive, but it's already out, so go ahead.

THE COURT: It is leading and suggestive, and you've also right, it's already been testified to, so there's no harm. You may answer.

THE WITNESS: Yes, I do place some significance upon the weight of this heart.

MR. CALLAHAN: And what is that, Doctor?

A As I mentioned or touched on before, this is at the—beyond the range of normal for a man of this age and for weight, according to reading, which I've done subsequently to examining the records the first time through and testifying at the deposition. I took the trouble to look up some weights just to reassure myself that my original thought that all the organs were normal, and in fact, I was wrong.

I discovered that the weight of this heart is outside the range of normal for this man's size.

Q All right. Now, Doctor, is it of any significance to you in forming an opinion, or in making a determination as to a cause of death from information that comes over a long period of time, that is, in this case, the occurrence as everybody knows took place some 12 years ago?

MR. HAYES: Well, your Honor, I object to that, calling upon this Doctor to evaluate the credibility of testimony. That is the jury's function.

THE COURT: May I have the question read back, please.

(Record read.)

THE COURT: Overruled. You may answer.

THE WITNESS: May I answer?

THE COURT: Yes, sir.

THE WITNESS: I think those, yes, that would be important to pay attention to, and it could affect an opinion, yes.

MR. CALLAHAN: All right. And is it a fact that some of the information came from persons who were children the age of thirteen or so at the time?

MR. HAYES: Your Honor, it is the function of the jury—

THE COURT: Objection is sustained.

MR. CALLAHAN: All right. Finally, Doctor, you testified on cross-examination to some questions as to a special type of staining of a segment of the brain and what may or may not have been of consequence. Now, in this case, in these hypotheticals as you understand, of course, we had no such specimens?

A We did not.

Q And we had no other tissues?

A That's right.

Q Is that correct? And we had nothing such as—

MR. HAYES: Your Honor, this is leading and suggestive.

THE COURT: As to form, sustained.

MR. CALLAHAN: All right. Doctor, were there any brain samples in this case?

MR. HAYES: Your Honor, this is obvious—

MR. CALLAHAN: Or specimens?

MR. HAYES: Why is this being prolonged? I object.

MR. CALLAHAN: All right. Doctor, in making a determination as to the cause of death, would you, as a pathologist, prefer to have, in addition to the autopsy that was done in this case, all the other tissue specimens from whatever—

MR. HAYES: I object to this, your Honor, what the preference would be. God, I dearly wish it had been taken, but I object to it.

THE COURT: Well, I'm going to let him answer. I think it's been covered before, but he may answer.

THE WITNESS: Yes, I would prefer to have all this. It would have added an element of completeness, which at this point, I have to deal with gross autopsy findings, that is, what you touch, see, feel, and there's nothing now that I can review other than that.

MR. CALLAHAN: All right. Thank you, Doctor. I have nothing further.

RE CROSS-EXAMINATION BY MR. HAYES:

Q Doctor, with respect to reading articles, you are, as a matter of fact, familiar with Dr. Joseph Segarra and articles that he has written on neuropathology, aren't you?

A I know who he is.

Q You've heard of the man?

A I know who he is.

MR. CALLAHAN: Your Honor, this is beyond the scope of my direct, and I would object.

THE COURT: Overruled. You may respond.

MR. HAYES: Q And Doctor, may I assume correctly that you are not a stranger to the witness stand, that you have testified in a number of cases before?

A I have, yes.

Q Doctor, lastly, will you read the title of the article from the English Journal?

MR. CALLAHAN: I'll object. That's beyond the scope.

MR. HAYES: He went into the cricket game.

THE COURT: Is that the one that has the cricket game in it?

MR. HAYES: Yes, sir.

THE COURT: Yes, you may read it, then. Overruled.

THE WITNESS: It is entitled, "Fatal Damage to the Brain by Epileptic Convulsions after a Trivial Injury to the Head."

MR. HAYES: Thank you very much, Doctor. No further questions.

MR. CALLAHAN: I do have one further question.

FURTHER REDIRECT EXAMINATION BY MR. CALLAHAN:

Q Doctor, have you ever seen anyone struck—incidentally, were the games that you saw, were these adults or children?

A These were—

MR. HAYES: I object.

THE COURT: Overruled. I was interested in that kind of a question myself.

THE WITNESS: Those were adults.

MR. CALLAHAN: I beg your pardon?

THE COURT: The games he saw were adults.

I take it none of them were thirteen-year-old children?

THE WITNESS: No way.

MR. CALLAHAN: And Doctor, did you ever have occasion to see a man rendered unconscious when struck by a cricket ball?

A Yes.

MR. HAYES: Your Honor, I'm going to object to all this. Okay. Fine.

THE COURT: If he saw it, he may so inform us.

THE WITNESS: I did.

MR. CALLAHAN: Q And what portion of the body was involved?

A The groin.

Q All right. Now, in your experience, Doctor, is it unusual, or do children on occasion exhibit unusual resilience or things like that in terms of injury that might have a different effect upon adults?

A Yes, they do. Children respond—

MR. HAYES: Your Honor, I object to this.

THE COURT: Sustained.

MR. HAYES: This is beyond the scope of direct and cross.

THE COURT: Sustained.

MR. CALLAHAN: I have no further questions.

MR. HAYES: I have nothing.

THE COURT: You may step down, sir.

(Witness excused.)

DR. JOHN R. HUGHES, called as a witness herein, having been first duly sworn, was examined and testified as follows:

DIRECT EXAMINATION BY MR. CALLAHAN:

Q Would you state your name, please.

A John R. Hughes.

Q Where do you live, sir?

A 720 Roslyn Terrace in Evanston, Illinois.

Q Would you tell us what your profession is?

A I am a physician and a scientist together.

Q What is your present occupation?

A I am Professor of Neurology at the University of Illinois Medical Center, Director of Electroencephalography, usually abbreviated EEG, and Director of the Epilepsy Clinic at the University of Illinois Medical Center.

Q Your offices then are at the University of Illinois Medical Center?

A Correct

Q Now, Doctor, I'm going to inquire briefly into your background. Would you tell us what college you graduated from, and the year you graduated?

A I graduated from Franklin and Marshall College, 1950, *summa cum laude*, Lancaster, Pennsylvania.

Q Did you have some subsequent additional schooling at other universities, Doctor?

A Yes, I did.

Q Would you tell us where that was?

A I was awarded two Fulbright Fellowships, allowing me to attend Oxford University in England where I went through their medical school program. I received two degrees from Oxford. Then I went back to Harvard.

Q Let me ask just a question or two about those two degrees from Oxford. Could you tell us what those degrees were?

A The degree is called BA, and the second degree is called MA, but it has no relevance or reference to the B.A. and M.A. of this country.

Q Would you tell us what the difference is, Doctor?

A The difference is that it is a very high degree in England, and it is also the degree that you get when you have completed your medical studies, before you go into what is usually called an internship. First of all, before those two degrees, if you are in medical studies, one usually receives first the Bachelor's of Medicine. I was excused from that because of my previous work and preparation for a medical career. So I went directly into the BA/MA program.

Q You did take some additional training, Doctor, did you not?

A Yes, between my junior and senior year, and also after my senior year, before going to Oxford. I had done eight months of research at Harvard University, and I had a fellowship awaiting me there. And I then entered Harvard for a Ph.D. program, after Oxford.

Q And when was that Ph.D. awarded, Doctor?

A 1954.

Q Now, could you tell us what kind of work you went into after receiving that degree from Harvard in 1954?

A First of all, I was on the staff of the Massachusetts Institute of Technology, M.I.T., in Boston, before going into the service in the form of the United States Public Health Service. For three years, I was at the National Institute of Health, doing work in electroencephalography, epilepsy, and neurophysiology, which means the study of the function of the brain.

Q Then, Doctor, did you subsequently come to the Chicago area and receive another degree from Northwestern University?

A Yes. I then received my M.D. degree from Northwestern University.

Q That is a little unusual for someone, after all the training you went through, to receive his M.D. degree at that point. Could you explain how that came about?

A Yes. It is unusual. When I was a high school student I decided that I wanted to work on brain and brain functions, but I did not think that I wanted to engage in the practice of medicine. Nevertheless, I knew that I needed a medical background in order to do the work that interested me, and so the Oxford career allowed me to get the medical school background with the two degrees.

But, I did not feel that I wanted to be licensed or practice. Therefore, I did not go that third step, which is like an internship, after which one gets the Bachelor's of Medicine, the second Bachelor's of Medicine. Then, later on in life, after I had been advising physicians for many years on epilepsy and writing many articles about epilepsy, I decided that I did want to be the treating physician, and actually be the one writing the prescriptions.

And of course, since I did not have a license for practice at that moment, I decided to leave my Professorship of Neurology at Northwestern, and become a medical student, after having studied, on my own, in the past, what is called the National Boards. Then, for 16 months, by an arrangement with the Dean of the Northwestern University Medical School, I did what is called Clerkships, of just being with patients on the ward, which then satisfied the M.D. requirements. And I was then given the M.D. degree from Northwestern, and I subsequently was given the license for practice.

Q Now, have you been given an honorary degree at the college that you attended as an undergraduate, Franklin and Marshall?

A I was given the Outstanding Alumnus Award a year and a half ago by Franklin and Marshall College, because of my work for twenty to twenty-five years in the field of epilepsy.

Q And, Doctor, did you receive an honorary degree from Oxford?

A I received an honorary degree from Oxford in 1976 called the Doctor of Medicine, rarely given, again because of my work in epilepsy.

Q Doctor, have you published any papers in connection with epilepsy and related matters?

A Yes. I have published about 160 papers on epilepsy and related matters.

Q And this goes back to about how long, Doctor?

A In 1949, I was working at Harvard on research, and that work eventually was published. And I think the publication was in the very early 1950s.

Q Have you published any books?

A Yes, three books.

Q They are related to the subject that you have been discussing here, I take it?

A Yes, that is correct.

Q There has been discussion here, Doctor, about boards, and board certification. Could you tell us what they are in relationship to your principle field of study?

A The boards in my particular specialty are the American Board of Qualification in Electroencephalography, and there is another board that deals with qualifications of electroencephalography called the American Board of Electroencephalographers, and in my interest in epilepsy and electroencephalography, those are the two boards that one usually seeks. The first board I have had, there were thirty-seven members in the United States, and I have served many years as examiner on it.

The second board was most recently established, and I have those boards and have been examining in those boards, also. They have been, after this time, independent of the American Board of Medical Specialists, and the American Board of Medical Specialists is the umbrella organization for most, but not all, American Boards.

I was Chairman of a committee, appointed by the American Board EEG Society, to look into the possibility of our electroencephalographic boards coming under the umbrella of the American Board of Medical Specialists. For various financial reasons, this was not immediately accomplished, but we are still pursuing it.

Q Finally, Doctor, are you a consultant to any national health organization?

A Yes. I am a consultant to the National Institute of Mental Health, the National Institute of Neurological Diseases, and also the National Institute of Arthritis, Metabolic and Digestive Diseases.

Q All right. Now, Doctor, I'm going to give you what has been referred to as a hypothetical question, and I'm going to ask you to assume facts that I give you, and then at the conclusion of that, I am going to ask you a question about those facts.

Assume, Doctor, that a thirty-six-year-old man, weighing some 160 pounds on December the 28th, 1967, was working as a railroad brakeman, and is alone in the caboose of a train, which is traveling on a line of track. Assume that, as that train is beginning to be slowed to make a regular stop, in order to make some switching movements, the train goes into emergency, which causes the train to stop perhaps a little more quickly but nevertheless, to come to a stop.

And assume that, at that occasion that this took place, the man in the caboose was "thrown against" or "slammed against" the side of the caboose, receiving, in the course of it, a cut on his ear, a bruised shoulder, and a bruised head. Assume that the man, thereafter, completed his tour of duty, that he was seen by the engineer of the train, who observed a small cut on the top part of one ear, and that the man in the caboose said nothing to the engineer about being knocked out or being unconscious.

Assume that, thereafter, having completed his tour of duty on December 28th, he also completed a tour of duty on December the 29th. Assume further, that he took off, or laid off, December the 30th, December the 31st, and January the 1st.

Assume further, Doctor, that on January the 2nd, 3rd, 4th, 5th, 6th, 7th, 9th, 10th, 11th, 12th, 13th, 14th, 15th, 16th, 17th, and 18th, he worked a regular schedule. And assume further that on January the 19th, while reporting for work in his caboose in Elkhart, Indiana, he entered the caboose, proceeded to fall on his right side and die within a few minutes thereafter. Assume further that, in the intervening period, in addition to the cut on the ear that I have described, he was observed in the intervening period—by that, I mean December 28th to January 19th—he was observed at different times by members of his family or relatives to exhibit periods during which he would appear to stare into space; that on New Year's Eve, at a party, he was observed by relatives to be "not himself," and on one or two other occasions, to have been staring into space.

Assume further, that from time to time, he was described by members of his family as appearing pale.

Assume further, that after his death, an autopsy was performed, and that the autopsy was performed after the body had been embalmed. Assume that the autopsy report was inconclusive in that the person performing the autopsy could not determine the cause of death.

Assume further that, if any slides, tissues, paraffin blocks, or such were taken or made in the course of that autopsy, none have been found or are available, and none have become any part of evidence in this case. Assume that the autopsy examination disclosed that there were no bruises or cuts to the body, that the ears and the auditory canal were normal and clear. There was no evidence of a severe blow to the body during the three weeks before the death. And assume further that the man who performed the autopsy found that there was no reason to ascribe trauma as the primary or secondary cause of death.

Now, Doctor, making all of those assumptions, do you have an opinion, based upon a reasonable amount of medical certainty, as to whether this hypothetical man's death could have been caused by a condition know as post traumatic epilepsy?

A I have an opinion.

Q And what is that opinion, Doctor?

A That it would not be.

Q All right. Doctor, now would you explain that?

A The term "post traumatic epilepsy" has the term "trauma" included within it. We have to decide what kind of trauma is ignored, when we use that word in reference to a particular individual.

Although, of course, there are exceptions in the medical world, most of the time epileptologists, the doctors interested in epilepsy, are not interested in trauma that is not severe enough to cause a concussion. And concussion usually is defined as an impact strong enough, secure enough, to cause unconsciousness. If we were concerned about all impacts to the head and any kind of head injury, everyone in this room would be a candidate for post traumatic epilepsy, since everyone in this room has received a blow to the head, if fact, perhaps hundreds of impacts on the head, mostly minor.

So, in view of the fact that we have no evidence at all of the hypothetical individual as having been "knocked out," which I believe is the term that you used, only a bruised head, we have no evidence of a significant trauma. And, as long as you don't have evidence of significant trauma, defined ordinarily by a concussion or unconsciousness, in the case of blunt head injury, and that I am referring to as injuries not piercing the scalp, then we do not have the evidence that we need, in order to establish post traumatic epilepsy.

The other part of that phrase is "epilepsy," and when we look for the evidence that there are epileptic attacks between December 28th and January 19th, we don't find the evidence. One suspicion could be staring, but everyone in this room has stared on many occasions, for various numbers of reasons. It is a common human endeavor to be staring from preoccupation or from just a feeling of malaise and for various other reasons.

So we don't have, between December 28th and January 19th, anything about staring in this hypothetical man, which is not common to all of us at one time or another. Furthermore, at the time of the death, we had no evidence of any definite convulsion or of any definite seizure.

So, in brief summary, we have no evidence of significant trauma. We have no evidence of definite epilepsy.

And so, therefore, my conclusion is this should not be considered, with all likelihood, with reasonable amounts of medical certainty, post traumatic epilepsy.

Q All right. Doctor, I am not certain if I did, but I intended to include, in addition to staring into space, and not being himself, an episode in which he was observed by his daughter, and I believe by his wife at some point, to be thrashing in his bed. If I did not, I meant to include that. Does that in any way change what you have told us about?

A That was not included, and let me speak to that. Thrashing in bed, especially now that electroencephalographers are frequently doing all night sleep records on patients, is now known to be very common. Actually, it has been known for years, but now it is being very well known, now that we are observing patients throughout the night.

And there are two phases of sleep. One is called a REM sleep, which stands for rapid eye movement, and that is the phase of sleep in which one dreams. The other phase of sleep is called non-REM sleep, and that is when you are more deeply asleep, not dreaming. In either phase of sleep, patients can be thrashing around. In the non-REM sleep, it is very common that they are changing their positions sometimes quite vigorously, and position change can occur twenty, thirty, forty times throughout the night in most individuals.

Now, the thrashing about is more likely characteristic of the REM stage, in which there is likely dreaming, and the reaction of the individual in this dream stage to what he is dreaming. As to the possibility of it being an epileptic attack, the one rule that we give our neurology residents when they are training is that, in epilepsy, if the patient is moving the head back and forth, and arms are moving in a uncoordinated fashion, it is not epilepsy. This comes into the differential diagnosis of what we call hysterical attacks versus real ones. One characteristic of attacks that may look like epilepsy but aren't, is the attacks in which there is thrashing about, head moving from side to side. That is not epilepsy.

Q All right. But then, do I understand, Doctor, what you have told us is, first of all, in the hypothetical question there is no evidence that any unconsciousness occurred, and, therefore,there is no basis for setting the stage for epilepsy in the first place.

A Correct.

Q And, secondarily, when I described in the hypothetical question staring in space, thrashing in bed, and so forth, none of those descriptions, in your judgment, fall into a characterization for which I believe you had used the term, "seizure"?

A They do not constitute seizure.

MR. CALLAHAN: All right. Thank you Doctor. That completes my questioning.

CROSS-EXAMINATION BY MR. HAYES:

Q Now, as I understand it, you started out with the proposition that the hypothetical individual was not unconscious for any period?

MR. CALLAHAN: By way of objection, that was my hypothetical question to him, so it is not—the witness did not start out with that. That was a hypothetical question put to him.

MR. HAYES: That is what I am asking him, your Honor. May I continue?

THE COURT: Yes, certainly.

MR. HAYES: You concluded that the individual was not unconscious; correct?

MR. CALLAHAN: Well, your Honor, I'm going to have to object. The doctor has nothing to work with but the hypothetical question.

THE COURT: He came to that conclusion, based upon the hypothetical question that was placed before him.

MR. CALLAHAN: All right.

MR. HAYES: You are dealing with the evidence that was given to you in a hypothetical question, and you were asked to assume that these things did indeed occur. And one of the assumptions that you made was that the individual was not unconscious; is that correct, sir?

A It was an assumption presented to me, that was part of the hypothetical picture.

Q And you were—in giving your opinion as to the causal relationship, that was the first thing that you said, that it was significant that the man was not unconscious; that is correct, you considered that significant?

A A significant fact.

Q And did you also conclude that the man had suffered no significant head injury?

A That is right.

Q Then you also concluded that the man did not have seizures; is that right?

A That's correct.

Q And then you concluded, lastly, that at the time of his death, on January 19, 1968, that he did not have a seizure; that was your conclusion; correct?

A Seizure of the brain; that is correct.

Q And a necessary corollary, then, of all that, if you make those assumptions, then, in your opinion, there is no causal relationship; correct?

A Between what and what?

Q Well, between—we are talking about a causal relationship between the incident on the railroad of December 28, 1967 and death on the 19th of January 1968.

A That's correct.

Q And the causal relationship therefore depends upon your consideration of the significance of those events; is that correct, sir?

A Yes.

Q Now, sir, is it your testimony that it would take a significant head injury in order to produce traumatic epilepsy?

A Of course there are exceptions in the medical world. There are exceptions in all aspects of the world. But, in most instances, we do not consider it a significant head injury unless there has been unconsciousness—with one great exception, and that is when there is a penetrating wound. There are exceptions in the literature describing trauma which did not produce unconsciousness, but these are the great exceptions. Furthermore, there are other reasons, other reasons why I concluded that this was not post traumatic epilepsy, as the cause of the death.

Q I am talking about, now, significant head injury.

A Yes.

Q A penetrating wound such as a bullet in the head, that you would consider a significant injury, would you not?

A Absolutely.

Q And sometimes a bullet wound in the head wouldn't produce unconsciousness; correct?

A That's correct.

Q And sometimes banging of the head, an acceleration type of banging on the head, will produce unconsciousness; correct?

A Oh, yes.

Q Do you consider confusion to be a sign of a post concussive state?

A Confusion at what point in time?

Q After the occurrence.

MR. CALLAHAN: Well, by way of objection, the doctor means,

"What point in time, in connection with the occurrence?" Do you mean immediately after the occurrence or later?

MR. HAYES: Let's stay with immediately after the occurrence.

A Confusion immediately after the impact does not establish concussion, by definition.

Q What is the length of unconsciousness that you were talking about in order to establish the definition of unconsciousness?

A A definite period of unconsciousness, and that can be for five seconds, if you like, or it can be for an extended length of time. But, in order to use the term "concussion," one must have a definite period of unconsciousness.

Q Wouldn't your fellow countryman, Dr. Simons, disagree with that, as to your definition of unconsciousness, as to a definition of a post concussive state? Are you familiar with Dr. Simons' writings?

A There are hundreds of Dr. Simonses. Which one are you talking about?

Q I am just asking you, generally, do you know what Dr. Simons has to say about this rigid definition of post concussive, post concussion state that you have given us?

A I don't know which Dr. Simons you are referring to. May I elaborate on my answer, which I would go further, and say that 99 percent of the neurological community would define concussion in terms of an impact severe enough to produce unconsciousness.

Q Doctor, is it also significant to you that, in terms of whether there can be post traumatic epilepsy in a given case, the duration of time from the time of the injury to the time when seizures can develop in a person?

A Yes, that is an important variable.

Q At the time of your deposition, you postulated as one of the reasons supporting your thesis that there was no causal relationship—was that you would have to postulate that there had been a seizure within three weeks after the injury, and you said, did you not, sir, that that was extremely rare, or it did not occur, I don't know which?

A I said that, in most instances of post traumatic epilepsy, there is more that three weeks between the time of impact and the time of the first seizure. And I further stated that, when seizures do occur within three weeks of the time of impact, they generally are associated with definite gross pathology, in particular hemorrhage in the brain.

Q Hemorrhage in the brain? You mean the pathologist opening the skull and looking at the brain and seeing hemorrhage?

A Yes.

Q Now, Doctor, what did you say is that percentage of people who develop post traumatic epilepsy less than months later?

A The figures on this are of the blunt head injuries. We are not talking about missiles, but blunt head injuries. Of those, four to six percent—other authors say eight percent—of those traumatic epilepsy, initially, within the first month. And that is the reason I said that it was relatively uncommon.

Q Now about all traumatic epilepsy; what percentage of those occur within the first month, sir?

A That is what I'm talking about. If one takes—

Q All cases of traumatic epilepsy, four to six percent occur within one month?

A Less than a month.

Q And that provides further support, you say, for your position that, since, in your opinion, first of all, that what were described as seizures were not, in your opinion, seizures, and further underpinning for that is the development of the seizures during the first month in cases of epilepsy—post traumatic epilepsy, is extremely rare, on the order of four to six percent; and that leads you also to the conclusion that what this man was having were not really epileptic seizures; is that correct, sir?

A That's correct. It makes it even more unlikely that the cause of death was post traumatic epilepsy. It makes it more unlikely.

Q Now, Doctor, is it possible for non-significant head injury to result in post traumatic epilepsy?

A As I said, there are exceptions to every rule and therefore, because there are exceptions to every rule that we use to decide on matters with reasonable medical certainty, the answer is, yes, there have been cases written up in the world literature of such exceptions.

Q Now, Doctor, you didn't tell us, in your very lengthy description of your background, that you were with the Cook County Coroner's Office, Medical Examiner's Office.

A No, I didn't because I am not.

Q Do you know Dr. Leestma?

A Yes.

Q And do you know him personally, sir?

A Very well. I was a Professor of Neurology for seventeen years, and he was a colleague of mine.

Q Doctor, can such a thing as burns cause epileptic seizures?

A Yes. I have written about that.

Q And burns—and that would be rare for burns to cause epileptic seizures, but it does occur?

A It does occur, and usually in infants.

Q But not always?

A Not always in infants.

Q As a matter of fact, you wrote that, in rare cases, adults sustain, incur epilepsy as a result of trauma of burns?

A Well—

Q Is that not correct?

A That is correct, but—

Q Doctor—

A —I have to, for the sake of clarity, include the fact that it is not only the trauma of burns, but sometimes the treatment of burns that may be implicated in the development of the seizure. I just wanted to clarify that point.

Q Now, Doctor, you also place significance on the fact that nothing was found at the examination of the patient's brain at autopsy; correct?

A I don't know exactly what you mean by "place significance."

Q Doctor, did you consider it significant in reaching your opinion that there was no causal relationship?

A Yes.

Q And is that—

A I wanted to elaborate. Although I must point out that there need not be any clear pathological change of the brain that is immediately visible to the pathologist or the neuropathologist in cases of post traumatic epilepsy.

Q Doctor, going now to the second thing, about the nature of these seizures, episodes of staring into space can be epileptic seizures; is that correct?

A They can be, under certain circumstances. And those circumstances are important to point out, to clarify that. In particular, staring into space, in a child, is known as absence seizures, although not every staring episode of a child is an absence seizure. So we have to confirm such staring episodes by the electroencephalogram, to differentiate between the daydreaming that all children do, and staring, and the staring that really is epileptic. Similarly, in an adult, staring can be a part of a seizure, as part of what is called temporal lobe epilepsy, epilepsy of the temporal lobe.

But staring, as a single manifestation of a seizure, is extremely rare. Ordinarily the patient will do other things that will make it clear that that staring is an epileptic attack, and such things are humming, mumbling, picking at the clothes, and what we call autonomisms, or automatic movements (indicating). So staring is a part of a constellation of symptoms that one could observe in a patient having a temporal lobe seizure, but rarely, rarely, does it ever occur by itself as part of a temporal lobe epilepsy.

Q Doctor, the last act was the falling over of a man in the caboose. Could not that have been a blackout?

A If one defines blackout as an episode in which an individual loses consciousness, yes, of course it was a blackout, because he lost consciousness.

Q Is not a blackout one of the manifestations of an epileptic seizure?

A Well, how do you use the term "blackout" in your question?

Q The common, ordinary thing of blacking out, and then something happening.

A Well, then I will have to say, yes, patients who have seizures, particularly generalized tonic-clonic seizures in which both upper and lower extremities are jerking. They are blacked out. Another way of saying they are unconscious at the time that they are having their convulsions, is to say that.

Q Doctor, you keep saying "most," and "great majority," and I take it, then, that there are exceptions?

A Well, as pointed out on about three occasions, we do know that there are exceptions to all the rules that we use to decide upon diagnoses.

Q And the exceptions are reported in—some of these exceptions are reported in the literature; is that correct?

A Yes.

Q And many others are disregarded by simply ascribing the cause of death to some other cause, without investigation?

A Many other what?

Q Many other sudden unexplained deaths following head trauma after several weeks or days; is that correct, sir?

A You would have to repeat that question.

Q I will withdraw the question. Doctor, you mentioned the American Board?

A Yes.

Q There is a publication, is there not, called the Director of Medical Specialists?

A That's correct.

Q And there are listed in here the boards that have been recognized by the Association, under the overall aegis of the American Medical Association, including the American Hospital Association, the Association of American Medical Colleges, the Council of Medical Specialty Society, the Federation of State Medical Boards, U.S.A. and the National Board of Medical Examiners; is that correct, sir?

A Yes.

Q Now, your specialty is the electroencephalography, is it not, sir?

A And epilepsy together.

Q Together with electroencephalography. Electroencephalography is used in connection with people who have epilepsy, of whatever form; isn't that correct?

A That is correct.

Q And the EEG is used to measure electrical activity; correct, sir?

A Yes.

Q And now the EEG sometimes, a person having, a person who has epilepsy may have a normal EEG; isn't that true, sir?

A Very rare, if—

Q Sometimes?

A Oh, yes, sometimes, but I would more accurately say very rarely, if the test was done completely and thoroughly. It is very uncommon to have a normal EEG, if the EEG is carefully and accurately done on an epileptic.

Q As a matter of fact, it is uncommon, very uncommon for a person to have a head injury and develop epilepsy; correct, you would agree?

A Oh, yes.

Q Very uncommon. And it is also, sir, especially uncommon, in your opinion, because of what you said, and then because of, in all cases of traumatic epilepsy, of any traumatic event, only four to six percent develop seizures within the first month, and the others are delayed for years?

A No, more than a month.

Q Now, do you include or exclude birth trauma in that?

A I am not including birth trauma.

Q So we are talking about the head trauma, not related to being born?

A That's correct.

Q Doctor, did you write a paper called "Electroclinical Correlation in Temporal Lobe Epilepsy with Emphasis…" et cetera, et cetera?

A Yes.

Q And did you write, in your paper, about thirty cases with a presumed etiology of head trauma?

A Yes.

Q And did you not say, sir, that of the thirty cases with presumed etiology of head trauma, twenty-nine percent had their first seizure within one month after the trauma?

A If you are quoting my paper, yes, I said that. I would use—

Q Are you inferring that I am misquoting it, sir?

A No. I would point out that this work was done—

Q Excuse me. I read from the paper, and you asked me if I were quoting you correctly. I ask you to look at what I quoted and tell us whether I quoted you correctly, sir.

A Yes. And I would like to explain why that figure is different from my other testimony.

Q Perhaps Mr. Callahan could ask you that question. I am sure he will.

MR. CALLAHAN: I certainly will.

(Laughter.)

MR. HAYES: Q Doctor, what is the explanation, sir?

A Yes. This work was done at a County Hospital in Buffalo, and you will see by the designation of my location under my name that that is true. And, therefore, I was dealing with cases with more severe trauma than in most instances. I included in those cases just exactly the kind that I was discussing with you, the ones that have severe enough head trauma that, at times, there were clear pathological changes in the brain, like hemorrhage, not yet determined by autopsies because these were not autopsied cases.

But, based on clinical findings, they were generally cases that had more severe trauma than the statistics I have quoted you would show. The statistics I have quoted you come from the Epilepsy Foundation of America, in which they are looking at many, many thousands of cases. And I was dealing with a rather special population of patients with rather more severe head trauma, as you get in County Hospitals.

Q Then, Doctor, these people that you were dealing with in this study—in the majority of them—even the EEG didn't show any seizure activity or any manifestation of seizure activity except during the sleep tracing; is that correct, sir?

A Well, that is exactly this case, in the huge majority of epileptics, that the epileptic manifestation in the EEG occurs during the sleep tracing period.

Q Now, Doctor, are you a member of the American Board of Neurology?

A No, I am not interested, and have not practiced general neurology.

Q And, Doctor, are you a member of any of the American boards approved by the organizations which I have mentioned to you, sir?

A No, but I would like to add that, as Chairman of the Committee of the American EEG Society, it looks into the possibility of our board—the American Board of Qualification in EGG is going to be part of the American Board of Medical Specialists. In meeting with Dr. Glenn Laymaster, the Executive Director of the American Board of Specialists, he indicated at our last meeting that the great likelihood was of our names being in that particular volume.

Q Doctor, the American boards go back for many years, and electroencephalography goes back for many years, but it hasn't been recognized as a board yet; is that correct, sir?

A Not at all. It is recognized as the board.

Q I am talking about the American Board of Medical Specialists.

A There hasn't been a request until recently. And when we did look into it, we were told of a likelihood that we would be included.

Q Doctor, is it true that it is possible that what happened, the episodes described to you, could have represented an epileptic type of activity?

A Which episodes are you referring to?

Q Let's take staring episodes.

A As I indicated, that is not at all likely.

Q Now, I am asking you whether it is possible, sir.

A Well, since all things are possible, I would have to answer, yes. But not probable.

Q Now, Doctor, you are familiar with retrograde amnesia?

A Yes.

Q And can retrograde amnesia follow a head injury—or concussion?

A Yes.

Q And a concussion then, in your definition, enough to produce loss of consciousness for whatever period of time, many also produce retrograde amnesia?

A That is correct.

Q Now, Doctor, were you given, in the hypothetical question, anything about the activities of the man from the time he hit his head, when he was slammed against the caboose?

A From what period of time are you referring to?

Q I am talking about being slammed against the caboose, and whenever the first so called seizure occurred. Were you given anything as to what activities the man engaged in between those times?

A When was that procedure that you are referring to?

Q From counsel's hypothetical question. I don't know. Have you made a judgment as to when the first episode occurred?

A Well, no—

Q The staring episode—

A My conclusion was that there were not seizures.

Q I am talking about the episodes, staring, thrashing about, the other things. Were you given any indication as to what had been the activities of the man, between the time of the injury and the occurrence of those seizures—or, strike that—those episodes?

A Not exactly, because no data was given for those episodes.

Q Okay, Well, with respect to what the man did between the time of the injury and the time of the death, did you make any assumptions as to what the man was doing during that period?

A What the man was doing?

Q Yes, between December 29th—

A Yes.

Q —28th, and January 19th.

A Well, if you mean what he was doing, I assume that he was eating and sleeping. I know that he was working many of those days. Your question is not clear to me. The only way I can directly answer it, is that I was told that he was working most of those days, with the exception of New Year's Day and the two days before that. And then, after New Year's Day, he worked nearly every day until the day of his death.

Q Did you make any assumption as to what he did after the accident and within the next several minutes?

A No. I wasn't told of anything, so I made no assumption.

Q You were told that the man had a bruised head?

A Correct.

Q Did you make any assumptions, sir, as to how the bruised head came about?

A Yes. We were told that the train was in a so called emergency, and it slowed down and stopped, and it was a reasonable assumption on my part that in the stopping of the train, he bruised his arm and he bruised his head.

Q Okay. Did you make any assumption about the seriousness of that incident from the description of the incident itself?

A I made the assumption, by the term "bruised" that it was not a very significant injury. And, furthermore, he included in the hypothetical that there was no evidence that the individual involved was unconscious.

Q Okay. Now, does retrograde amnesia, is that necessarily dependent upon there being a significant head injury?

A What do you mean by "significant head injury"? The same thing I do, namely, unconscious?

Q Okay. Say unconscious.

A Yes. Ordinarily, ordinarily—ordinarily, and we always have to speak in such terms—ordinarily retrograde amnesia does not occur unless unconsciousness has occurred.

Q Doctor, if you assume that the man had some period of retrograde amnesia, would that lead you to conclude that he did have a concussion?

A It would be a reasonable assumption, if it could be clearly shown that he had retrograde amnesia, that then the term concussion would be likely.

Q What do you mean by clearly shown?

A That there would be clear evidence that he had retrograde amnesia.

Q What do you consider to be clear evidence that he had retrograde amnesia?

A It can only come from the patients, of course. If you believe what he says, if he seriously tells you that he has no memory of certain spaces of time.

Q Measured in seconds or minutes or whatever?

A Measured in minutes and hours or whatever.

Q Okay. And, Doctor, you have testified a number of times, have you not?

A Yes.

Q You are not a stranger to the witness stand, are you?

A That's correct, I am not.

Q And you have testified in Chicago and in other states, have you not?

A Yes, that is correct.

Q When you are engaged in testifying on all these trials and other matters, you are paid a fee, are you not?

A Yes, we are always paid for the time and effort.

Q Doctor, I was interested in something about these articles. You said you have some 160 publications?

A Yes.

Q Doctor, the vast majority of those are on electro-encephalography, are they not?

A Yes, many of them are. As it relates to epilepsy, in many instances.

Q You keep saying that, sir. But, for example, "A Brief Noninjurious Wave Form for Stimulation of the Brain." Is that related to epilepsy, sir?

A Absolutely.

Q Anything dealing with electroencephalography deals with epilepsy?

A No, not particularly, but that paper was very much related to epilepsy, because we were using the wave form to study epilepsy.

Q Now, Doctor, there seems to be a lot of publications. Are they all separate articles?

A Oh, in some instances, in a group of publications you will find an abstract, which means that it is a summary published in one journal, and then the full length article will appear in another journal. But, in one's bibliography, you include both of those.

Q So, as a matter of fact, many of those articles among the 160 are printed, the same articles will be in more than one publication, and sometimes the conclusion of one article is printed somewhere else; is that correct, sir?

A That is a little misleading to put it that way.

Q Let me ask you—

A May I answer that?

Q For example, at the Annual Ski Meeting of the Eastern Association of Encephalographers. Was there a note that was included as one of those 160 publications?

A Which ski meeting are you referring to?

Q The ski meeting at Saint Marguerite in Quebec.

A I was there many times. I don't know which one you are referring to.

Q The Eastern Association of Encephalographers Annual Ski Meeting.

A Yes. It's held every year.

Q "A Statistical Analysis on the Location of EEG Abnormalities?"

A Yes. I presented the paper there. The abstract is then published in the International EEG Journal. And then the full length article will appear, perhaps, in another journal or that journal.

Q So there are two, that this article or what appeared here at the Ski Meeting of the Eastern Association would also be presented in two others in the same or similar form?

A Not two others. Characteristically the abstract will be published where you print the paper, and the full length article may be published in the same or a different journal. That is characteristic in medicine.

Q Doctor, there is mediation of cardiac activity through the brain, is there not, sir?

A What do you mean by "mediation"?

Q Okay. I'm going to withdraw that question, sir. I have no further questions.

MR. CALLAHAN: Your Honor, I have no questions.

THE COURT: You may step down, sir.

Chapter Eight

Summary of Testimony of Certain Witnesses

That which is obvious need not be proved.

— Bracton, *Note Book Case* (1222)

It is impractical to include the complete testimony of all of the witnesses to this trial. Set out in the following pages is a summary of the testimony of the witnesses other than the four expert witnesses in the *Mohler* case whose testimony is transcribed in the prior chapter.

It will be noted that several of the witnesses whose testimony is summarized are children of or are otherwise related to Harold Mohler. Witnesses such as these are sometimes referred to as "safe" or "free" witnesses because they can be attacked on cross-examination only at great risk. If they are cross-examined at all it is usually merely for completeness or to make a minor correction.

DELAND BURNS, called as a witness by the plaintiff, identified himself as a physician who received his medical degree from Loyola School of Medicine in Chicago and took a one year residency in pathology at Illinois Research and Education Hospital in Chicago. He became board certified in pathology in 1962. He took a position at Riverside Hospital in Kankakee, Illinois, as Director of Laboratories and continued there until 1968. He then took a residency in ophthalmology at the University of Chicago, which he completed in

1971. Since that time he has limited his practice to ophthalmology. He is board certified in ophthalmology. He testified that he has performed perhaps three or four thousand postmortem examinations.

In January of 1968, he performed a postmortem examination on the body of Harold Mohler. He determined that the body had been embalmed before his autopsy, testifying that the embalming involved the use of a trocar, an embalming tool which inflicts a great deal of tearing and ripping and penetration of the viscera. He described the trocar as a large, pipe-like device that embalmers use to inject embalming fluid into various parts of the body cavity. He testified that the heart was of normal size and weighed 370 grams. He stated that the heart was penetrated by the trocar and sustained postmortem damage.

Dr. Burns testified, based upon his examination of the heart, the arteries and tissues involved in the heart, and the coronary-arterial system, that they were non-contributory to the cause of death. Everything else was normal—kidneys, liver, pancreas, ear canals, spleen, brain, et cetera. He testified that he had no microscopic slides of any tissues. He stated that he had no recollection of any tissue slides or paraffin blocks being made. He said that his autopsy was performed at the request of Dan Hackett, the brother-in-law of the deceased.

Dr. Burns stated that he was unable to come to a certain diagnosis as to the cause of death. He further stated that he found nothing in the anatomic examination of the remains that would support heart disease, lung disease or primary disease of any other organ as the cause of death.

On cross-examination, he stated that he did not know when the autopsy was performed. He admitted that the exhibit from which he was testifying did not have a date on it. He also said that, although the exhibit did not have a name on it, he had an independent memory of it. He agreed that he would not ordinarily have such an independent memory of any of the three thousand to four thousand other autopsies he performed. He stated that, as a pathologist, he would have preferred that the body had not been embalmed.

He reached no conclusion as to the cause of death, and none was indicated on the exhibit. He conveyed to the family that he was unable to establish an anatomic cause of death. He explained anatomic as meaning, "a cause of death which shows abnormalities of the organs that are identifiable by an autopsy examination." He testified that the trocar went through all the chambers of the heart, multiple times. He conceded that if an arrhythmia developed quickly and the person died in, say, three minutes or so, death could be so quick that there would be no palpable change in the heart myocardium. Finally, he repeated that he found no evidence of trauma.

On re-direct examination, Dr. Burns restated that, in his opinion, the death of Harold Mohler was not a coronary related death.

On re-cross, he repeated that a trocar would dislodge any structure in its way. He knew, or had read of, cases of death as a result of heart disease prompted by constriction of the blood vessels, but upon autopsy examination, there was nothing evident to show that this was the cause of death.

RENE BENOIT, called as a witness for the plaintiff, testified that he lives in Bourbonnais, Illinois, is employed by Conrail as an engineer, and has been so employed for the past twenty years. He was in charge of the engine on the run from Kankakee, Illinois to Zearing, Illinois on December 28, 1968. On that run there was a "break-in-two," which means that the train broke into two separate sections. At that time, the train went into an emergency stop, which involves a loud exhaust of air through the air brake lines on the train. He testified that the break-in-two was caused by a broken "knuckle" on the coupler mechanism. A replacement knuckle was provided by a Conrail train travelling in the opposite direction on an adjacent track. Harold Mohler came up on the engine after it was stopped to repair the broken knuckle; asked what had happened, and said, "I hit my head on the caboose wall."

On cross-examination, Benoit stated that his train was being slowed for a stop at the time the brake-in-two occurred. He also testified that trains operating with steel wheels on steel tracks cannot stop quickly, the way automobiles do. His train was going about ten or fifteen miles an hour when the break-in-two occurred. He never left the engine and had no direct knowledge as to just what happened to cause the break-in-two. Nor did he do anything about getting the new knuckle. Benoit also testified that Mohler never told him that he lost consciousness during the break-in-two.

ROBERT SHEARER, called as a witness for the plaintiff, stated that he lives in Kankakee, Illinois, and was employed by the railroad as a brakeman on the date of the break-in-two. He identified Harold Drazie as the conductor. He testified about the break-in-two. After the stop, he and the conductor got off the engine, and walked back to the point where the train was separated. They received a replacement knuckle from another train and installed it on their train. He stated that he saw Mohler after the break-in-two, and observed that he had dried blood in his ear, perhaps as much as a tablespoon. He noticed that Mohler seemed very tired after the occurrence. He attempted to communicate with him but Mohler didn't seem to respond too much. He later suggested to Mohler that he see a doctor. Mohler did not respond.

Shearer worked with Mohler the following day on the return to Kankakee. He said that Mohler seemed to be very tired and "not too conscious of what he was doing." Shearer also worked with Mohler on January 11th, didn't remember observing him at that time, but did not recall anything unusual occurring.

On cross-examination, he testified that the conductor on the December 28th run, Harold Drazie, has since passed away. He explained that it is the air pressure that keeps the brakes from being applied. When there is no air pressure in the air line, the brakes are applied. He stated that the brakes can be applied by the engineer, and also from the caboose, and that if a piece of debris were to sever the air line, there would be a sudden, automatic application of the brakes.

He said that he was located on the second unit, the second engine, when the train went into emergency, and that from that position, he would have no way of knowing what caused it to go into emergency. He then corrected himself to say that, before the train went into emergency, he went forward to the lead unit, the head engine. He testified that the train was being slowed down by the engineer before it went into emergency. He agreed that it was possible that the train went into emergency for another reason, such as someone putting it into emergency from the caboose.

He stated that he found part of the coupler about eight or ten feet behind the car on which it was broken, and agreed that it was unlikely that the train would have traveled only about eight or ten feet after losing the coupler. He also agreed that it was Mohler's duty to stay in the caboose, so he wasn't surprised that Mohler did not come forward to the head engine. Shearer testified that they made the run the following day back to Kankakee. On that trip, Mohler was the conductor. He noticed nothing unusual about him on that day. On redirect, he stated that the knuckle that he saw eight or ten feet from the car must have been from some other train and that the train he was on traveled several hundred feet after it went into emergency before coming to a stop.

MICHAEL KENNETH MOHLER, eighteen years old, one of Harold Mohler's sons, testified that he was eighteen years old, that he had finished high school, and that he lived in Kankakee. He had gone to grammar school at St. Theresa, and high school at Bishop McNamara which had previously been named St. Patrick's. He remembered good times with his father. He remembered going out to McDonald's and a White Castle, and to drive-in movies with his father. His father took him for a ride on a train. He had a bicycle, which his father kept in good repair. He remembered that his father always had a smile on his face. His memories of his father were good.

NORMAN PHILLIPS, called as a witness for the plaintiff, testified that he lives in Bourbonnais Illinois, that he was subpoenaed to testify, and that he is employed by Conrail. He started on the railroad on November 11, 1963, and Mohler started on the railroad at about the same time. He is currently working as a brakeman. He described the type of work being done on the runs out of Kankakee—industries, steel companies, grain elevators. He stated that the run from Kankakee began on January 17, 1968, and arrived in Elkhart, Indiana on January 18. They were off duty until 3:00 a.m. on January 19, 1968.

Phillips stated that he was in the caboose, waiting to start the trip back to Kankakee, when Mohler came in, walked past him, put his grip down on the floor and keeled over. Phillips took him by the shoulders, rolled him over on his back, and saw that he was not able to speak, was gasping for air, and was emitting what sounded like a choking noise. He put his coat under Mohler's head, and yelled for a worker outside the caboose to get an ambulance and a doctor right away. He tried to get some response out of Mohler, but was unable to do so. He was still making the same choking sounds. He tried to feel for a pulse, but could get none. Then a trainmaster got on the caboose, felt for a pulse and heartbeat, and then said, "This man is dead." Three to five minutes had passed.

Phillips described Mohler as a good friend and a good railroad man. He explained the difference between being in an engine and being in a caboose, when the train goes into emergency. In the engine, it will be a gradual slow down to a stop. In the caboose, because of slack action between the cars, there is usually a pretty good jolt. He further testified that he and Mohler did the same work, and had the same seniority, and that he (Phillips) earned the following gross income in the years indicated:

1968 - $12,856.55

1969 - $14,069.65

1970 - $12,688.09

1971 - $15,467.01

1972 - $16,849.43

1973 - $16,379.55

1974 - $17,660.88

1975 - $22,613.28

1976 - $23,941.00

1977 - $27,503.31

1978 - $31,860.38

1979 - $36,593.17

On cross-examination, it was developed that the income shown were gross income figures and show no deduction for federal and state income tax.

Phillips did not know when he last worked with Mohler before January 17, 1968. He went over the duties of a brakeman and a conductor, and their mutual responsibility to protect the rear of a train when it is stopped.

A five-page statement was marked, "Defendant's Exhibit #1."

Phillips stated that he gave the statement to attorney John Hayes on January 21, 1968, and that he (Phillips) signed each page of it. It was given in an office building in Kankakee. Using the statement to refresh his recollection, he stated that he had seen Mohler having a cup of coffee in the Elkhart Hotel on the 18th of January. Mohler went to bed between 8:00 and 9:00 on the night of the 18th, and Phillips went to bed a little later.

They received a call to go to work at 1:00 a.m. on January 19, 1968. They went to the Railroad YMCA Hotel for coffee at about 2:00 a.m. Mohler never mentioned the occurrence of December 28, 1967, to him. Phillips stated that Mohler collapsed at about 4:40 a.m. Thereafter, the train departed Elkhart at 5:55 a.m.

LEE MOHLER, twenty-one years old, one of Harold Mohler's sons, testified as to his memories of his father and their relationship.

KATHLEEN ANN TOMASIEWICZ, twenty-eight years old, one of Harold Mohler's daughters, testified as to her memories of her father, and the things they did together.

She recalled that after the accident, he had a very severe headache, and he refused his wife's advice to take some medication for it. He also refused her recommendation to see a doctor. On cross-examination, she stated that she had not seen any blood on her father's face or body. On redirect examination, there was a question as to whether she had heard a conversation concerning the presence of blood in his ear. The question was objected to by the defendant, and the objection was sustained.

CAROLINE JANE MOHLER, twenty-five years old, one of Harold Mohler's daughters, testified that she lives in Wheat Ridge, Colorado. She stated that she remembered going to the circus, the zoo, and the Museum of Science and Industry and the Planetarium with her father. She also remembered when he operated a bar and grill. Defendant's objections to this testimony were overruled by the trial court.

She remembered when he had been injured on the caboose. She noticed blood on his arm. Conversation between Caroline and her father was objected to, and the objection was sustained. She testified that, on one occasion, she attempted to get her father's attention about a book she was reading, but was unable to do so. Another time, she heard her father making incoherent noises and rolling in bed. She recalled that he was very listless during a New Year's Eve party. "He just wasn't himself." He was staring blankly, like in a trance. She related that she was in the eighth grade when her father died. On cross-examination, she stated that her mother was upset about her father's unusual behavior. She did not remember a doctor being called.

MILDRED MOHLER, Harold Mohler's mother, testified that her son was born August 16, 1931, in Kankakee, Illinois, and that he went to St. Patrick's grammar and high school. She stated that he went into the Air Force, and that after that he owned a bar and grill, and then became employed by the railroad. She said that she saw blood coming out of his ear after the accident. She also noticed that he wasn't acting like himself. She testified that she had asked him to put some screws in a strip of metal between her carpeting and the kitchen and, while doing so, he suddenly put his hand to his head and said, "Oh, that damned accident. Ever since then—" She said, "Well, you better not go out on the road," and he replied, "Well, I got to make this trip." Defendant's objection to this testimony was overruled.

On cross-examination, she stated that the blood she had seen was coming from her son's right ear, and was flowing down his cheek. She testified that she told her son to see a doctor, but did not know if he did so. Defendant's question inquiring into the death of another child of Mrs. Mohler was objected to. The objection was sustained and the jury was instructed to disregard it.

THOMAS ANTHONY MOHLER, twenty-four years of age, one of Harold Mohler's sons, testified that he lived in Kankakee, Illinois, and that he played basketball in grade school and that his father, who had played in high school, helped him to learn the game.

VIRGINIA MOHLER, Harold Mohler's widow, testified that they were married in 1951, that he was stationed in Germany in the Air Force, that she went there and lived with him, and that their daughter, Caroline, was born in Wiesbaden. She stated that he went with the railroad after running the bar and grill. She said that, on occasion, her husband would take the children on the train. She testified that he loved the railroad; one Christmas he played with a toy train set that had been given to one of the children.

She said she was awakened early in the morning of January 19, 1968, and a Mrs. Balosso and Father Anzak had come to her home to tell her of her husband's death. She stated that her husband was "a fair, a just man," and that he was always good with the children. She said that they had a good marriage, and that they loved one another.

After the accident, she saw the dried blood in his ear. She also noticed that her husband slept a lot. He did not get up on New Year's Eve in time to go skating with the rest of the family. He was very quiet. Later in the evening, she noticed him missing, and found him lying down in one of the bedrooms. He was just not like himself. She identified Plaintiff's Group Exhibit #20 as her husband's railroad book, which shows his record of trips and runs. It shows the time on duty, the time off duty, the place he reported, the number of cars, et cetera. He would also calculate the pay to which he would be entitled.

She testified that on one occasion after the New Year's Eve party, when she was taking down Christmas decorations, he came in and sat down and complained that his head hurt. Another time he struck one of his daughters, which was very unusual. She also saw him rolling around in bed and groaning. She stated that she wasn't sure whether or not she should call a doctor. She decided against it.

The last time she saw her husband alive was January 17, 1968. He had come in about eight o'clock in the morning, took a shower and went to lie down. She noticed later that he was lying on his back on the bed, staring into space. It looked unnatural to her. Later, he got up to go to work. She thought he looked all right to her at that time.

She identified Plaintiff's Exhibit #22, the W-2 form for 1965, showing her husband's earnings in that year of $9,636.94 and Exhibit #23, the W-2 form for 1966, showing earnings for that year of $10,930.02 and for 1967, $11,540.29.

Mrs. Mohler testified that she authorized an autopsy to be performed on her husband's body. The body was taken to the Clancy Funeral Home, where the autopsy was performed. She received a copy of the autopsy report from Dr. Burns of Riverside Hospital.

On cross-examination, she testified that the blood she saw in her husband's ear was in the right ear. She did not recall seeing any bruises. From the trip book, Mrs. Mohler was able to state that her husband worked on December 29, 1967. He next worked on January 2, 1968. She testified that at no time during the period from December 28 to January 19, did her husband see a doctor. Referring to the autopsy report, she agreed that she was not familiar with the medical terms used in it. She agreed that there was no conclusion to the report. She testified that her impression was that there was no conclusion. She said that Dr. Burns gave her no additional information as to the cause of death. She stated that her husband had never complained to her of chest pains before his death, nor did anyone mention to her that he had complained of chest pains. On redirect, she testified that Dr. Burns told her that her husband did not have a heart attack.

SUSAN FISHER, called as a witness for the plaintiff, testified that she was employed as a pathology medical secretary at Riverside Hospital in Kankakee, Illinois. She stated that she conducted a search for any documents, slides, paraffin blocks or notebooks relating to an autopsy performed on the body of Harold Mohler, on or about the month of January, 1968, and found no such records. She did know that Dr. Deland Burns was a pathologist at Riverside in 1968.

On cross-examination, she testified that the records of the hospital would show the name and date of such an autopsy and the name of the physician performing it. When shown plaintiff's Exhibit #1, the autopsy report, she stated that the report looked similar to the form

Riverside used, but that the exhibit did not state a name nor an autopsy number, and that the exhibit appeared "to be only a gross autopsy description." She also stated that the exhibit did not bear a date, and that it was signed, Deland J. Burns.

DAN HACKETT, testified that he was Harold Mohler's brother-in-law. He stated that he knew of Harold Mohler's accident on the railroad, and that the Mohlers attended his family's New Year's Eve party. He said that Harold Mohler was always athletically active and in good health. He said that he did not feel that Harold Mohler was his usual self at the party.

It was Hackett's suggestion that the autopsy be performed and recommended that it be performed by Dr. Deland Burns.

On cross-examination, he stated that he suggested to Harold Mohler that he see a doctor, but to his knowledge Mohler did not do so.

VIRGINIA MOHLER, was recalled to testify as to Harold Mohler's personal expenditures. She stated that he spent very little on himself. He was not a drinker. He gambled only for penny ante stakes. He was at home most of the time when he wasn't on the railroad. He had no expensive hobbies. He enjoyed gardening. He did contribute to church, to the United Fund, the March of Dimes, the Heart Fund and union dues. They had never taken an exotic vacation.

She identified a cancelled check for $50.00, paid to Dr. Deland Burns for the autopsy. It was dated March 16, 1968. She identified a home movie film of her husband and some of the children, which was taken in the summer of 1967. The film was shown to the jury.

At the conclusion of the film, the plaintiff rested.

GEORGE S. WESTFALL, called as a witness for the defendant, testified that he is a physician and lived in Goshen, Indiana and was a graduate of Indiana University School of Medicine. He stated that he interned at Methodist Hospital in Indianapolis. He was the Elkhart County Coroner in 1968. As Coroner, one of his duties was to determine the cause of unattended death, and to rule out unnatural deaths. He was called to the scene of all fatal accidents. Dr. Westfall identified Defendant's Exhibit #2 as an inquest and summary of the death of Harold A. Mohler. He stated that he had no independent memory of inquiring into the death. He read his findings as follows:

"This thirty-six-year-old man collapsed and died suddenly at the Robert Young Railroad Yard in Elkhart. I pronounced the victim dead shortly after, beside the tracks near the caboose in the railroad yard.

There was no evidence of violence or foul play. I ordered the body moved to the funeral home pending further arrangements.

The said deceased being a male of the age of thirty-six years, six feet and one inch in height, black hair, gray eyes, medium complexion, nativity white."

On cross-examination, the witness testified that it would have taken him about forty-five minutes to get to the railroad yard from Goshen.

[An offer of proof of the portions of Dr. Westfall's evidence deposition, which had been excluded by the Court, were put into the record outside the presence of the jury. The offer included Dr. Westfall's findings that Mohler had died of a heart attack. The offer was denied.]

[After the testimony of Drs. Leestma and Hughes, set out in the chapter on expert witnesses, the defense rested. The plaintiff then offered a rebuttal witness.]

DONAL E. O'SULLIVAN, called as a rebuttal witness by the plaintiff, testified that he lives in Oak Park, Illinois, and is a physician. He received his medical degree from Stritch School of Medicine, Loyola University, Chicago, Illinois. He did his internship at Madigan Army Hospital, Tacoma, Washington, and took a residency in pathology at Mercy Hospital in Toledo, Ohio. He did a two year residency at St. Joseph's Hospital in Chicago, and, from 1977 to 1979, was a fellow in oncology and hematology at the Chicago Medical School, University Health Services. He also was graduated from Loyola University Law School in 1971, but is not engaged in the practice of law.

He stated that he had been certified by the American Board of Pathology and subsequently was certified by that Board in Hematology. He has also been certified by the American Board of Nuclear Medicine.

Dr. O'Sullivan was given an extensive hypothetical question and testified that "primary cardiac cause" means that the cause arises within the heart, and that primary "CNS" means that the cause of death arises within the central nervous system. He said that the brain was part of the central nervous system.

In his opinion, the death was not of a primary cardiac cause. His opinion was that the death was primarily a central nervous system death. He stated that a heart weighing 370 grams is not abnormal in a man six feet one inch in height, weighing 160 pounds.

Dr. O'Sullivan testified that persons who suffer from an increased amount of lipid or fat in their blood are said to have a condition called hyperlipidemia. This is a serious condition. He said that a bolus of fat can obstruct a blood vessel and can cause death. But it would produce anatomic changes, which are clearly observable on gross examination. A blood pressure of 134 over 80 for a man who is thirty-two years old is within normal limits.

On cross-examination Dr. O'Sullivan stated that there is no American Board of Hematology itself, nor is there a board of oncology. He conceded that the limits of a person's heart weight, as compared to his height, are the limits that he would apply, as opposed to standards set by a medical specialty such as cardiologists or pathologists. He stated that there are many studies of such matters and that some studies differ from others.

He testified that different persons have different amounts of fat in their blood. It could be compared to the difference between skim milk and cream. He agreed that a physician would be concerned if he found an elevated amount of fat in a patient's blood. In response to a hypothetical question, the doctor testified that the most likely cause of death from such a condition would be cardiac arrhythmia.

On re-direct examination, adding evidence of mucus in the bronchial tree, the doctor stated that, under these circumstances, the cause of death would be primarily respiratory. He elaborated further that the blow to the head set in motion a chain of events, "that lead to a conclusion that a central nervous mechanism led primarily to respiratory failure, and subsequent cardiac failure." He used the term laryngospasm and defined it on recross-examination as an acute medical emergency, in which the entire space through which a person breathes is occluded, and the mechanism of death is anoxia due to laryngospasm, a natural form of strangulation.

CHAPTER NINE

Jury Instructions

A drunken man is as much entitled to a safe street as a sober one, and much more in need of it.

— Heydenfeldt, J., *Robinson v.Pioche*, 5 Cal. 460, 461 (1855)[1]

The jury is the sole determiner of the facts of a case while the Court rules on all questions of law. The law of the case is contained in written instructions. Those instructions are read to the jury by the Court at the conclusion of the closing arguments, before the jury retires for its deliberations. In some jurisdictions, the jury receives a set of the instructions for its use in the jury room. In other jurisdictions, the instructions are read to the jury but the jury does not receive a copy of them. The jury is given forms of verdict, one of which is to be signed by the jury foreman and by each individual juror.

Pattern or model jury instructions have been developed in many jurisdictions. They are revised from time to time to conform to changes in law or practice. Illinois has developed its separate and individually numbered Illinois Pattern Jury Instructions (I.P.I.). These instructions have been approved by the Illinois Supreme Court with the direction that each proposed jury instruction (except the original,

[1] *This is considered to be the first product liability case. The opinion is notable for its brevity, its acuity and its wit.*

which goes to the jury) be individually numbered, be identified as to the party submitting it, and also bear its identifying I.P.I. number. If the proposed instruction is modified in some way or is not contained in I.P.I., it should so indicate. Thus:

Plaintiff's Instruction No. 3
I.P.I. 1.07

Plaintiff's Instruction No. 4
I.P.I. 20.01 (Modified)

Plaintiff's Instruction No. 5
Not in I.P.I.
Evans v. Barnes, 133 Ill.2d 128, 136 (1971)

At some time early in the trial the Court will direct counsel to exchange their proposed jury instructions in anticipation of the conference on instructions which is usually held a day or two before the case is submitted to the jury. At the conference, attended by the court reporter as well as the Court and counsel, the Court considers each instruction in order, beginning with those of the plaintiff and then going on to those of the defendant. The opposing attorney is given an opportunity to object to any of the instructions which he finds erroneous, or in some way wanting. The Court decides which instructions will be given, which refused, and which he directs be modified.

All objections are made of record and may form the basis of a subsequent appeal. The Court requires two copies of each of the proposed instructions, one marked with the identifying information set out above, and the other without it. It is the unmarked set that is given to the jury. Many of the instructions are "standard," and are given in every case.

The instructions which commonly give the most difficulty are those delineating the issues raised by the pleadings, and those dealing with the plaintiff's burden of proof. These instructions go to the very heart of each case, and they can directly affect its outcome.

Having met with the Court and knowing what instructions will be given, the attorneys base many of their arguments on those particular instructions which they consider favorable to their case. This was done in the summation in the *Mohler* case.

The following are the jury instructions given by the Court:

Faithful performance by you of your duties is vital to the administration of justice.

The law applicable to this case is contained in these instructions and it is your duty to follow them. You must consider these instructions as a whole, not picking out one instruction and disregarding others.

It is your duty to determine the facts, and to determine them from the evidence produced in open court. You are to apply the law to the facts, and in this way decide the case. Neither sympathy nor prejudice should influence you. Your verdict must be based on evidence, and not upon speculation, guess or conjecture.

The evidence which you are to consider consists of testimony of the witnesses and the exhibits offered and received. The production of evidence in court is governed by rules of law. From time to time it has been my duty, as judge, to rule on the admissibility of evidence. You must not concern yourselves with the reasons for these rulings. And you are not to consider exhibits to which an objection was sustained or testimony or exhibits which were ordered stricken.

Arguments, statements, and remarks of counsel are intended to help you in understanding the evidence and applying the law, but are not evidence. If any argument, statement or remark has no basis in the evidence, then you should disregard that argument, statement or remark.

The corporate defendant in this case is entitled to the same fair and unprejudiced treatment as an individual would be under like circumstances, and you should decide the case with the same impartiality that you would use in deciding a case between individuals.

Neither by these instructions nor by any ruling or remark which I have made, do I, or have I meant to indicate any opinion as to the facts.

In determining whether any proposition has been proved, you should consider all of the evidence bearing on the question, without regard to which party produced it.

A fact may be proved by circumstantial evidence. Circumstantial evidence consists of proof of facts or circumstances which give rise to a reasonable inference of the truth of the facts sought to be proved.

In considering the evidence in this case you are not required to set aside your own observation and experience in the affairs of life, but you have a right to consider all the evidence in the light of your own observation and experience in the affairs of life.

You are the sole judges of the credibility of the witnesses, and of the weight to be given to the testimony of each of them. In determining the credit to be given any witness, you may take into account his ability and opportunity to observe, his memory, his manner while testifying, any interest, bias, or prejudice he may have, and the reasonableness of his testimony, considered in the light of all the evidence in the case.

An attorney has a right to interview a witness for the purpose of learning what testimony the witness will give. The fact that the witness has talked to an attorney and told him what he would testify to does not, by itself, reflect adversely on the truth of the testimony of the witness.

In deciding whether any fact has been proved, it is proper to consider the number of witnesses testifying on one side or the other as to that fact, but the number of witnesses alone is not conclusive, if the testimony of the lesser number is more convincing.

The credibility of a witness may be attacked by introducing evidence that, on some former occasion, he made a statement or acted in a manner inconsistent with his testimony in this case, on a matter material to the issues. Evidence of this kind may be considered by you, in connection with all the other facts and circumstances in evidence, in deciding the weight to be given to the testimony of that witness.

When I say that a party has the burden of proof on any proposition, or use the expression "if you find," or "if you decide," I mean you must be persuaded, considering all the evidence in the case, that the proposition on which he has the burden of proof, is more probably true than not true.

In deciding whether Harold Mohler's death resulted in whole or in part from the occurrence of December 28, 1967, it is not a defense that Harold Mohler failed to seek medical attention, nor is it a defense that the widow failed to provide medical attention for her husband.

I have determined as a matter of law, that the cause of the occurrence of December 28, 1967, was the violation by the defendant of the Federal Safety Appliance Act.[2]

The plaintiff claims that the death of HAROLD MOHLER resulted, in whole or in part, from the occurrence of December 28, 1967, and that his widow and children have suffered pecuniary loss as a result of his death.

The defendant denies that the death of HAROLD MOHLER resulted in whole or in part from the occurrence of December 28, 1967. The defendant further denies that his widow and children have sustained pecuniary loss to the extent claimed.

The plaintiff has the burden of proving that the death of HAROLD MOHLER resulted, in whole or in part, from the occurrence of December 28, 1967.

If you find from your consideration of all the evidence that this proposition has been proved, then your verdict should be for the plaintiff; but if, on the other hand, you find from your consideration of all the evidence that this proposition has not been proved, then your verdict should be for the defendant.

If you decide that the death of HAROLD MOHLER resulted, in whole or in part, from the occurrence, then you must decide what amount of money will reasonably and fairly compensate the widow and children for the damages resulting to them from the death.

If you decide that the death of HAROLD MOHLER did not result, in whole or in part, from the occurrence of December 28, 1967, then you will have no occasion to consider the question of damages.

[2] *The plaintiff made a motion for a directed verdict on the issue of a violation by the defendant of a federal law. The Court granted the motion over the defendant's objection.*

To determine the pecuniary loss suffered by each survivor, as a result of the death of Harold Mohler, the decedent, you should consider what benefits of pecuniary value, including money, goods and services, the evidence shows that the decedent customarily contributed to each survivor. You should also consider what the decedent was earning, and what he would have been likely to earn in the future, in view of his earning capacity, habits of industry and thrift, his health, his age, and life expectancy at the time of his death. You should also consider the personal expenses of decedent, and other deductions from his earnings. Consider also how long each survivor would have been likely to receive pecuniary benefits from the decedent, if he had lived. Consider, also, all other facts shown by the evidence which aid you in determining what pecuniary benefits it might reasonably be expected that each survivor would have received from the decedent, if the decedent had not met his death.

Some of the survivors were the minor children of the decedent. As to these survivors, you may award an amount to compensate those children for the pecuniary value of any loss of care, attention, instruction, training, advice, and guidance the decedent would have been likely to give the children during their minority, if decedent had continued to live.

The contributions and benefits which you may consider, must be only those contributions and benefits upon which a money value can be placed. You are not permitted to award any amount for the grief or loss of society and companionship, caused to any survivor by the death of Harold Mohler.

If you find for the plaintiff, then in assessing damages you may consider how long the widow and children would be likely to have received pecuniary benefits from the decedent, considering how long he was likely to have lived, and how long they are likely to live.

According to a table of mortality in evidence, the life expectancy of a male person aged 36 years is 36.8 years. That of a female person aged 48 years is 32.1 years. These figures are not conclusive. They are the average life expectancies of persons who have reached those ages. They may be considered by you, in connection with other evidence relating to the probable life expectancies of the decedent and his widow, including evidence of the decedent's occupation, health, habits and activities, bearing in mind that some persons live longer and some persons live less than the average.

In calculating the amount of these pecuniary benefits, you must not simply multiply the life expectancies by the annual benefits. Instead, you must determine their present cash value. "Present cash value" means the sums of money needed now, which, together with what that sum will earn in the future, will equal the amounts of the pecuniary benefits at the times in the future when they would have been received.

If you find in favor of the defendant on the question of liability, you will have no occasion to consider the question of damages.

If you find in favor of the plaintiff, the damages you award are not subject to income taxes and you should not consider such taxes in fixing the amount of the award.

Forms of verdict are supplied with these instructions. After you have reached your verdict, fill in and sign the appropriate form of verdict and return it into court. The verdict should be signed by each of you. You should not write or mark upon this, or any of the other instructions given you by the Court.

If you find for the plaintiff and against the defendant, then you should use the form of verdict which says:

"We, the Jury, find for the plaintiff and against the defendant. We assess the damages in the sum of $_____."

If you find for the defendant and against the plaintiff, then you should use the form of verdict which says:

"We, the Jury, find for the defendant and against the plaintiff."

Verdict Forms

We, the Jury, find for the plaintiff and against the defendant. We assess the damages in the sum of
$_____________ .

____
Foreman

____
____
____
____
____
____
____
____
____
____
____

We, the Jury, find for the defendant and against the plaintiff.

____
Foreman

____
____
____
____
____
____
____
____
____
____
____

Chapter Ten

Closing Arguments—Summation

There is an idiom in truth which falsehood never can imitate.

— Napier, L.C., *Low v. Holmes*, Drury Cases, Temp., 290, 323 (1858)

At the conclusion of all the evidence, when both parties have rested, the case is ready to be submitted to the jury. Once again the plaintiff has the right to open and close. The plaintiff goes first, and has the right to answer or rebut anything the defendant argues in his closing. The Court will ask each side how much time he will require, and will see that the attorneys comply with whatever limitations are established.

In conference with counsel, the Court will also decide at what time the case goes to the jury. As a rule, judges dislike having a case go to the jury late in the day because it could mean that jurors will have to travel home late at night. For that reason, the most desirable time for closing arguments is in the morning. On occasion, the question of sequestering the jury will arise. A jury is sequestered by placing it in a hotel or motel overnight, so that the jurors do not talk to other persons. The alternative is to permit the jurors to go home and return the next day for further deliberations. Once again, the Court and counsel will confer and decide how to resolve such questions, should they arise.

The jury usually will have developed strong feelings about the case by the time both parties have rested; however, the closing arguments are an important part of the trial and can be critical in determining who wins or loses. The plaintiff's right to open and close is a significant advantage. When he attempts to minimize that advantage his opponent may respond with humor, pointing out that, "You don't have to be a lawyer to understand the advantage of the last word. You only have to be married."

The difficulties presented to the defendant in not being able to respond to the final argument of the plaintiff can be dealt with along the following lines:

> As I have already mentioned to you, this is the only opportunity I have to address you at the close of the case. My opponent will have the opportunity to talk to you again and although I may sit here and want to respond, the rules of court prohibit me from doing so. He may say things that I think are untrue or unreasonable or simply wrong, but I must remain silent. I can ask you the jury, however, to be my silent advocates in your position as jury members. If my opponent says things that do not seem reasonable to you, keep that in mind when you retire to consider your verdict. If there are arguments or points of evidence I might have made, make those arguments yourself after you have retired. In other words, to be sure that the process is fair, that it is what it should be, make certain that no argument goes untested. In the pursuit of truth, be advocates yourselves, advocates for the truth. In that way, I am confident that you will answer my opponent's arguments better than I could.

It is a phenomenon that has occurred too often to be chance that a lawyer spills a glass of water or has a briefcase fall from his counsel table during the most highly charged emotional point of his opponent's closing argument. The effect of this is to interrupt the proceeding entirely and to break the rhythm and emotional pitch of his opponent's strongest argument.

The way to respond to such a tactic is to take your time when you resume your argument. Go back to a part preceding that in which the interruption occurred. When you reach the point where you are getting into that part of your argument which was interrupted, you pause, glance over your shoulder in the direction of your opponent and say, "I trust we will not be interrupted again."

Arguing Damages

Inexperienced defense lawyers are reluctant to talk about damages in their closing argument. They fear that by discussing damages they implicitly concede liability: "If I argue damages, I necessarily admit that my client is liable." Not only is this not the case, arguing damages often can be turned to advantage in the argument on liability. A persuasive, convincing argument on the damage issue, made first, can cause the jury to be more receptive to the argument on the liability issue.

It is an error not to argue damages. The failure of the defendant to argue damages permits the attorney for the plaintiff to assert that since defense counsel did not argue damages, the jury is obligated to accept his damage figure because no other has been offered. The defendant's closing argument should discuss damages first and liability second. It can be approached in the following manner:

> The job of the plaintiff's attorney is to win the case and to get you to give the plaintiff as much money as possible. My job is slightly different. There are two issues presented to the defense. One is liability; the other is damages. While I may be thoroughly convinced, as you will see from my comments on liability, that your verdict should be in favor of the defendant and against the plaintiff, I have an obligation to my client to cover both issues. That is because no matter how convinced I am that your verdict should be for the defendant on the issue of liability, I may find that my persuasive powers fail to rise to the level of my personal conviction. If that is the case, I will not have discharged my responsibilities to my client if I do not address the issue of damages. You can imagine how embarrassing it would be for me to lose the case and have a huge amount of money given as damages against my client and when asked the question, "Did you argue damages?", to have to respond, "No." Therefore, I am going to talk to you about damages as well as liability, and I am going to begin with damages.

It is helpful to the jury to repeat and restate the important points in your argument. This can be done by making the same argument or arriving at the same conclusion in two or more entirely different ways. It can also be done by simple repetition.

* * * * * *

"The plaintiff testified that he never saw the red marker. He never saw the red marker."

* * * * * *

"The evidence is that there were twenty-two shipments but only twenty bills of lading. Twenty-two shipments; twenty bills."

* * * * * *

"The testimony was that the porthole was open. Everyone said that the porthole was open."

* * * * * *

Go over every possibility which could explain how or why the occurrence took place, each one, of course, pointing to the conclusion which you believe is the one which should be reached. Then invite the jury to consider any other possibilities which they might come up with. The effect of this is to draw the jury into your reasoning process while at the same time being fair by encouraging them to consider other possibilities. Your analysis, of course, should have concluded that there are no other possibilities.

Contrary to common assumption, the closing argument is not a speech in any conventional sense. It is more like conducting a group discussion in which you lead. That is one of the reasons that it is not only acceptable but necessary to repeat yourself. You do it for emphasis and to insure that everyone is following your reasoning. Equally important, use the personal pronouns "we" and "us."

* * * * * *

"What are we to make of the evidence which appears to show that there were not three but only two persons in the room? And if that is true where does it lead us?"

* * * * * *

"How are we to deal with the repeated and apparently true statements that the plane was approaching from the North, not the East?"

* * * * * *

"Is there a way to interpret the conflicts in the testimony that will still enable us to believe that each of the witnesses is testifying truthfully?"

* * * * * *

If it is consistent with your style, it is appropriate to quote poetry, or passages from the Bible or lines from a song or saying to make a point. It is not necessary that you quote chapter and verse. In discussing the testimony or making your point, merely allude to your saying generally, perhaps as follows, "I recall some lines from Scripture … "

There are certain quotations that could be helpful and no doubt have been used by both plaintiff and defendant. The plaintiff's attorney might like the following:

> "I expect to pass through this world but once; any good thing therefore that I can do, or any kindness I can show to any fellow creature, let me do it now; let me not defer or neglect it, for I shall not pass this way again." [1]

For the defendant there is the admonition in the saying:

> "To be generous with one's own funds is a blessing;
> To be generous with the funds of another is a curse."

* * * * * *

A country judge received a question from the jury after it had retired to consider its verdict: "If we find in favor of the defendant, can we still give the plaintiff some money?" The judge responded by saying to the jury, "First, return your verdict, and then I will answer your ques-

[1] *Stephen Grellet [Etienne de Grellet du Mabillier] (1773-1855)*

tion." The jury quickly returned a verdict in favor of the defendant. The judge entered judgment on the verdict and then pulled a hat from beneath his bench, handed it to the foreman and said to the jury, "Now, in answer to the question, you may pass this hat among you and each of you is welcome to give the plaintiff as much money as you would like."

* * * * * *

Counter Arguments

It was observed in the chapter on cross-examination that an advocate's most powerful weapon often can be turned against him, sometimes in quite unexpected ways. The same can be true in closing arguments. In a case involving an action for damages arising out of a derailment and resulting fire and explosions of tank cars carrying liquid petroleum gas, the operating railroad claimed that it had been supplied with a defective railroad car by the railroad which owned it.

The evidence showed that the railroad car which failed was one of a series that had been built in 1954 and rebuilt in 1992. The essence of the plaintiff's case was that the railroad car which had its wheel bearing overheat and fail, causing the derailment, was defectively rebuilt. The car was refit with friction bearings, when at a relatively small additional cost, the car could have been rebuilt with more modern and safer roller bearings. While there were many defenses to the case, the defense most relied upon was that had the plaintiff railroad installed "hot box detectors" along its right of way prior to the accident, the "hot box" (overheated wheel bearing) which caused the derailment would have been detected and the accident would have been prevented.

As it happened the hot box detectors were installed on the right of way of the plaintiff railroad some six months after the accident and the defense urged throughout the trial, particularly in its closing argument, that had the plaintiff installed the hot box detectors six months earlier, the accident never would have occurred.

After each side had made its closing argument but before the plaintiff's final argument, the court took a fifteen minute recess. At this point the defense pretty clearly had the better side of the case. Unless the plaintiff could come up with a very powerful final argument it could not hope to win. So in the brief recess the plaintiff's lawyer sought some inspiration, and in a sudden epiphany it came to him.

In his final argument he addressed the jury as follows:

> Sometimes when looking back at the end of a long complex trial with numerous exhibits, much expert testimony and a great deal of other evidence, the smoke begins to clear a little and things can be seen in better perspective. If we reduce each party's argument in this case to its essentials, could not they be that the plaintiff argues that had the defendant put roller bearings on its cars when they were rebuilt, the accident would never have happened. For its part, the defendant argues that if the plaintiff had installed hot box detectors before the accident it would never have occurred.
>
> So what has taken place since the accident? Well, the plaintiff installed the hot box detectors six months after the accident. And what about the defendant? Well, it was thirty-eight years before it rebuilt its cars and if that is any guide to what we can expect, it will not be until the year 2030 that the defendant finally installs roller bearings on its cars!

And so the hot box detectors, used so powerfully and effectively against the plaintiff throughout the trial, suddenly, and in a wholly unexpected way, became the primary weapon aimed directly back at the defendant. And the argument carried the day.

The counter argument principal can be extended with equally devastating effect into the appellate process. Take, for example, the child trespasser who was severely injured while jumping on and off of a moving freight train on a railroad right of way in a large city. Under an attractive nuisance theory[2] his attorney brought suit against the operating railroad and the railroad which owned the tracks on which, under a contract between the two, the operating railroad's train was moving. The theory of liability against the operating railroad was negligence. The theory of liability against the railroad company owning the tracks was that it was "vicariously liable" for the negligence of the operating railroad which it permitted to use its tracks.

---

[2] *The child was irresistibly attracted to the moving train. The tracks should have been fenced.*

The verdict was against both railroads. After the trial the operating railroad settled the case against it by paying the plaintiff one-third of the judgement in exchange for a "covenant not to enforce the judgement against it." But on appeal the owning railroad argued that if it was only vicariously liable for the negligence of the operating railroad and if the operating railroad was protected from the judgement because of a covenant not to enforce the judgement against it, it necessarily followed that the owning railroad was equally protected!

Multiple Defendants

In cases with multiple defendants, it is common for the defendants to attack one another in an effort to avoid liability, or to insure that the others share in any adverse verdict. Agreements are often entered into among the defendants in such cases that they will not act in that manner. Unfortunately, no matter how firmly such agreements are made they tend to come apart as the time of closing arguments approaches. It is a great help to the plaintiff when defendants attack each other because that provides assistance in proving the plaintiff's case.

* * * * * *

This was perhaps best exemplified in a case tried by the well regarded aviation disaster attorney, John J. Kennelly, in a suit against Northwest Airlines and McDonnell Douglas Corporation arising out of an airplane crash. Northwest was charged with negligence in the operation of the plane and McDonnell Douglas, as the manufacturer, was charged under a product liability theory.

In his final closing argument, Kennelly addressed the jury as follows:

> Ladies and gentlemen of the jury, you have just heard the attorneys for Northwest and McDonnell Douglas make their closing arguments to you. If I understood them correctly, the attorney for McDonnell Douglas says the fault for the crash was that of Northwest and the attorney for Northwest says the fault was that of McDonnell Douglas.
>
> Ladies and gentlemen, I agree with both of them.

* * * * * *

The following are the closing arguments in the case we have been following.

THE COURT: Good morning, ladies and gentlemen.

THE JURY: Good morning.

THE COURT: Are you gentlemen ready to proceed?

MR. CALLAHAN: Yes, your Honor.

MR. HAYES: Yes, your Honor.

THE COURT: Mr. Hayes. Please observe your time.

MR. HAYES: I shall, sir.

CLOSING ARGUMENT BY MR. HAYES:

May it please the Court, Mr. Callahan. Good morning, ladies and gentlemen.

THE JURY: Good morning.

MR. HAYES: It's been awhile since we last talked. We have reached that stage of the trial in which the lawyers have an opportunity to sum up the evidence or, if you will, to argue the case. I would ask you to bear in mind that nothing which has been said in this case by the lawyers in the opening statements is evidence, and cannot be considered by you to be evidence. The oath you took as a juror was to decide this case according to the law and the evidence in this case, and that law is the law that comes from Judge Norman. That evidence is the testimony that comes from the witness stand, or through documents which were received in evidence.

Before I sum up the evidence on behalf of my clients, the seven Mohler children and Mrs. Mohler, I want to express our appreciation to you for the attention that was paid through sometimes difficult evidence and through some long, but unavoidable, delays.

It is the function of the summing up of the evidence or arguing the case, if you will, to persuade you that the evidence has justified a certain result, if indeed the evidence does justify that result. But before we talk about lawyer's arguments, I think we should discuss the law. The law will come to you after the lawyers have argued, and before you retire to the jury room to deliberate upon your verdict. That law will come to you in the form of the judge reading instructions of law to you, and sending those written instructions with you when you go in to deliberate on your verdict. There is no longer, I believe the Court will instruct you, any issue as to whether the railroad violated the Safety Appliance Act.

As you may recall from the opening statements, there was discussed the existence of federal law, the Federal Safety Appliance Act, which applies to railroad workers. It provides those workers their only compensation for injuries, and their widows and children their only compensation for the loss of a husband and father. I believe the Court will instruct you that the Court has found, as a matter of law, that the railroad violated the Federal Safety Appliance Act on December 28, 1967. Now, in addition to having denied that originally, the railroad has also denied that the death of Harold Mohler resulted, in whole or in part, from the occurrence of December 28, 1967; in addition, the railroad denies that the widow and the children have sustained pecuniary loss to the extent claimed.

The issues then are: Did the death of Harold Mohler result, in whole or even in part, from the occurrence of December 28, 1967, an occurrence which happened because of the railroad's violation of the Federal Safety Appliance Act, and if the death of Harold Mohler resulted in whole, or even in part, from that occurrence, then it is your obligation to determine that amount of damages which will fairly and justly compensate the widow and children for the pecuniary loss sustained by them. Now, the law does not expect you to consider evidence in a vacuum. For example, the law does not expect you to set aside the ordinary observations and affairs of life that you have made and the judgment that you have brought with you to this jury room from your years of life. I believe the Court will instruct you also that there is such a thing as circumstantial evidence. Circumstantial evidence is that evidence which, by proof of facts from which something can reasonably be inferred, is to be considered by you.

In determining the credibility of witnesses—that is to say, how much weight is going to be given to the testimony of a witness—

you may consider, in determining that credibility, whether that witness on some prior occasion made a statement or acted in a way which is contradictory to the testimony given by him in this trial. That is called impeaching the credibility of a witness.

Now, as you were informed during the jury selection, and as the Court will instruct you, the plaintiff has the burden of proving that the death of Harold Mohler resulted, in whole or in part, from the occurrence of December 28, 1967; and the burden of proof in this civil case is not to convince you beyond a reasonable doubt. The burden of proof that Mrs. Mohler and her children have is to persuade you that, on that issue, it is more probably true than not true.

I would like to review the evidence. Has not this case come down to this? Was Harold Mohler's death, in whole or in part, related to what happened on December 28, 1967, or did Harold Mohler die of a heart attack, wholly unrelated to the occurrence of December 28, 1967? The evidence on this issue has been given to you. We've had medical evidence from eight physicians, and let me detail for you what those eight physicians' evidence has been. It's mainly in inverse order.

Dr. Donal O'Sullivan, the board-certified pathologist, board-certified in general pathology, anatomic pathology, clinical pathology, and hematology, also board certified in nuclear medicine, and Dr. Hughes, not certified by one of the accrediting boards, but a member of another board, the American Board of Electroencephalographers. Dr. Leestma, board certified in pathology, in neuropathology.

Dr. Segarra, board certified by the American Board of Neurology, and certified by the American Board of Pathology in neuropathology. Dr. Burns, board certified in pathology and general pathology. Dr. Westfall, the coroner from Indiana, who pronounced Harold dead, and then two others.

Almost one year to the day before Harold Mohler's accident, he was examined by a railroad doctor, and found to be in excellent health. Before that, when he applied for the job at the end of 1963, he filled out a long questionnaire, and was examined by a railroad doctor and found to be fit for Class A service on the railroad; and that, ladies and gentlemen, has been the medical testimony.

The testimony as to those activities of Harold Mohler, between December 28, 1967 and January 19, 1968, came from the widow, children, and from Dan Hackett, the brother-in-law. There are certain things I made notes of, and I would like to bring them to your attention by some kind of key words that people have said. Dr. Westfall's testimony was that Harold Mohler died suddenly and he was pronounced dead beside the railroad car.

(Writing on a blackboard)

MR. CALLAHAN: Your Honor, I object to this. The jury heard the evidence and the jury can remember what they heard and counsel may comment upon it, but to write it down here as if it's somehow another record, it's improper.

THE COURT: May I see it? Objection is overruled. Proceed.

MR. HAYES: Now, we've heard the term "inconclusive" used and I will remind you, particularly that in the hypothetical questions that were posed by the railroad to Dr. Leestma and to Dr. Hughes, that not once were they given Dr. Burns' findings on the autopsy.

MR. CALLAHAN: I object to this. Counsel had the right to examine this doctor. I can ask the questions I want to and I'm not obligated to ask the questions he wants me to.

THE COURT: Overruled. Counsel, you'll have an opportunity.

MR. CALLAHAN: This is improper argument.

THE COURT: Counsel, the objection is overruled.

MR. HAYES: What was said was that the autopsy was inconclusive—that's not what Dr. Burns testified to. Dr. Burns testified as to the autopsy he performed and he testified that, in his opinion, there was nothing in the autopsy that at all related to a cardiac cause of death, and, in his opinion, the cause of death was not related to a heart attack.

It is also true that he testified that he could find no evidence of trauma as a cause of death, but it is different to say that an autopsy was inconclusive without giving what those findings actually were and what they suggest to the man who was actually doing the cutting out and the examination of the tissues of this man. Now, that's what Dr. Burn's testimony was.

It is also omitted from the hypothetical question given to Dr. Hughes and Dr. Leestma—

MR. CALLAHAN: Your Honor, I'll have to make the same objection, to protect my record. I know what your ruling is going to be.

THE COURT: Very well. Yes. Go ahead.

MR. HAYES: —that the finding of the mucus obstructing the tracheal bronchial tree—that was not given to Dr. Hughes or to Dr. Leestma. Now, Dr. Segarra is called on behalf of the plaintiff after the testimony of Dr. Burns had been received and Dr. Segarra, if you'll go back with me to when he testified—it was, frankly, difficult to bring out how really well trained this man has been. He wasn't there saying, "I'm a big shot neurologist or neuropathologist." I remember, for example, when I asked about whether he had had a scholarship to study at the Sorbonne, and did he get a diploma and he answered, "Oh, yes. They give a very nice piece of paper."

Some of you people may recall that; and he was modest about his contributions to the knowledge of the modalities and the mechanisms of epilepsy and death, and, yet, we learned he lectures annually to such organizations as the World Neurological Congress on the modalities and mechanisms of death.

Now, Dr. Segarra has that unique combination of a man who has been recognized by his peers as having made valuable contributions to the literature of neurology and neuropathology, as Dr. Leestma recognized, but also he brings to that combination of the real treatment, observation, his taking bedside care of patients, and the science of neuropathology. Dr. Segarra told us that, in his opinion, the probable cause of death was related to the injury received December 28, 1967. In his opinion, as he stated on cross-examination, when asked about "Well, would you accept the word of a thirteen-year-old or would you accept this?" He said, "First of all, I prefer to have lay words rather than big long medical words. It is lay people who describe what they see. They don't describe it in long medical words; they describe it in the ordinary words that you and I use every day to describe what we see and what we hear, what we feel, and that is what is assessed by the clinician."

And he testified that, in his opinion, the occurrence of December 28th probably caused—as a matter of fact, he said the death of January 19th and the probable mechanism of that death was that, as a result of the injury, he developed minor epilepsy, minor epileptic attacks manifested by such things as were described by the family members, and a constellation of which on January 19, 1968, when he keeled over, caused laryngospasm, leading to the man's choking to death on his own mucus, an opinion supported by the finding of the mucus obstructing the tracheal bronchial tree.

Now, it is true that Dr. Segarra was asked his opinion as to, "Well, couldn't he have died of a heart attack?" And Dr. Segarra said, "Very unlikely." However, he said, "I am not a general pathologist and I would not like to hold myself out an expert on that." Now then, what has the railroad offered? The railroad has offered Dr. Leestma and Dr. Hughes. I'm going to take them in inverse order.

No. I'll take them in the order in which they came. Dr. Leestma is board-certified in neuropathology. As Dr. Segarra told us, neuropathology is that branch of science which deals with the brain, spinal cord, peripheral nerves, and deals with the microscopic evidence of the pathological processes of neurological diseases, but what was the question asked by the railroad of Dr. Leestma, a neuropathologist?

"Question: What, in your opinion, was the cause of death?"

"Answer: A heart attack."

After his testimony, I then made inquiry of Dr. Leestma about his opinion as to whether that was described by the family could represent minor epileptic attacks, and Dr. Leestma at this time said, "I would prefer not to talk about that," but in his deposition he was not at all reluctant to offer opinions. This same Dr. Leestma who has collaborated with Dr. Hughes in articles; they worked together for seventeen years at Northwestern University, Dr. Leestma at the time of his sworn testimony under oath in his deposition said—"As to every one of those incidents, could they represent a minor epileptic seizure?" And he answered, "Yes." And he also admitted on the stand that the cause of death could be related to the injury of December 28, 1967, because of the development of minor epileptic seizures as a logical alternative to the cause of death by heart attack.

Now, Dr. Hughes' testimony, I think, was characterized by some words that I recall: "usually ... uncommon ... rarely ... It is the exception, when dealing with minor epilepsy following head injury the time of the appearance of the epileptic seizures, and the relationship to a cause of death." Usually, people who receive a minor head injury do not develop minor epilepsy, and that's agreed. Usually, people who have minor epilepsy do not die of it. There's no doubt about that.

As Dr. Segarra said, millions of people are hit in the head every day. They don't all die, but many do, for reasons that are not exactly known yet, but has been demonstrated through the work of Sabina Stritch and Dr. Oppenheim, in developing sophisticated techniques for staining brain tissue to show how the mechanism of these minor attacks leads to death or can lead to death and sometimes even when the injury is not a, quote, "significant injury," and sometimes, as Dr. Segarra said, shrapnel will literally penetrate a man's brain and yet nothing happens.

It is a constellation of events that leads to the disastrous catastrophe of which Dr. Segarra spoke. Now, the person who did testify as to the cardiac death was the neuropathologist, but he also said a couple of other things, like "enlarged heart."

If there is an enlarged heart, that could lead to high blood pressure, and high blood pressure, et cetera, et cetera, et cetera, could lead to arteriosclerosis, and that could cause death. Besides the enlarged heart, some people die of fatty blood. This is, remember, the neuropathologist.

I ask you, ladies and gentlemen, when measured against that testimony, how does the testimony of Donal O'Sullivan, board certified in hematology, stand up to you? I ask you how does the testimony of the general pathologist, Dr. Burns, as to what he thought of a heart attack as the cause of death and the testimony of Donal O'Sullivan, who did a residency for two years in internal medicine, including cardiology and other diseases?

Ladies and gentlemen, I suggest to you, it is more probably true than not true, that that constellation of events occurred in this case, and that's why Harold Mohler is dead, and that's why we're all here twelve and one-half years later, and if you agree that it is more probably true than not true, that that occurrence of December 28, 1967, in whole or in part, led to his death on January 19th, 1968, the it will be your obligation to determine the amount of damages.

We have offered the testimony of Professor Walter Johnson to assist you in determining something that is going to be a significant thing in the lives of many people. Now, let's talk about what you cannot consider. You cannot consider grief and sorrow, that consuming sense of loss of a good father and a good husband. The law says that you may not consider that in determining damages.

The law says that you shall consider only pecuniary loss. However, the law says that you shall recognize, on the part of the children, the pecuniary value of the loss of advice, counsel, et cetera, of their father. Now, with respect to the pecuniary value of a man, the loss to the widow and children, there are several earnings.

There are the earnings that this man contributes to the family. These are the fringe benefits that come from the earnings, or flow from it, and there are those future loss of earnings and those so-called fringe benefits, which are reflected in a pension for himself, till he dies, if he puts thirty years in on the railroad, and to his widow till she dies. Lastly, as we will discuss, the question of advice and counsel, et cetera. Now, this is somewhat complicated, but I want you to bear with me because I have tried to reduce the testimony of Dr. Johnson to some things that I hope will show you visually, in the hope it will be of some assistance to you in determining the question of damages, if you should find that they are entitled to damages.

Now, the first thing I want to be kept in mind is that money has an earning power, as Professor Johnson said, but in all of Dr. Johnson's calculations, he took account of the income taxes that Harold Mohler had to pay. He took the lowest possible deduction that he could, the standard deduction, and that's because he did not know, and could not know what Skip would have done, had he earned this money.

We know this. We know Norm Phillips. We know just about what Skip would have earned, because we know what Norm Phillips earned, and Norm Phillips was hired on the road within three days of Skip, and, as a matter of fact, Norm Phillips was the brakeman on the run where Skip was the conductor, so he was the conductor, making more money than Phillips, so we know pretty good, maybe minimum, what Skip would have earned. We also know this: that even though Norm Phillips had only four deductions, by using the standard deductions, Skip pays more income tax with his seven children under Dr. Johnson's recapitulation than Phillips did. It doesn't seem fair, but that's the way Professor Johnson did it.

His figures were, in every instance, ladies and gentlemen, the conservative figures. Now, after income taxes, after deductions from January 1968 to July 1, 1980, we have $247,282.

There is a contribution made by the employer during those years, and we can think of that in terms of when a working man, individually or through a labor union, is given an employer contribution or pension or for hospitalization costs. It is something that he receives in lieu of wages, so the past loss is $247,282.

Now, that money was never received by Skip, never received by his widow or children. The money was theirs but they didn't get it and that money had earning power, but the law does not permit, in this case, what we call "interest before judgment." It's not permissible under the law relating to railroad workers, so this is the net. $247,000 is the loss to date and that is not to be reduced to present cash value.

Now, from Skip's earnings, without fringes, from July 1, 1980 to age sixty-five, reduced to present cash value—that is to say, the amount of money needed now, which, when added to what that amount of money is able to earn, will equal the amount of loss in the future when the money will have to be paid back that present cash value is $621,300, if he only works to age sixty-five. Therefore, without fringes, the past loss and the future loss to age sixty-five is $868,582.

Now then, we'll talk about what Skip could have earned if he worked to age seventy, and this railroad had a seventy retirement age, not sixty-five. Some railroads have sixty-five; this had seventy. If he had worked to age seventy, the present cash value of the earnings that this man would have received is $984,000, reduced to present cash value. If he worked then to age seventy, the total loss would have been, with the past up to date, the future to age seventy, $1,231,000.

Now then, let's talk about the pension. Now, the way it is figured is a little unusual, as you heard from Walter Johnson, but we do know this: That at age sixty-five, if Skip worked till sixty-five, he would have already had his thirty years in, so he would get the full pension. From Skip's age sixty-five to his life expectancy at age seventy-four, the pension loss to Virginia would be $301,843, and then, under the law, she's entitled to one-half of that total pension, and so that would still be, from the time he died, to the time that she dies. If she lives her life expectancy to eighty, or if she lives beyond, it's more; if she dies before eighty, it's less. The total loss of pension in dollars is $611,567, to Virginia.

However, maybe he would work to seventy, and if he worked till seventy, obviously the pension would be less in number of years, and that total, using those same figures, is $512,978. That's working to age seventy. However, that must be reduced to present cash value, and here is where the economist, using the railroad's way of figuring things, determined the present cash value of what the railroad would have contributed; he said that if he retired at age sixty-five, the present cash value would be $99,000, and if he worked to age seventy, the present cash value would be $145,000.

Well, that doesn't make sense when we are talking about not what he would have gotten or not the value of the contribution by the employer, but when you have to make provision for the future. Walter Johnson was asked, "Is there any annuity company in the world that would write a policy from ages sixty-five or seventy, that would return those benefits which she would have received if Skip had lived for $145,000?" And he said, "No." The total loss then, if Skip were to work to age sixty-five and if we accept that somewhere, somehow, there would be an annuity company that would generously say to Virginia, "If you give me $145,000 tomorrow, I will guarantee that you will get those pension benefits that you have lost in the future," assuming that that could be done, the total loss is $1,013,936, if he retires at sixty-five.

And if he retires at seventy, it is $1,331,154.

Now there's something that $1,331,000 does not recognize and that is the children and what a father means to a child, and this isn't something on which the Court, I believe, will instruct you. The children are entitled to recover the pecuniary value in dollars, of a father's care, attention, instruction, training, advice and guidance. Now, in determining the value of that, you're going to have to make an assessment of what kind of person Skip Mohler was. You've heard from his children, most of them, and I didn't especially like parading children to the stand, but it's something that you have to live with, and, therefore, I have to address, and that is the value of Skip Mohler to these children. It's been twelve and a half years since this man died, and twelve and a half years that those children, then ranging from the ages of five to fifteen, have been deprived of the advice, counsel, et cetera, of their father, and I am not going to suggest what that is, expressed in dollars.

I am going to suggest to you, ladies and gentlemen, that Skip Mohler was probably summed up best by Norman Phillips, the man who saw him live and watched him die, and he said, "One hell of a guy," and we're not talking about a marriage that's on the rocks, or divorce or separation; we're talking about a marriage that was a good marriage. They even had arguments. The thing that they had, and that this family had, was good communication. "We loved him and we knew he loved us."

I ask you this; can the dollar value of those things that a father can give to his children, can it possibly be less than his value as a person who provides food, shelter, and clothing? Will you value that aspect of a father as a provider, less than that of a counselor and guardian? Ladies and gentlemen, I know that we're talking about what, to you, may seem to be a very substantial sum of money, into the millions, but each and every one of you, under oath, said that if you found that it was justified by the law and the evidence, you would not hesitate to sign your name to a verdict that would reflect those substantial damages, and I suggest, ladies and gentlemen, that this amount of money that you may award in this case—it is not subject to income taxes. We have already deducted income taxes from his earnings, and the award that you made is not subject to income taxes. It is an award that will be shared by eight people.

Thank you very much.

THE COURT: We'll take a short recess. Remove the jury, please.

(Recess taken).

* * * * * *

(Whereupon the following was held in the presence of the jury)

THE COURT: Mr. Callahan

MR. CALLAHAN: Thank you, Your Honor. May it please the Court.

THE COURT: Counsel.

MR. CALLAHAN: Mr. Hayes. Ladies and gentlemen of the jury.

FINAL ARGUMENT BY MR. CALLAHAN:

This is my opportunity to argue the case on behalf of the defendant. And when I said in my opening comments that I would have only one opportunity to address you, I believe that I covered that at the end of this the plaintiff will have another opportunity to rebut anything that I have said here. That is, he can comment upon what I say to you.

Now, the reason I have made some notes here—you will see me referring to them from time to time—is that I don't want to overlook or forget something that I have noted here. As chance would have it, sometimes we do anyway, because as I become involved in making these comments, I tend to skip to things I have already made notes about, and sometimes, later, I find that I overlooked some of them.

But you are the people who heard the evidence. You are the jury in this case. What you heard, what you understood, the impressions you got, are what is really important here. And when I comment upon the evidence, or when Mr. Hayes does, if I say anything that isn't consistent with what you understood, then, by all means, follow your understanding of the evidence from the witness stand and follow what you remember, not what I say.

One of the reasons that I alluded briefly in my opening statement to the fact that the plaintiff is given the right to open and close, is because he has something which is different from what the defendant has in this case. That is, the plaintiff has the burden of proof. And we are going to be talking about burden of proof. And, incidentally, that gives him, then, the way this operates, that gives him the right to open and close. And he will have a right to comment upon what I have had to say to you.

But the burden devolves upon the plaintiff to prove his case. We have discussed from the beginning, in the opening statements, the big question which is: Was there a connection between the injury of December 28, 1967,and the death of January 19, 1968? I will discuss that and discuss the testimony of specific witnesses in the course of my comments.

Now, as I say, when I am through here, that will be the end of my comments. I may want to get up and say something when the plaintiff again addresses you, but the way the system works, I cannot do that. Now, as to the burden of proof, I want to go back to that again, because I think it is important that we understand just what it is the plaintiff has to prove here in order to recover. And we understand that if he has not proved that, he is not entitled to recover.

As you have already seen in these discussions, there are two elements to a case. The first element is liability. And I'm going to discuss that not first, but second. The second element is damages. You will see from my discussion of the liability issue in this case that I feel very strongly that the verdict should be in favor of the railroad and against the plaintiff on that issue and you will see why. It has an awful lot to do with the credibility of the plaintiff's witnesses, and the distortions and untruths that have been brought into this case.

Nevertheless, I cannot assume, no matter how strongly I feel about what the verdict should be in this case, that you will fully agree with me. I have an obligation to my client to discuss damages, whether I think there should be a damage award or not, and if I didn't discuss damages and you did find against the railroad and my client asked me later on, "Did you discuss damages?" and I had to say, "No, I didn't," I would feel like a fool and I would look like a fool.

Therefore, no matter how strongly I feel that the verdict should be for the railroad, I'm going to discuss damages, because it would be irresponsible not to do so.

First of all, let me say this: One of the difficulties with a defendant discussing damage is that there is a concern that the jury, in dealing with damages, may say: "Maybe we ought to go half way between what the plaintiff says is the right amount and what the defendant says it should be. Let's be fair; we'll split the difference."

In that case, no matter what I say in terms of damages, what figure I might suggest, I'm just arguing against myself. It makes no sense, if immediately, no matter what figure I use, somebody says, let's split the difference or find in that area. I have argued against myself.

Let me put this in a different context. In Europe, and in many other countries in the world, when you go to buy something there isn't a price on it. If you go to Marshall Field's or Sears or wherever else here in the United States, it's $29.95. You want the item, you pay $29.95.

Even over on Maxwell Street here in Chicago, there's a certain amount of negotiated sales. There's no price on it, but in that kind of context, somebody comes in—let's use as an example a pair of shoes—let's say the pair of shoes is worth twenty dollars.

That's the value of that pair of shoes. There's no price on it. And let's say there is one exchange for the sale. So the prospective purchaser comes in and says to the seller, "How much do you want for the shoes?"

Well, if the seller said eighty dollars and the prospective purchaser only has one opportunity to offer something for the shoes, the only thing that would make any sense would be to say, "I offer you minus sixty dollars."

That's the only way you can get it down to twenty dollars. That's an absurd argument and I'm not going to insult your intelligence and my own by making that argument here, but I merely use the illustration to demonstrate to you how difficult it is for me to talk meaningfully about damages.

At the conclusion of my comments, and the plaintiff's comments in rebuttal, the Court will give you various instructions that will be read to you from the bench, and one of them is going to be an instruction on what the burden of proof is. I believe that instruction will be as follows: When I say that a party has the burden of proof on any proposition or use the expression "if you find," or "if you decide," I mean that you must be persuaded, considering all of the evidence in the case, that the proposition on which he has the burden of proof is more probably true than not true. "More probably true than not true." This is the burden of the plaintiff, to show that the death was connected to the incident of December 28, 1967, that it is more probably true than not true. You also will be instructed that your verdict may not be based upon speculation, guess, or conjecture. It may not be based upon speculation, guess, or conjecture.

Now, you have heard various doctors testify here as to what they thought or didn't think about this. In each case, after a hypothetical question was put to a doctor, this question was put: "Do you have an opinion, based upon a reasonable amount of medical certainty?"

"A reasonable amount of medical certainty." Now, when we put these phrases together, we have these ideas to relate: proving that this death was connected to the incident of December 28, 1967, more probably true than not true, not based upon speculation, guess or conjecture, and a reasonable amount of medical certainty.

That is the test. That is what is on the plaintiff, and that is why it is called the burden. And it is a burden, and he has to meet that burden and persuade you that his case is more probably true than not true. And your verdict must not be based upon speculation, guess or conjecture. And we are talking about medical certainty. And when we combine these instructions, these requirements, I submit to you that the plaintiff has simply not established his burden in this case.

And, incidentally, I think that it is appropriate to point out—Mr. Hayes used the phrase "twelve and a half years." There has been twelve and a half years in which the plaintiff had an opportunity to develop his case. And, as a matter of fact, the plaintiff was in the hands of a highly skilled, and very capable trial attorney. He has demonstrated those skills and abilities to you in these last two weeks, here in this courtroom. And we know that because when Norman Phillips testified in the course of some questions, a statement that he made some time ago was marked. We asked what the date of the statement was. The date of the statement was January 21, 1968.

And when I asked who was present, the answer was, "Mr. Hayes was present." Well, that means that this case has been in the hands of a highly skilled, competent trial attorney for twelve and a half years. And that burden has now come to issue. And the question is: "Has that burden been sustained?" And I submit to you that it has not.

Now, the plaintiff has been discussing the facts of the case; let me make some comments about them.

The plaintiff could have asked any questions he wanted to of any witness that was put on that stand in connection with the hypothetical question. If he was unhappy with the facts that I gave, he was entitled to ask his own questions. He could have subtracted some of the facts. He could have added to them. He could have asked his own questions, just as I asked mine.

When I put Dr. Leestma on, and when I put Dr. Hughes on, and when I said "No further questions," when cross-examination begins, and on cross-examination, the examiner is entitled to inquire into whatever he wants, and to add facts, assuming that they are available, and in evidence, or subtract them. So if he wanted answers to any particular questions, he could have asked them, and you could have heard the answers.

One of the instructions you will be given uses the phrase, "… in whole or in part …" and there has been reference to "in whole or in part," and I think there will be some instruction about it; but the burden of proof, to return to that, is more probably true than not true, and your verdict is not to be based on speculation, guess, or conjecture, and there must be a reasonable amount of medical certainty.

Now, there was a statement made by the attorney for the plaintiff in his comments that Doctors Leestma and Holmes worked together for seventeen years. My memory of Dr. Leestma's testimony was that he graduated from the University of Michigan Medical School in 1964. So if you added seventeen to sixty-four, that would be 1981. But, if I recall correctly, he said he spent three years at the Armed Forces Medical Institute, and he said he took further training at, I think it was, the Einstein Institute in New York. So that statement, based upon what we have heard from both these doctors, simply does not seem to me to be accurate.

There was some criticism of Dr. Hughes' testimony, using the words "unusual," "uncommon." And I will deal with Dr. Hughes a little further in a minute. But Dr. Hughes was one of the most precise persons I have ever seen on a witness stand. And when he gave an answer, he wanted it to be exact, he wanted to be precise, and he wanted it to be just what the fact was. And if he used the word "uncommon," it was because he meant uncommon. And if he used "usually," he meant usually, and he didn't want to say anything but that.

Finally, we hear some statements about staining brain tissue, and that you then make a determination. We never had any tissue in this case. And I am going to say a few words about that. Dr. Burns told us that the pathologist did not know the cause of death. He also stated that he wasn't certain if tissue or slides were taken.

Both Segarra and Leestma said they could have made a better autopsy if the embalming had not occurred. Both Leestma and Segarra said it would be helpful if they had the slides. Segarra referred to them as the histology. Now, in examining Dr. Burns, the question arose from the attorney for the plaintiff, whether his office had been in contact with Dr. Burns over the past ten or twelve years concerning this tissue and these paraffin tests. And Dr. Burns said yes.

Dr. Burns also stated that there was nothing unusual in the ear nor in the ear canal, no cuts or bruises. He conceded that if an arrythymia developed quickly, it could be so quick that there would be no evidence of it in the heart. He said that he saw no signs of blows to the body, and, I believe he said that he had no reason to ascribe trauma as the primary or secondary cause of death.

But let's get back to the autopsy. All we had was the autopsy report, which was marked and which the doctor referred to when he testified. And when I asked both Doctor Burns and Mrs. Mohler about what information was transmitted from the doctor performing the autopsy, I never really got a very clear answer. And, once again, I am deferring to your memory of this, but it just didn't come across. We heard that the heart weighs 370 grams, and the term cardiopericardial was used. What does that mean to the ordinary person? That doesn't mean anything. So, it seems to me that it would be more reasonable for some other communication to have passed between these two people in the course of giving this report. Giving this report to a lay person is just like giving you or me an X-ray and saying, "Read it yourself." Well, we can't read X-rays. That is why there are doctors and experts. And that is how you get the results.

We even had someone from Riverside Hospital, a Miss Susan Fisher who said that there was nothing found in Riverside Hospital. We find out, as a matter of fact, that the autopsy was performed elsewhere. So it would not have been reasonable for there to be anything there in connection with whether tissue, paraffin blocks, or whatever those things are that we have heard a lot about—if they were taken. Evidently, they would have been of great assistance to Dr. Segarra and Dr. Leestma, and the doctor says he is not certain if they were taken. Nobody could find them. And an awful lot of fuss was raised about their existence or nonexistence. We know we don't have them, and this smacks of, "Methinks he doth protest too much." Maybe if we had them, we would know more about this death then we do; then maybe we would be able to reach a conclusive decision as to what caused the death.

Finally, although this came out almost by chance in the beginning, here is a man who performed between three and four thousand autopsies, yet on my cross-examination, he says there is no date on this. He says there is no name on it, except his own signature. And he says it doesn't even show where it was performed. And yet he says he has a distinct, independent memory of this. Well, I wonder; without something further, I wonder.

Now, let me turn to Dr. Segarra. First, it is interesting to find out that we have an expert right here in Chicago. As a matter of fact, Dr. Segarra says there probably are a lot of neuropathologists around. But, in proving this case, we go to Boston to get a doctor to come here to testify about this tenuous connection. And, evidently, if I recall the examination of Dr. Segarra, it appears that he has testified on other occasions, in a case in which he was involved with Mr. Hayes.

But, if this is so clear, why couldn't we have gotten a doctor from around here to testify to that? We have a doctor who went to medical school in Barcelona, Spain, and who came to the Boston area some years later; currently, from what he has told us, he is practicing in Boston. My own view of his attitude in testifying, the word that comes to mind, is "cavalier": "You want me to testify? I will testify. I think there might have been a connection. Who knows? There might have been a connection."

And I got that impression about my first question. I walked up to him and said, "What was the date of the accident?"

And he said, "I don't know."

And Mr. Hayes supplied him with December 28th, the date of the accident.

Now, here is a doctor who comes in here, and is going to testify specifically to a hypothetical question, and my first question to him on cross-examination is, "What was the date of the accident?"

And he says, "I don't know."

That is one of the reasons that I question both his competency and his testimony. Then there is another area. And I am not going to discuss everything these witnesses said. Once again I said to him, "Does it trouble you, Doctor, that a lot of the evidence that you are using in this hypothetical question comes over a period of twelve years, much of it supplied by people who, at the time of the occurrence, were only thirteen years old?"

His response to that question was interesting. In effect, he said, "That is your problem. If that goes into evidence, that is a legal problem. I am just here to give testimony." And, as far as I can tell from his answer, it didn't bother him at all—didn't make any difference where or how competent that evidence might have been. And there was another interesting area that I covered with the doctor. In discussing blows to the head, he said, "It doesn't make any difference how severe it was." He didn't care how fast the train was going. That wasn't important. He didn't care how severe the blow was.

Finally, in a kind of desperation, when you are asking questions of somebody whose answers don't make sense, you are trying to figure out something, and I said, "There was a big boxing match up in Montreal, north of Boston, about three weeks ago. And it went fifteen rounds. It was an incredible fight, and every kind of blow you can imagine was thrown." I asked, "Why don't boxers come down with post-traumatic epilepsy? They are exposed to this all the time." And I don't know exactly what his answer was, but he couldn't explain it. Finally I asked, "Do you know of any papers that anybody has written, dealing with post-traumatic epilepsy in boxers?" And he said no, no he didn't. I would like to just generally compare the testimony of Dr. Segarra with that of Dr. Hughes; just their manner in testifying, their knowledge of the facts, their determination to tell exactly what the situation is. But, let's return for a second to Dr. Leestma, who happens by chance to be another local expert. We don't have to go to Boston from Chicago to get people to testify about things like this. There are a lot of competent people around here, as we all know.

Dr. Leestma is on the faculty of Northwestern Medical School, a graduate of the University of Michigan, board certified. That board certification became interesting, and I will have a few words to say about it.

Dr. Leestma tells us, first of all, that the hypothetical man had a heart attack. To bring us a little closer to the situation, Dr. Leestma had occasion to perform an autopsy on a man who, while he was hooked up to an electrocardiogram device, or whatever, had a heart attack and died. And Dr. Leestma said he performed an autopsy and found there was no way to find out from that autopsy the cause of death, although they all knew he had died from a heart attack.

So he testified that, in about 50 percent of cases in which people die of heart attacks, the autopsy doesn't show it. And this, of course, was consistent with what Dr. Burns said, arrhythmia develops, the heart attack comes quickly, and you can't tell from the autopsy.

And, by the way, I don't think I mentioned, in connection with Dr. Burns, and I meant to, that he said that if the trocar had penetrated the heart, and he seemed to say that it could have, it could have or might have dislodged any occlusion that would have been there. Now, in my questions to Dr. Leestma, I went over the dissolution of a blood clot. I asked him questions about constriction of blood vessels. I even got into fatty blood. I am not saying this man died because of fatty blood. I am trying to bring out, in an effort to seek the truth of this matter, that there is more than one kind of heart attack, and more than one way in which a person can die of a heart attack.

This is twelve and a half years after the fact, and we are limited by an autopsy that wasn't complete, or at least the slides weren't taken. So we are doing the best we can. I am not saying he had fatty blood. I am just asking the doctor, while he is here, to give a little more information about how this occurrence could have taken place.

Now, I want to turn to Dr. Hughes, and let me say, as I have earlier, I was impressed with Dr. Hughes, and I would have been impressed with him whether he was my witness or was testifying against me. Here is a guy, about whom the phrase came to my mind, "A Yank at Oxford." I think there was a movie about that. Here is a man who gets a Fulbright scholarship to Oxford University from his undergraduate school. Oxford University is one of the great seats of learning of the Western World. It is one of the great seats of learning of the English speaking world,and it pre-dates, by centuries, Harvard and other schools that we, in this country, think of as great centers of education.

He went over there and got both his BA and his MA, and he explained to you that those degrees are more significant from that university than they are from universities in this country. He told us that he decided in high school, if I am not mistaken, to make the study of the brain and brain functions his life work.

I used him because he was an expert from the Chicago area. But after his testimony here and the way he comported himself, my suspicion is that he is probably the preeminent expert on brain and brain function in the world. Later on, he obtained his Ph.D. from Harvard, then his M.D. from Northwestern. He received a special award from Franklin and Marshall for his work in epilepsy and electrocephenology. Thereafter, he received an honorary doctorate from Oxford for the same thing. With a background like that, I believe that he probably is the most expert person in the world on this particular subject.

Now, what did he say to us? First of all, he said there has to be some evidence of unconsciousness, and there wasn't any. So he said you have to start with evidence of unconsciousness before you get into the area at all. And he said that everybody in this room has received hundreds of blows to the head, and if you don't presuppose some way of measuring this—a period of unconsciousness—you don't have anything to begin to work with.

Incidentally, after I gave him all those assumed facts, my question was not, "What was the cause of death?" My question was, "Do you have an opinion as to whether the death in this case could have been caused by or as a result of post traumatic epilepsy?"

He said that, "Yes, I have an opinion."

I said, "What is it?"

He said, "It could not have been."

It was then that I said, "Well, Doctor, will you tell us why?"

And it was then that he said, "First of all, there is no evidence of unconsciousness. Therefore, we can't even set the stage for post traumatic epilepsy, because there was no unconsciousness." And, by the way, as to that, there was no evidence of unconsciousness. One of the things that was put into evidence was a report of Mr. Mohler, who related this occurrence, and said that he received a cut ear, bruised arm, and he continued to work.

That was what went into those hypothetical questions. And based on what he said, there is no evidence of unconsciousness. So the stage wasn't even set, as the doctor said, for the post-traumatic epilepsy. He said that only 4—as I recall—4 to 6 percent of persons who suffered from post-traumatic epilepsy had seizures within the first month.

And then he added that some writers would say 8 percent. That is the kind of person he was. "I say 4 to 6, but concede that some writers would say 8 percent."

Dr. Hughes said that early seizures are almost exclusively involved in very severe head injuries. You may recall that Mr. Hayes had the article, and asked him on cross-examination if he had written the article. He said, yes, he did. And Mr. Hayes brought out some statistics that would put it much higher, and the doctor—that was an interesting exchange. Maybe we all remember it, because the doctor said, "Well, I want to add something, in explanation," and Mr. Hayes said, "Perhaps Mr. Callahan will ask you that question." And I said, "I certainly will." But I didn't have to, because at that point, Mr. Hayes decided that maybe he ought to let him answer.

He said that that study was carried out at a county hospital in Buffalo, New York, and every one of those people had received very severe head injuries. And that is what he testified to. That was absolutely consistent with what he had said in the beginning.

So it was not post-traumatic epilepsy, and it could not have been. There was no unconsciousness. There was no significant head injury. Then he said there were no seizures. He said that staring into space is not a seizure. He said that people stare into space for various reasons, and various periods of time, and they do not constitute seizures.

That is not absolutely 100 percent. More than once he said, in the sense that anything is possible, this or that, but he said that staring into space, as a single manifestation, is not a seizure. It is extremely rare. Usually, there are other things, humming, mumbling, and here he imitated picking at the clothing, and none of those were indicated.

And I simply say, on cross-examination, he was splendid. And finally the plaintiff's attorney was reduced to trying to question his competency because he wasn't board certified in pathology. If I am not mistaken—well, let me say it this way—he is as competent a doctor as I have ever seen on the stand, and that was demonstrated by his testimony.

Now, in closing, I want to refer again to the question that I asked each one of you, I think, when you were being qualified, and that is the question of sympathy. And I said, "We don't expect you to put aside your natural sympathy for someone who has lost a loved one in an untimely death." And just because I represent the defendant here, that doesn't mean I don't have natural human feelings of compassion for someone who has suffered a loss.

But that is really not what we are here for. If that was what we were here for, we could have all stipulated that this was a tragedy, and we wouldn't have to have listened to all of this testimony. That is not the question.

The word "verdict" is a combination of two Latin words which together mean, "to say the truth." And that is really what we are dealing with here.

And it is interesting to me to realize—and I have said this before—the burden is on the plaintiff to prove that this is more probably true than not true. And those words are particularly pertinent when we realize that what we are dealing with is a verdict. That is what you are going to be asked to sign, and that is your attestation to the truth of the matter.

So, we are going to be dealing with a proposition that the burden of the plaintiff is to prove that it is more probably true than not true. You may not base your verdict on speculation, guess or conjecture, and the testimony we heard here must have been based upon a reasonable amount of medical certainty.

Finally, let me say this. I represent a corporate defendant and we often are concerned that, if a jury is uncertain, there may be a tendency to say that, well, the plaintiff is an individual and the defendant is a corporation, so why don't we just find against the corporation.

Now, I don't have to say to you, and I don't want to appear to be critical, but I know and you know that that is not your job. And if it were, if that were the way those things were resolved, we wouldn't need a jury. We would just need somebody to pass out the money.

So, in conclusion, ladies and gentlemen, I ask you to return a verdict in favor of the defendant.

THE COURT: Mr. Hayes

FINAL ARGUMENT BY MR. HAYES:

Thank you, your Honor.

Skip Mohler died on January 19, 1968. A friend of their father is a lawyer, named Paul Davidson, in Kankakee.

Nobody could understand how this healthy, happy, robust, hard working man, how he came to his death. And they asked me—

MR. CALLAHAN: Your Honor, I am going to object to this. This is not proper rebuttal.

THE COURT: Yes. Sustained as to such conversation.

MR. HAYES: A report of injury of December 28, 1967 was made by Skip Mohler. It was made on a form provided by the railroad, which says you have to make a report of injury. And if it is a serious injury, the report is to be a telegraphic report. And the report that was made was a telegraphic report of injury.

In Exhibit—

MR. CALLAHAN: Your honor, I am going to have to object. That particular Exhibit was identified by Mrs. Mohler. There is no evidence to telegraphic things or anything.

THE COURT: What is the document?

MR. HAYES: It is the railroad form. It says—

THE COURT: May I see it?

MR. HAYES: (tendering document.)

THE COURT: Is it received in evidence?

MR. CALLAHAN: Yes, it is, your Honor, but I am saying there is no evidence as to what the railroad's custom is or anything.

THE COURT: Sustained. Confine your argument to the evidence.

MR. HAYES: On January 22, the report of injury to persons or property was made by a Mr. Strickland, the Trainmaster. Mr. Strickland is the same man who went to the house to inform Mrs. Mohler of the death of her husband. And on this it says, "In addition to immediate telegraphic report, GAS-1 must be made in all injury or death cases except those of slight injuries to employees." And at the bottom it says, "Send original to the Chief Claim Agent immediately."

MR. CALLAHAN: Your Honor, I am going to have to object to this. This isn't rebuttal, and he sounds like he is making a brand new argument.

MR. HAYES: I will tell you what it is about.

MR. CALLAHAN: I have no opportunity to answer his argument. None of this was made in his opening argument.

THE COURT: The objection is overruled. Confine your arguments to proper rebuttal—

MR. HAYES: I am.

THE COURT: —within proper scope. Thank you.

MR. HAYES: What he suggested is that there is something wrong with a lawyer representing a widow and their children—

MR. CALLAHAN: I object. I am not saying that there is anything wrong. I am merely saying that the lawyer was involved in the case from January 21st. I am not saying there is anything wrong at all.

THE COURT: Very well. Proceed, please.

MR. HAYES: And the railroad was involved in it from that twelve and a half years as well.

MR. CALLAHAN: I am going to object to this line—

MR. HAYES: Your Honor—

MR. CALLAHAN: It is not proper rebuttal.

THE COURT: Counsel, a document is in evidence. The report was made. Counsel can draw reasonable inferences from evidence. The objection is overruled. Proceed.

MR. HAYES: Now, every doctor who has testified in this has said, the defense doctors have said, that it is possible that Harold Mohler died as a consequence of the injuries sustained on December 28, 1967. It is possible, they testified. Dr. Leestma testified, question after question, from his deposition, where he finally concluded that the cause of the death being the result of that accident of December 28, 1967 is a logical alternative.

MR. CALLAHAN: Objection. I don't think that is a proper summary of that doctor's testimony. And I don't think it is proper for counsel to argue this way.

THE COURT: Overruled.

MR. HAYES: It is said, your Honor, that the time that a man spends fishing is not deducted from his allotted time on earth. May my time be without the objections?

MR. CALLAHAN: Well—

THE COURT: I am not a fisherman. Proceed, counsel.

MR. CALLAHAN: Your Honor, I have a right to make objections.

THE COURT: You certainly have. Each of you has the right to object, and I rule on them expeditiously.

MR. CALLAHAN: Thank you, your Honor.

MR. HAYES: Now, let's talk about Dr. Segarra.

I have a friend in Chicago who is a neurologist, not a neurosurgeon, a neurologist. That was brought out by Dr. Segarra on cross-examination. And I asked my friend, who is a very competent neurologist, who was the best. And he told me, "There is a man under whom I studied at Tufts University in Boston, whose name is Joseph Segarra."

Not only is Joseph Segarra board certified in neurology, but also board certified in neuropathology, bringing together that, dealing with real people on a treatment and diagnosis basis, but also well-learned in the pathologic aspects of how diseases occur, and investigating the mechanisms of death. And there is one other thing. He studied under Denny Brown. That is D-e-n-n-y Brown. Denny Brown is probably the most revered figure in American neurology. He was, as Dr. Segarra said, the granddaddy of American neurologists, even though he himself came from England.

And, ladies and gentlemen, my clients are entitled to the best. Whether they have had the best is a matter for you to decide.

When the question of this so-called heart attack being testified to by a neuropathologist, and a person who talked about enlarged hearts and fatty blood was brought up, there was produced for you a man, boarded by four, including nuclear medicine by five, of the American boards, for the benefit of his opinion.

Now, in every case, when the doctors took the stand on behalf of the defense, I was asked to hand over some documents. One of the documents I was asked to hand over was Skip's time log. And I am going to digress a moment. I am going to ignore the innuendo about that autopsy. Dr. Burns performed a lot of autopsies at Riverside Hospital, and an inadvertent slip was made, saying it was performed at Riverside Hospital. And I knew the railroad would pick that up.

And that is why you had the people from Riverside Hospital to say, "No, it wasn't performed here." Mrs. Mohler knew where it was performed, but the railroad is going to say, "Well, why do you believe her? She is a party to the lawsuit. Here is her check to pay Dr. Burns."

MR. CALLAHAN: I object. That is improper.

THE COURT: Overruled.

MR. HAYES: As if it had been performed at Riverside Hospital. He wouldn't have been paid because he was a salaried pathologist at that hospital. And this he did as a private case. And he got paid by the check from Mrs. Mohler. But to get on to the book, every time when those two doctors took the stand I was asked to provide the book.

I would assume—

MR. CALLAHAN: By way of objection, that is in evidence. I have a right to use it. It isn't as if I am asking him to hand over something—

THE COURT: The document was in evidence and available to both sides, that is correct.

MR. HAYES: But the curious thing is it wasn't used, it wasn't used by the railroad. It was used by me on behalf of the Mohlers. And Dr. Segarra testified that he had examined the book and that there was something about the book that suggested to him that something was happening in this period, some of what he called those subtle changes in cognitive ability.

That kind of thing, like, well, maybe only the family would recognize; that he isn't acting exactly the same as he was, ever since that accident. That is what Mrs. Mohler said, when he mentioned, "that damned accident." Now, here is something from Skip's own hand. I am going to take you—the whole book was examined, and the whole book has been in evidence, and it shows all of the times. The date is the first column, job number is the second column, the engine number there may not be stated. "On duty at Kankakee." That is—

MR. CALLAHAN: Your honor, I object to this as improper rebuttal. I made no reference to that book. If he had made those comments in his opening statement I would have had an opportunity to say something about it. It is improper now.

MR. HAYES: The time off-duty, the time on-duty, the destination, Elkhart, time off-duty 11:30, class of service, freight, car rate, number of cars, 126 cars.

And going over here, room and meals allowance, et cetera, things like that.

Now, we get to—this is in December, December 7, '67.

"One, Job number, et cetera, et cetera."

And we go on down in this book to December 24.

MR. CALLAHAN: Your Honor, I think that the record should show that what is going on here, is that Mr. Hayes, certainly without my knowledge, has had enlargements made of this book, and he is now testifying or talking to the jury about these enlargements.

This is improper rebuttal, I have no opportunity to say anything about these exhibits.

THE COURT: May I see the exhibits at a side bar, please? (Whereupon, the following proceedings were had at side bar out of the hearing of the jury)

THE COURT: It would have been appropriate to have the blow-ups marked with the number for identification so counsel would have the opportunity to offer what objections he had.

MR. CALLAHAN: And brought it out in your opening statement.

MR. HAYES: I have never heard of an objection being made to using a blow-up.

THE COURT: Counsel may make an objection if he wishes to, whether you have ever heard of it or not. But it would have been appropriate to have it marked for identification in order to give him an opportunity to preserve an objection.

This is the first time anybody has seen these blow-ups, and that is what his objection is to.

MR. HAYES: Your Honor, I am sorry. I didn't—I wasn't aware this had to be done.

We have made blow-ups of evidence all the time.

THE COURT: That doesn't deny the fact that counsel has a right to offer an objection.

MR. HAYES: Am I then to have to go to the jury, and have them go along, the twelve of them? This is just a demonstrative aid to the jury, just like those charts.

THE COURT: But his objection is, he never had an opportunity to offer an objection, and I have to honor that.

MR. HAYES: What would have happened if it had been objected to? It is a true representation.

THE COURT: I would have ruled on it, but he would have had an opportunity to preserve the record.

I am going to sustain the objection.

(Whereupon, the following proceedings were had in open court in the presence of the jury)

THE COURT: Objection sustained.

MR. HAYES: I am sorry, ladies and gentlemen.

Now, inadvertently, I forgot to mark those and they will have to be dispensed with.

As we said—I hope you can see—this is December 7th, and you will note that the first entry, December 7, you note that the column way over to your left is—

MR. CALLAHAN: Your honor, I hate to belabor this, but this should have been brought out in his opening, at the start of the closing statements. Then I could have said something about it. This way I get no opportunity to do that.

MR. HAYES: Your Honor, counsel asked for this book before his argument, and I gave it to him. This is evidence that is in the case and has been brought out by the two witnesses on behalf of the defense.

And this is rebuttal argument to suggestions made in the counsel's argument.

THE COURT: The objection is overruled. Counsel, proceed.

MR. CALLAHAN: Well, let me say for the record, that it is not rebuttal to anything I said. I am not going to get an opportunity to talk about it.

THE COURT: I believe he is leading to that, counsel. Proceed.

MR. HAYES: Now, we go to the 25th. He didn't work Christmas. He worked the 26th and the date is in the column. The job number where he was going from is here, and then we get down to, ladies and gentlemen, the 31st of December. On the 31st of December—first of all, he laid off for two days which was unusual for Skip, to lay off two days, but he did lay off the 30th and the 31st and the 1st, but he may have been off on the 1st anyway.

But on the 31st, something happened. In the first column is the job number, 791, and then in the second column, under job number, is the 31st. But it is more than that, if you will see that there is something as you can progress down to the 8th. He has the 7th and the 8th not only in the wrong column but in the same box.

MR. CALLAHAN: Your Honor, this cannot be proper, for him to do this without me ever having had a chance to rebut this. It just is not proper rebuttal.

THE COURT: Counsel, it would have been proper to refer to it in your opening remarks. I would have agreed to that. But if you are leading to a response, I think you should get to it immediately.

MR. HAYES: All right. Over the 8th and 9th, the 10th; and continually, over to—I am going the wrong way—oh, over to the last day when he misses days and puts dates in the wrong place, and then finally puts the 17th back into the right column, there is a pattern that emerges.

Now, there is some evidence that was not given to the doctor who saw him; who testified on behalf of the railroad. You remember Dr. Segarra testifying to, that it is an unusual type of thing? The point of it is this, ladies and gentlemen. You have been asked, in argument by the railroad, to disregard all of those things that happened to Harold Mohler within days after the accident of December 28th, 1967, to disregard all of those episodes that are—that were observed by the family.

MR. CALLAHAN: Your Honor, I am going to have to object. I specifically put those so-called episodes in. We talked about staring in space and thrashing in bed. Those were in my questions. And I did not ask anybody to disregard them.

THE COURT: Sustained. There was no such comment that they disregard those. Proceed.

MR. HAYES: Ladies and gentlemen, will you disregard all of the evidence of something happening to Skip Mohler within days after the 28th of December of 1967? Will you say that these things, which had never occurred before, and which occur within days—as a matter of fact a couple of days—are things you are not going to give any weight to? Are you going to say that this is unrelated to, not even in part, to the death of Harold Mohler on January 19, 1968?

Or are you going to say, ladies and gentlemen, that, yes, it is uncommon for death to occur as a consequence of head injury; and, yes, it is unusual for a person to die of an epileptic seizure; but, also, are you going to say that all of those things that happened to Skip Mohler only after the accident, and from that time to the time of his death—and had never occurred before—you are going to ignore and disregard and say, statistically, he didn't die in an epileptic seizure because, statistically, most epileptics do not die of seizures? But we know that many do. And if you were to make this a statistical cause of death you would deny everybody who would not fall within that statistic. The little boy who was playing cricket and got hit in the head and got a bruise on the head.

There is one more thing that struck me as kind of unusual. Getting to what Dr. Hughes said, talking about the necessity of a significant head injury, and that this was not a significant head injury, I asked him about retrograde amnesia. Retrograde amnesia is a lack of memory for some events that preceded the event that causes trauma, and sometimes includes the event itself. You know, the thing like, "What happened?" Or, "I know what happened, but what happened before?" You remember when Harold Mohler—the witness Benoit testified that Mohler went to the engine at Streator and at Streator—

MR. CALLAHAN: Your Honor, this is improper rebuttal. There is nothing about Mohler and Benoit and what have you. How can I answer these arguments?

MR. HAYES: It is significant of the evidence, your Honor, in rebutting the suggestion of counsel.

THE COURT: Overruled. Proceed.

MR. HAYES: He asked Benoit what happened, and Benoit said, "We went into emergency."

Now, everybody in the world who has ever worked on a railroad knows that when a train goes into emergency there is an explosive blast of air. Yet, there was something about Mohler, when he talked to Benoit, that made Benoit tell him that, "We went into emergency."

Now, I am going to talk to you now about the cricket case, and the cricket case is only one of many cases recorded in which catastrophic events occur because of minor injury, for reasons that are not absolutely known, except that we know that they are related.

It is that constellation of events in a thirteen-year-old boy that was hit in the forehead by a cricket ball. He went on about his business the whole evening, the whole day, joked about the bruise on his head, and then had the first attack 24 hours later and ultimately died of an epileptic attack.

The title of the article, ladies and gentlemen, as Dr. Leestma was asked—I don't know if the words are exact—"Fatal Damage to the Brain by Epileptic Convulsions after a Trivial Injury to the Head."

MR. CALLAHAN: I would object, your Honor. That was a single instance in an article. It was not plural.

MR. HAYES: I didn't say it was.

THE COURT: Proceed. That's correct.

MR. HAYES: Ladies and gentlemen, the evidence, I suggest to you, is more probably true than not true, that the death of Harold Mohler on January 19, 1968, resulted, in whole or in part, from that injury sustained on December 28, 1967, and that it is more probably true than not true, that these unusual events occurring, coupled with the negative findings at autopsy, lead to that conclusion that it is more probably true than not true.

And if you find that, though you may be beset with doubts as to whether that is absolutely fact, Virginia Mohler and her seven children are satisfied that that burden was proved, and then it will be your job to assess fair and just compensation on behalf of the family.

I thank you once again, and the next stage will be the Court giving you the instructions of law.

On behalf of myself, as well, thank you.

(Whereupon the Court read the instructions to the jury; thereafter, the jury retired to the jury room for its deliberations.)

CHAPTER ELEVEN

The Verdict

What is truth? (Pontius Pilate)

— John

Arranging for the Verdict

When the closing arguments are completed, the judge reads his instructions to the jury, gives the additional direction to first choose a foreman, and the jury retires to consider its verdict. Thereafter, the foreman will be the person who communicates to the Court on behalf of the jury, if necessary. And it is the foreman who responds to the Court's question, "Ladies and gentlemen of the jury, have you reached a verdict?" "We have, Your Honor."

After the jury has retired, the Court usually asks the lawyers to give his clerk a telephone number where each can be reached. It is often agreed between the Court and counsel at what time they will return to the courtroom to discuss the various alternatives presented if it appears that the jury may not arrive at a verdict until late in the evening. Upon reporting back, consideration needs to be given, for example, to whether to order dinner for the jury. Until they receive a call from the Court, or until they report back at the appointed time, the lawyers are free to do as they wish.

Occasionally, the jury has a question for the Court. When this occurs, the Court is under an obligation to communicate with counsel before responding to the jury's inquiry. The parties have a right to be consulted and to be heard by the Court as to any proposed response or other communication with the jury. They also have the right to be present in the courtroom when the Court responds to a question from the jury. It is improper for the Court to communicate with the jury without the knowledge and consent of the attorneys for the parties.

On those occasions when you have a question from the jury after it has retired to consider its verdict, or when the jury is brought into the courtroom for questions from the Court as to whether they are close to reaching a verdict or for other reasons, you will have an opportunity to see the jury after it has been deliberating for awhile. There is a well-accepted way in which it can be determined which jurors favor you or your opponent. Those who look at you as they return to the jury box are those who support you. Those who look at your opponent support him.

Return of the Verdict

On the day of victory no one is tired.

— Arab Proverb

When the jury has reached a verdict, each juror must sign it. This is explained to the jury in the course of the Court's instructions. The jury indicates that it has reached a verdict by sounding a buzzer, audible to the bailiff, who notifies the judge. If the attorneys are not in or near the courtroom, they are contacted by telephone, and the return of the verdict must await the arrival of the attorneys.

On occasion, when it appears that the jury will not reach a verdict until late at night, the parties may agree, through their attorneys, that the jury return a sealed verdict. This is not opened until the following day when the attorneys are present in court. It may also be stipulated that the verdict be delivered to the judge, who opens it, and has his clerk or bailiff advise the attorneys by telephone. Although most jurisdictions require the traditional unanimous verdict, ten to two or even nine to three quotient verdicts are the rule in a few jurisdictions.

Most commonly, the verdict is returned in the courtroom, in the presence of the Court and counsel and the parties to the suit. The jury comes out and take their seats in the jury box. The Court asks, "Ladies and gentlemen of the jury, have you reached a verdict?" The foreman of the jury stands and replies, "Yes, your Honor." Some judges then direct the foreman to hand the verdict to the clerk, who hands it to the judge, who opens it and reads it aloud. Other judges have the foreman read it aloud, and then direct the foreman to hand it to the clerk. Still others have the clerk read the verdict.

In the case we have been following, the jury returned a verdict in favor of the plaintiff and awarded damages in the amount of $500,000. In view of the economic testimony showing a monetary loss of more than $1,330,000, this was clearly a compromise verdict. Nevertheless, because of its belief that there were serious errors in the trial, the railroad filed an appeal to the Illinois Appellate Court. The appellate court affirmed the judgment.[1]

Polling the Jury

A liar will not be believed even when he speaks the truth.

— Aesop

At this point, each party has the right to ask that the jury be polled to confirm that the verdict which was read aloud was, in fact, their verdict. The Court sometimes invites such a motion by asking, "Any motions, counsel?" Although either party has the right to make the motion requesting that the jury be polled, it is commonly made by the attorney who is unhappy with the verdict. It gives him an opportunity to express his displeasure. The procedure is as follows:

Attorney: Your Honor, I request that the jury be polled.

COURT: Very well. The clerk will poll the jury.

CLERK: (reading from the jury cards) Mr. Smith, was this and is this your verdict?

MR. SMITH: Yes.

CLERK: Mrs. Brown, was this and is this your verdict?

MRS. BROWN: Yes, it is.

---

[1] *Mohler v. Blanchette et al.*, *106 Ill.App.3d 545, 435 N.E.2d 1161 (1982). Leave to appeal to the Supreme Court of Illinois denied.*

The clerk reads each of the juror names, and asks the same question. It is rare for a juror to change his vote. Even though, on occasion, jurors may be seen to weep with frustration or futility, they rarely change their vote.

Once this process has been completed, the Court will enter judgment on the verdict. It is common at that time for the Court and counsel to thank the jury for serving. The Court then discharges them. The Court may also tell them that they do not have to discuss the case with anyone if they do not wish to, but once discharged they are also free to do so if they choose.

* * * * * *

In the *MCI v. AT&T* antitrust suit, the jury had returned a verdict in favor of MCI in the amount of $600,000,000., which when trebled as required by the antitrust law reached the amount of $1,800,000,000. Since the verdict was returned late in the evening the trial judge indicated he would follow his normal practice of having judgment entered on the verdict on the next business day of the Court.

It happened that there was a legal holiday being celebrated that weekend which meant that the next business day of the Court was three days away. Before leaving his chambers that night the judge heard a knock on his door and upon opening it there appeared the attorneys for MCI. They were very deferential but were concerned that he was not entering judgment on the verdict on the day it was returned. The judge pointed out that he was simply following his normal procedure of entering judgment on the verdict on the Court's next business day. The MCI attorneys explained that their concern was that since interest on a verdict does not begin to run until judgment is entered, their client would lose some $1,500,000. in interest over the weekend!

The judge agreed to enter judgment on the verdict that day.

Conclusion

This above all: To thine own self be true …
Thou canst not then be false to any man.

— Shakespeare, *Hamlet*

This, then, is a summary of the jury trial process. It will be recognized that much of what has been written here is mere common sense. To advocate without alienating, to contest without seeming petty, to object without whining, to play your role simply and unpretentiously and earn the respect of the jury: that is what you are really about.

Experience teaches us not to argue about insignificant matters. Inexperienced lawyers argue and contest everything. To gain experience you must be prepared to look like a fool from time to time. Not intentionally, of course, but you will find yourself in situations, usually of your own making, in which you look foolish. The best way to deal with this, as pointed out earlier, is with a sense of humor. Do not take yourself too seriously.

The price of experience is practice. The way to learn how to try a lawsuit is to try lawsuits. To gain experience you must be prepared to go to trial. But of course, the decision to go to trial brings out all your insecurities and fears of losing. You must discipline yourself to stand by your convictions and try the case to verdict.

One way to deal with the prospective loss in the course of trying a case is to confront yourself, quite specifically, with what the worst result might be. A defense lawyer in a tort action should articulate to himself that, "If everything goes against me, the jury could return a verdict as high as six million dollars," or whatever the case may be. If the consequences are even more devastating, he should deal with that in the same way: "If I lose, I will never make partner. I will have to look for another job." The point is: It is better to recognize and identify the consequences of losing the case than simply to have a feeling of vague, unarticulated apprehension. To place oneself in the position of believing that, "I must win, because I cannot even think of losing," is dangerous in the extreme.

The lawyer for the plaintiff is in a different, if even more threatening, situation. He takes his cases on a contingent fee basis. If he loses, he sees years of time and effort evaporate before him. All is for naught. But there is more. If there has been a substantial offer of settlement, and his client has refused it, the client's decision is necessarily based upon his lawyer's advice. A loss, then, may often bring out, after the first shock, an enraged, accusatory client who is almost impossible to handle.

The trial of lawsuits always brings forth the unexpected. No matter how well you have prepared your case and your witnesses, things do not always go according to plan. Testimony can come out on cross-examination which was never expected. Perhaps worse, on occasion your own witness will surprise you by his answers on your direct examination. These unexpected developments do not necessarily mean that you have lost the case, but they do require adjustments, a change of emphasis, sometimes a change in your theory of the case.

The trial lawyer needs a sense of balance, the ability to adjust to changes, a recognition and acceptance that the best laid plans of mice and men oft go astray. If you believe that you can plan and control a trial so that nothing unexpected will come up, I suggest you pursue a different career.

A number of attorneys will be excluded from becoming trial lawyers by an inappropriate temperament. Many lawyers are unable to argue and contest without suffering emotional exhaustion. But argument and contestation are fundamental to trials. And you must be prepared to engage in it for days, or weeks, or even longer. If doing this is draining and exhausting to you, this is not your game.

And you must be prepared to lose. You must be able to take a loss, even a staggering one, and come back to try other cases without being adversely affected by it. Like the great golfers, you must be able to concentrate and play effectively the hole after the one you've just played so terribly. This is not to say that you shouldn't think about the case you've lost. The cases you learn from are those that you lose. When you win, it's only natural to think that you did everything right and to bask in the reflection of the splendor of your talents. You do not, you cannot, look critically at your performance. After all, how could you? You were victorious, and you achieved the victory through your brilliance and hard work.

You learn from your losses. It is then that you go over the entire trial with critical insight to determine just what happened, where the case was won or lost, and what you could have done differently. Determining why the jury could not, or in any event did not, accept your view of the evidence and, instead, accepted your opponent's. It is then that you learn.

In both plaintiff and defendant alike, there is always the use of the appeal to blunt the sting of a loss. Based upon the narrow likelihood of prevailing on appeal, one is tempted to conclude that the process is often misused, even abused. It does serve, nevertheless, to take attention away from the hurt of a loss in the trial court, and focus it on the appellate process.

Finally, the need to win, and the fear of failure—the thrill of victory and the agony of defeat—may bring forth the temptation to interfere with the trial process. The ways in which this can be done need not be set out here. Suffice it to say that they are limited only by man's imagination.

Which leads us to where we began; a trial is a search for truth. That places the advocate in that forum in a role that demands honor and dedication. It is a high calling. This is not to say that one should not be a vigorous advocate of his side of the case; rather, that the drive to win should always be subordinate to the overriding importance of the pursuit of truth. Success is gratifying; winning is exhilarating; fame is intoxicating.

Truth is sacred.[1]

[1] *Veritas, a quocunque dicitur, a Deo est. (Truth, by whomsoever pronounced, is from God.)*

4 Justinian's Institutes, 153 (A.D. 534)

Index

081579